SOLUTIONS
FOR A
TROUBLED
WORLD

John
Thanks for your statement
which captured the mood and
intent of this book so
well. Best wishes.

Mark M.

SOLUTIONS FOR A TROUBLED WORLD

Edited by Mark Macy

Peace Series
Volume One

Earthview Press, Inc.
Boulder, Colorado, USA

To the future

Cover design and mechanical specifications: Clyde Mason.

Printed in the United States of America

Inquiries can be addressed to Earthview Press
P.O. Box 11036, Boulder, Colorado, 80301

Library of Congress Cataloging-in-Publication Data

Solutions for a troubled world.

  (Peace series ; 1)
  Bibliography: p.
  Includes index.
  1. Peace I. Macy, Mark, 1949-   . II. Series.
JX1963.S64524 1987   327.1'72   87-8859
ISBN 0-930705-03-3

0-930705-04-1 Peace Series
0-930705-03-3 Volume One (Solutions for a Troubled World)

CONTENTS

INTRODUCTION

Overview

Peace is possible if we can all get in the habit of fostering such basic ingredients of peace as clear communication, equity and sensible regulation . . . in our personal lives, our social groups and our world.

Clearer communication. If people in the same household or nations in the same world don't share ideas and information regularly, they gradually grow apart, and eventually become incompatible. So among the first things we need to do as individuals is learn to express our ideas and feelings clearly and get in the habit of talking to people. Meanwhile, technology is making the world seem smaller, as we can call someone up or send a flood of computer information next door or halfway around the world in a matter of seconds. Clear communication within us is also important to peace. For centuries people in the Far East have been practicing meditation — an important means of opening communication paths between the conscious and unconscious mind. Now meditation is readily available and useful to people in the West as well.

Bridging the gap between our conscious and unconscious mind, between the many diversified nations of our world, and between ourselves and the people around us, all lead to clearer communication . . . and that means greater peace.

Equity. But communication is only one basic peace issue. Another is equity, or fairness. Being equitable is important, whether we're talking about children in the same family, families in the same community, communities in the same nation, or nations in the same world. Rampant poverty and starvation must not be allowed to exist while some people indulge in conspicuous consumption. Solving this problem may require different efforts in different parts of the world. People in the Third World may need to more fully understand and appreciate the benefits of education, development and technology. We in the West certainly need to rethink our consumer lifestyle. Many of us have been brought up to believe in the ethic of "buy this, buy that . . . keep the economy growing. Buy-buy-buy." That ethic lent itself to an era fifty or a hundred years ago when there were a lot of resources and not too many people. It's not like that anymore. Things have turned completely around, so now we need to turn our attitudes and our behavior completely around . . . and that doesn't mean sell-sell-sell. Rather, today we have many more people in the world and not as many resources, and so we need to learn self-restraint and moderation.

Perhaps Gandhi summed it up best: "There is enough for everyone's need but not for everyone's greed." If we want equity in the world around us we must learn to control the desires within us. That is a basic ingredient of peace.

Sensible regulation. A third basic peace issue is regulation or management. Sensible regulation is initiated at the lowest or most local levels of society, but high enough to account for everyone affected. Imagine a large office space filled with a hundred partitioned cubicles. The general neatness of each desk is managed at the personal level because only the person who works at the desk is affected by how neat or how cluttered the desk is.

Cigarette smoking is another matter. Smoke from one cube wafts into other cubes. If twenty smokers are scattered throughout the area, everyone is probably affected by their smoke . . . so that situation needs to be managed at a higher level, by an authority that can account for all 100 workers.

So again, regulation needs to take place at the lowest levels of society, but high enough to account for everyone affected.

Let's apply that to our nations and our world. How about toxic wastes in one country? Who should regulate that? Certainly not somebody from another country halfway around the world. Nor the United Nations. As long as the waste affects only *that* country, (as long as it is not sent down the river or shipped by truck across borders), then that country needs to regulate it. But what about acid rain? The poisons from industrial smokestacks waft across the borders of many nations, and so acid rain must be managed at a higher level — an international level.

The most crucial decisions facing us today have to be made at the world level. For example, oceans and rain forests provide the very basis of life on our planet. They transcend national borders. But the oceans are being poisoned. Rain forests are being stripped out from under us. These deteriorating conditions threaten the future of everyone in the world, and for that reason they must be managed at the world level, along with nuclear weapons, and other issues that can affect all of us. Right now there is a continual dispute among nations over the question of who should regulate what. The fact is that the time has come for *all* nations to relinquish some small portion of their authority to a world body. Today's world cannot find peace without sensible guidance from a knowledgeable world body. We need sensible guidance at *all* levels of our lives, from self-control to world governance.

Dealing with conflict. Clear communication, equity, and sensible regulation . . . these and other basic peace issues to be explored in future volumes of this series can bring greater peace to our lives and to our world. Hopefully as we address these basic issues in the coming years, the obstacles to interpersonal and international peace will gradually disappear. Meanwhile we are left to deal with many existing obstacles, painful reminders that we have ignored the basics long enough. Most notable among these is conflict. Grassroots conflicts disrupt our day-to-day lives while international conflicts threaten the future of our planet. It would benefit each of us to learn the skills of conflict resolution — skills that have taken peace professionals decades to piece together yet are easily learned, understood and applied. A general knowledge of how to resolve conflicts effectively would cause a rapid, substantial easing of tensions throughout our species.

Moving toward a world of peace will require some significant changes in our lives and our world. For many, perhaps a few compromises. For some, a few sacrifices. But the needed changes *will* come. Many are now in the works.

Background

Originally — before any articles were received from the authors — the aim of this book was to present a collection of global standards and values . . . a set of social mores, political regulations, economic objectives, technological standards, and other tools of order that could help steer a volatile world to a peaceful state. Such an effort, if successful, would have produced a multi-volume encyclopedia.

•All religions and cultures possess written and unwritten codes of ethics and morals, many of which overlap with those of other religions and cultures on various points that most of us generally consider to be proper or improper behavior.

•There are already comprehensive world laws dealing with international politics and economics, most notably in the legal documents of the United Nations, World Bank and World Court. There are also private efforts moving toward the same end. For example, the World Constitution and Parliamentary Association, a private transnational organization propelled by the boundless energy of professional peace researcher Philip Isely, has written and adopted a complete constitution for world government . . . so that if and when the time comes for the world to be steered by a strong government with well thought-out legislation (ranging from the replanting of rain forests to the banning of nuclear weapons), the WCPA constitution may provide a model or framework.

•Meanwhile, many technical organizations are busy writing international standards for science, industry and technology. The most important of these may prove to be the ISDN standard (a subject of Chapter 3) now being developed by a UN organ (the CCITT) which may someday link all telephones and computers into a compatible global telecommunications network.

These and other global standards and values that are now being developed at a dizzying pace will someday soon have to be catalogued in an orderly fashion.

We certainly need such a comprehensive collection of global standards and values. Just consider our priorities: There are 4,000 peace researchers in the world today, but 400,000 military researchers and engineers employed by national governments, according to Jan Oberg, research director at the Transnational Foundation for Peace and Future Research in Lund, Sweden. Apparently we are preoccupied by military dealings because our nations distrust each other. The mistrust seems to exist because our nations are incompatible with each other in many ways. These incompatibilities are at the very root of our conflicts. Global standards and values are starting to erase those incompatibilities, and we can expect the trend to continue. That, in turn, is starting to lessen the need for military endeavors. As that trend accelerates in the coming years we can expect to see our nations expending more energy and resources toward cooperative pursuits. That is the premise on which this project began.

However it has evolved into something substantially more timely and perhaps more important. This book and the Peace Series (of which the book is the first volume) has become a voice of leading thinkers from around the world and a means of deriving a general consensus of their views. What our diversified world seems to need now more than anything else, is consensus . . . agreement on the most sensible means of solving today's troubles. If the Peace Series can help draw that consensus, it will have provided a valuable service.

A Promising Future

One final note: There is reason for optimism. As I was completing this introduction in March (1987) I received a letter from Caesar Voute (author of Chapter 6), who had returned from the Moscow Forum held in February. Soviet Premier Mikhail Gorbachev in an address to the international guests had expressed many of the views and reflected the general mood of this book. From Professor Voute's letter:

"Gorbachev in his address made one statement which I found nowhere quoted in the media — that confidence, its creation, consolidation and development come from common endeavor, emphasizing that we all must begin with ourselves . . . . He mentioned global relationships between humanity, society and nature and the consequences of material activities, of man trying to dominate forces and processes in nature without due regard to the effects. He referred to the unprecedented diversity and increasing interconnection and integrity of the world . . . the world being a multitude of states, each having its unique history, traditions, customs and way of life. Each people and country having its own truth, its national interests and its own aspirations. He stated that no nation has the ultimate answer to all questions, no government commands the ultimate truth, offers the final solutions."

It would seem that the socialist world is indeed (as predicted by author Jozsef Bognar, Chapter 14) entering a new age. If so it might provide a great opportunity for the USA to join in a series of social, political and eonomic talks with the USSR. If the two superpowers can become reasonably compatible in these areas, their current preoccupation, nuclear weapons, will dramatically shrink in importance . . . and East and West can begin talking about tools of development rather than weapons of destruction.

— Mark Macy

ACKNOWLEDGEMENTS

Special thanks to:

My wife Regina for support, assistance and discussion of ideas throughout the project.

Clyde Mason for providing the skills to make the book visually appealing, cover to cover.

My parents Blair and Gen who, retired from careers in journalism, provided their expertise in typesetting, proofreading and editorial matters.

The authors, whose articles and correspondence broadened my understanding and view of the world.

The readers who use the ideas to achieve greater peace in their lives and their world.

PART ONE:
CLEARER COMMUNICATION

*P*erhaps the biggest step toward peace is to achieve smoother, clearer communication at all levels of our lives — within us and among us, throughout our social groups, nations and religions . . . and among them.

Inner personal communication — or meditation. Jan van der Linden starts us off with an article about "ourselves," and about a way of inner action to unblock the communication channels between the conscious and unconscious minds, for deepened insight and intuition. Building toward a better and wiser future may well depend indeed upon an opening up to our inner sources of vision. The author heads a school where students are trained in advanced meditative techniques over a period of many years and learn to apply their growing spiritual abilities to world-serving. There is no better subject to start our book, as well as our quest for world peace, than meditation . . . because enhanced communication and peace must occur within us before they can occur around us.

Interpersonal communication. Ideally, any two people in the world should be able to exchange greetings and ideas clearly. In reality, of course, there are barriers to clear interpersonal communication. Not only do we humans speak some 5,000 different languages, but even if two of us do happen to speak the same language, our messages are often garbled . . . our intentions misunderstood. What we *meant* to say is not always what they *heard* us say. There are proven methods to improve communication, and for the sake of peace they should be given more attention in today's troubled world.

While technological aspects of communication have advanced by leaps and bounds, the more subtle, social factors have been left far behind. World Educator Prachoomsuk Achava-Amrung observes social scientific factors in communication technology, namely languages that link communicating parties, and an act of will to cooperate and understand.

These are the aspects of communication that deserve considerable attention today in order to bring peace to the world. Educators and psychologists should play a more active and constructive part in language learning, for abstract words like "human rights" and "democracy" lack clearly defined concepts and hence are not easily put to practice. Both fields — Education and Psychology — can also help toward developing an attitude against discrimination in all forms, as well as creating a psychological state of acceptance among all types of audiences. The teaching of history in particular should neither arouse one's feelings of hatred and vengeance, nor destroy one's national or cultural pride.

Global telecommunications. Telecommunications technology is quickly leading us to a digital world of bits, bytes and formatted data transmitted as tens of thousands of light bursts per second and streaming through optical fibers among telephones and computers in homes, stores, offices and classrooms around the world. In a matter of years you will probably have (if you haven't already) a telephone and personal computer, interconnected — maybe even built into the same cabinet — sitting together on a table or desk at home.

This is your electronic link. Through it you have instant access to an ocean of human knowledge — library books, current events, college courses, medical breakthroughs . . . not to mention conversations with friends and loved ones.

But before that can happen, a global transformation, now underway, must be completed. There are new networks to be built, old networks to be completely restrung with glass cable replacing the expensive old copper wires, new telephones and desktop computers to be designed which are inexpensive and easy to use.

And it all must take place in an orderly fashion . . . in such a way that when the global network is complete and operating, all parts are compatible. What good is a global communication network if the people and computers can't all talk to each other?

The article by Keith Clarke and Jon Chidley of British Telecom give readers a taste of what is just around the corner in the world of telecommunications, with special attention given to the "ISDN" standards that are now being developed by an international body to ensure that the global network now under construction grows in an orderly, compatible fashion.

Even readers with no technical background will draw a general impression of this global project that will soon greatly enhance our lives.

Chapter 1
The Way of Meditation

by Jan van der Linden
Director, School for Esoteric Studies
New York, NY, USA

Background. Has been involved since 1945 in in-depth study of metaphysics and spiritual wisdom, as well as with the social psychology of industrial life. Spent 25 years in corporate management training and development in The Netherlands. Studied psychosynthesis with Roberto Assagioli, Italy. Co-founded a worldwide meditation group focused on spiritual laws and right human relationships. Since 1976, active full-time in the field of spiritual development, guiding an international program of training through correspondence.

His article. There are proven, effective methods to free up the communication paths between our conscious and unconscious minds. If we are to achieve peace in our world, we must first find peace within ourselves . . . and one step in that direction is to clear out the psychological, emotional and spiritual blocks that cause most of our internal conflicts and frustrations, while responding to the light, love and wisdom of our higher self. There is perhaps no more effective way to do that than to embark on a program of daily meditation. Truths found deep within can be used to improve the outside world.

Through meditation one may feel better, one may feel "high," one may stand in the light . . . but that is not the final goal. Those who are beginning to contact their souls will face the question: How can we make use of what we have seen?

The Way of Meditation

by Jan van der Linden

*T*he Western world in the last few decades has shown a growing
interest in meditation. This could be explained as a result of greater
contact between East and West. Some eastern teachers, such as the
Maharishi Mahesh Yogi, have indeed done much to popularize the
idea of meditation in the West, not only with the "hippies" (starting
with the Beatles) but with other categories of people as well.
However, the deeper approaches, as practiced in the more esoteric
groups, are receiving increasing interest too. In addition, meditation
has become the subject of scientific (i.e., psychological and
physiological) investigation in universities and other research
institutes.

There are two major reasons for this development. First, there is the
inner need. We are discovering that we are more than we seem to be.
A whole part of our inner being is still unknown; why should we cut
ourselves off from it? Just as we have begun to explore outer space,
we have a need to explore our inner space. Also, as human beings we
possess higher faculties and powers within ourselves, higher
possibilities which we want to explore and use. We always (generally
speaking) tend to actualize ourselves as fully as possible; we have an
inherent human need to "fulfill" ourselves. Through meditation we
find a way to be more truly ourselves.

Secondly, there is a very real *outer* need for meditation in the world
today. Looking at our present international problems, the difficult
situations in our society and the big questions to be solved in
economic, political and other fields, it is quite clear that these cannot
be dealt with adequately from the level of the rational mind only.
Many begin to realize that we need to go beyond that, we need
another dimension to our thinking in order to find the wisdom to
solve these problems.

Perhaps this second reason, the demands of our outer world for a truly creative response, relates more clearly to the theme of this book. However, the inner and the outer worlds as well as our inner and outer needs cannot really be separated. Before elaborating on meditation as a path to creating a more peaceful world, we must go a little further into investigating the inner need first.

Meditation: Toward More Complete "Being"

There is a tendency in modern man to think that we are no more than that which we are consciously aware of in our rational mind: our body, our feelings, emotions and thought life. However, depth psychology (Freud and others) has made it clear that, as with an iceberg, the largest part of our nature — our *unconscious* — is invisible, yet it influences our acting and thinking in many ways, often more than we realize.

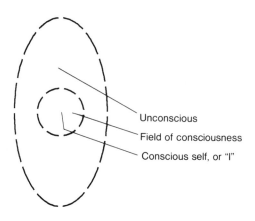

Unconscious

Field of consciousness

Conscious self, or "I"

Our conscious being is embedded as it were in a much larger, unconscious part of our nature. This may reveal itself through the symbolic language of our dreams, for example, and through the often unexplained impressions and impulses that affect us from "inside." The parts of ourselves that we deny or do not admit entrance into our consciousness (because we fear them, or don't know how to cope with them) are continuing their existence "invisibly" nevertheless. Thus, what is drawn in this diagram as a little dotted circle around the "I" can, through repression and a "shutting off" of oneself, easily become a "closed" line, blocking the harmonious communication with one's deeper nature or with large parts of it. It should be stressed, however, that what is commonly "repressed" does not just concern our sex drives or our libido (as Freud emphasized) but can also be our feelings (the feminine aspect in man, for example), our religious nature, our creative urges and our intuitions.

Roberto Assagioli, M.D., the father of psychosynthesis, has made a helpful distinction between different levels or regions of the unconscious, as in the following diagram:[1]

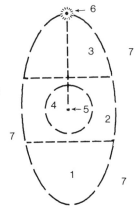

1. Lower unconscious
2. Middle unconscious
3. Higher unconscious, or superconscious
4. Field of consciousness
5. Conscious self, or "I"
6. Higher self
7. Collective unconscious

The *lower unconscious* is related to the functioning of our biological life; it contains our fundamental drives and primitive urges; also many complexes, pathological urges, phobias, etc.; it is the source of our dreams and imaginations of an inferior kind.

The *middle unconscious,* directly surrounding our field of consciousness, consists of those psychological elements which are of the same kind as our daily awareness and can easily be recalled by our conscious mind. It is the inner region where our various experiences and thought activities are digested and assimilated.

The *higher unconscious* is the area from where we receive our intuitions, inspirations, enlightenments, heroic impulses; it is the source of the higher feelings, such as altruistic love; also of genius. This region is sometimes called the "super-conscious," for it is felt to be "beyond" our conscious range, containing elements we have not yet fully and consciously mastered, but toward which we are growing and into which we seek to penetrate. It is this area to which Abraham Maslow refers as "the farther reaches of human nature."[2] In terms of human evolution one could say the lower unconscious represents the past, the middle unconscious the present and the superconscious the future — that which is still to be.

High up in the region of the superconscious abides the higher Self. The dotted vertical line linking the personal self to this higher center symbolizes the way of ascent.

Glimpses of this area of the higher unconscious and of our true Self come to us usually only in "peak-experiences" — those higher moments of realization, of love, of wisdom, strength, insight, beauty, creativity. Such peak moments come to us as a gift, a "grace." However, there is a *path* upwards, and the *outstanding way to deliberately communicate with and raise our consciousness into our higher nature is meditation.*

Meditation indeed is our "Jacob's ladder," the way by which to ascend to the world of meaning, and the approach to contact the higher, true Self or Soul. It makes it possible then, to see ordinary life from the viewpoint of that Self, and in its light, with the beneficent and liberating effects this has to our insight, understanding, and life. Meditation implies developing the mind in such a way that it opens itself to its higher dimension which functions normally in these higher regions — the higher mind and intuition.

Meditation, in this sense, is more than just stilling the mind or finding inner peace — although these aspects are part of its practice. The first step is always right preparation: quieting the body, the emotions and the mind, and aligning them as far as possible with one's inner being, the Self. Pure stillness and full presence to oneself! Then, through concentration on a well chosen "seed thought" for example, the meditator gradually seeks to penetrate into the deeper meanings behind the words — first through reflective meditation, then "receptive" meditation and, ultimately, that deeper stage of contemplation which essentially means viewing from the angle of the true Self.

It is not possible on this "way upward" to climb immediately to the top of the mountain, but there are several plateaus in between from where one can have a wider look-out than from "below." If a regular practice of meditation is established, more and more often such vistas give one the reward of new insights of "truth, goodness and beauty," to be carried back to daily life. The realization dawns that the closer we come to our true Self, the closer we are to all; for (as Maslow pointed out so clearly), in that point of being where we are most uniquely and fully ourselves, we know ourselves at the same time to be one with all others, and the dichotomy disappears.[3] True *group consciousness* therefore is experienced on this level of the higher Self. It is from this center that the illusion of alienation and separation falls away and that a more inclusive way of thinking and being begins to influence the life of the individual. Looking beyond again, the Self or Soul is also that "divine spark" in the human being which knows itself to be part of a greater Whole and can relate to the Divine.

It is not possible in the scope of this article to go further into detail about the practice of meditation — how to learn its skills and avoid its pitfalls. There are training courses and good books that can give guidance, according to the different background and motivation of the student. Some recommended books are by Alice A. Bailey[3], Michal J. Eastcott[4], and Robert Leichtman, M.D. and Carl Japikse[5].

Two aspects of meditation however will be considered more closely here, because they are the consummating stages which give meditation its meaning in creative living and bring it into the category of service to humanity. These stages are those of *illumination* and *precipitation*.

The Physiological Side of Meditation

The brain operates at different speeds, from very slow during a deep sleep, to very fast when we are excited. Measured in cycles per second (cps), brain activity is often classified as follows:

BRAIN SPEED	MENTAL STATE	
	NICKNAME	COMMON NAME
2-4 cps	Delta level	Deep sleep
4-7 cps	Theta level	Normal sleep
8-13 cps	Alpha level	Unconscious dream state
14-25 cps	Beta level	Awake
30-50 cps		Hysteria
50+ cps		Psychosis

Normally when the brain slows down to speeds less than 14 cycles per second, the conscious mind switches off and we fall

Illumination and Precipitation

What is meant by illumination? A few points could be made that might help to convey the idea, though words are very limiting to describe what is happening.

First, illumination occurs in *various degrees*. It not only refers to that enlightened state of being that may finally be achieved after a life of spiritual aspiration and struggle (such as when we speak of a person who is "illuminated"), but it also is that brief flash of light which may enter or pour into the mind during meditation and by which Reality is seen in true undistorted perspective. At such a moment it is as if the sun breaks through the fog and clear sight suddenly replaces the partial or distorted view.

asleep. Physiologically speaking, meditation is simply the practiced skill of preserving a degree of conscious thought as the brain slows down; instead of entering a sleep state, we enter a meditative state, and a number of changes take place in our bodily routines, such as breathing.

So, the trick with meditation is to slow the brain down without nodding off . . . while staying somewhat alert. Usually all it takes is relaxing the body and clearing the mind, then the brain slows down by itself. These simple steps can be used:

•Get comfortable in a sitting or lying position and close your eyes.

•Starting at the toes and working slowly upward to the top of your head, concentrate on relaxing all your muscles.

•Clear your mind of random thoughts. This is sometimes easy, sometimes difficult. It may help to count slowly, silently backwards from 50, or visualize a pleasant situation like a sunset, or repeat a relaxing phrase such as, "slow, smooth, relaxed; slow, smooth, relaxed . . . ."

Benefits of meditating once or twice a day include diminished stress, a more relaxed demeanor, improved intuition and insight, more reliable "hunches," a higher proportion of correct decisions, better organized thought processes, a capacity to sense when others are troubled (and why), and much more . . . all the result of cleared communication paths between the conscious and unconscious mind.

— *Adapted from existing Earthview Press publications.*

Technically speaking, illumination is the *result of contact* with the higher Self or spiritual being, the Soul, in which is light. The Soul is light and so, if in meditation one approaches the Soul, there might come a flash of contact giving the experience of standing in a totally new light, different from that of intellect or of normal thinking.

This conscious contact with our true Self or transpersonal being can be developed through a regular practice of meditation. At first it may be rare — just a brief flash — but later on, as one progresses on the path of meditation and consequent service, this contact may gradually become more frequent. It can then be "induced" and become more permanent.

Second, illumination can take place on *various levels* of our inner nature. It can occur in the emotional nature, which is our life of desire, feelings, and aspiration, but it can also primarily affect our mental nature. The results of the two are different, and they can happen in combination, too. If illumination takes place on the emotional level, it gives that wonderful experience described by many mystics as the transcendence of all desire, a surrender of all personal selfishness and of all personal ego. One is raised *inwardly* to a level where there is union with all. There is a realization of love and compassion. In mystical literature there is much testimony of a sense of exaltation, of mystical ecstasy. All this is the result of illumination on the level of the emotional life, the feeling or desire life.

On the mental level illumination is realized as the irradiation of the mind, and this is happening increasingly through our modern meditation practices. It means an enlightenment of the intellectual nature and thinking; showing all previous thinking to be only preliminary and partial in comparison with the flood of light coming in. It is here that there can be true intuition — a seeing of things in their wholeness, not limited by time and space. One is perceiving things not in a logical sequence as in ordinary thinking, but all at once, in a synthetic and comprehensive way.

Abraham Maslow found that in the "peak experience" there is a totally new way of cognition, which he calls "Being-cognition."[6]

It is impossible to describe fully what illumination is, but here, the more important question is: What does it lead to? What comes after? Is the receiving of light, is illumination, the final goal in meditation? One may also ask: What are we really meditating for? Is our aim to bathe in light for our own pleasure? Is it to find salvation? Is it to find a place where we would like to be eternally? Of course, through meditation one may feel better, one may feel "high," one may stand in the light. This certainly is all in the process, but is it the final goal? To be sure, from the angle of the higher Self it is NOT the goal at all. It is not the end — it is only the beginning, because light is the normal state of the true Self or Soul, and illumination means that one is nearing the region where one is the true Self. Thus, in the light we begin to function as the Soul.

Of course, from the point of view of the "little" personal self, one may consider illumination as the end. It *is* the end in a very literal sense, because the personal self seems to be ended, seems to be transcended; it ceases to be the center of the universe. It gives way to another center where one is much more truly "oneself."

What then is the work that comes next, after reaching — perhaps momentarily — that flash of light? One may remember that Buddha, after achieving illumination, went back to the world and gave out a new teaching. He served the world with the fruits of his illumination; he showed man the cause of suffering and he taught the noble eightfold path. Another ancient example, Moses, went up the Mount of Sinai, where he experienced the light, the countenance of God. However, he did not sit there in idleness nor did he come back with empty hands to the people of Israel. Indeed he brought them the Ten Commandments — the laws for their social and spiritual life.

Thus today, all who have learned to work deliberately and knowingly toward the "light," and who are beginning to contact their Souls, will face the question: How can we make use of what we have seen? How can it be made effective and practical to others?

This brings us to the next stage, which could be called the work of *precipitation.*

We find that what is realized "in the light" is of a different, more subtle, nature than what is experienced in everyday life where things are more concrete, more dense. Often it is found to be very difficult to convey to the world of daily life what has been realized in that peak moment of light. In trying to explain to other people, the chances are that they cannot understand. Many who have had great and revealing experiences of light have found themselves unable to express to others what they have seen. Some, then, may fall into the trap of isolating themselves with their experience, separating themselves within a little circle which they think is their new world. But such a reaction, of course, is of no practical value and will only create another problem. In fact, it should be realized that one has *omitted* a stage of meditation, and not done the whole job!

The difficulty of this stage, as we have seen, is that on that higher level there is a different "wave length" in comparison to our ordinary way of thinking and our ordinary way of living and speaking to each other. It is as if we have contacted a high voltage power, while in our normal homes we can only use a lower voltage electrical current. What is needed therefore is a transformation of the energy; we have to step it down from that high voltage level to the understandable and practical lower voltage use of the ordinary plane. We have to "bring it down" from the level of subtlety to the level of increased density. And for this process the word "precipitation" is a very apt word.

What has been seen in the light, in meditation and in the peak moment of deep being, is in fact formless, intangible, abstract. What is needed is the added mental work of letting it precipitate into the alert, concrete mind as concepts and practical truths that can be used in daily life and in any field of service one finds oneself engaged in.

This "downward approach" of seeking to "ground" and make of practical value the results of deeper insight reflects a major cultural-spiritual change at this time. "Spiritual" life during the past 1500 or 2000 years has emphasized first of all a rising upwards, symbolized by the towering spires of our gothic cathedrals. "If you want freedom, . . . flee the world and seek God," as Guido Gezelle, a Flemish mystical poet expressed it. The emphasis however seems to be changing in this century to a more downward direction: rather than on rising to heaven, there is a focus on bringing paradise *on earth*. As a potent modern invocation has worded it: "Let Light and Love and Power restore the Plan *on Earth.*" While the past era has produced and strengthened the higher vision, the next stage and emphasis may well be to bring that vision to manifestation, here and now. "Bring down to earth what you have seen in heaven" is therefore a very apt keynote for meditation today.

Also, for meditation to be a safe and psychologically healthy process, it is desirable that it is accompanied by a life of service. This will insure that the energies invoked through meditation will find an outlet, and overstimulation or mental indigestion will be avoided. At the same time, the intention to serve provides the right motive for the practice of meditation. How rightly it has been said: "The way to the inner sanctum is the way of outer service."

Meditation for the World We Live In
Now let us consider the objective need for meditation in relation to our present world situation. I would like to give a few practical examples to illustrate what forms such meditation may take.

Meditation and the resolution of conflict. Our world today is in a state of flux. Great changes are taking place — and are needed in response to new emerging realities. The unparalleled acceleration of technological development has brought to the foreground the actual global interdependence of humanity. However, the lagging behind of moral vision and of education in large parts of humanity has created enormous tensions and conflicts. These tensions in themselves are a healthy reaction for they stimulate the attainment of greater consciousness and vision. Our natural longing for peace should not make us fall into the trap of merely "wishing these conflicts away" and seeking to restore the comfort of the status quo. Conflict, through all evolution, has been an impetus for change and growth.

A *spiritual approach* to the conflict (such as through meditation) therefore accepts the fact of tension between polar opposites, but then seeks to raise the level of its resolution to a point beyond them.

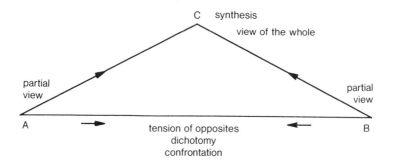

Instead of confrontation between the opposites A and B on their existing "horizontal" level — which usually would mean a seeking of mutual annihilation — there will be a search upward for a viewpoint that is more inclusive. This will imply, for instance, the renouncing of mere physical plane confrontation and focussing the consciousness on a more creative, mental level. The synthesis (C) (sought for often only under great pressure) is to be found by *rising* beyond old levels of thinking. It will be clear how *meditation* can be of help here in "holding the issue in the light." If enough thinking people will take an objective stand, and in the silence of their meditative thought bring the principles of the higher realm to bear upon the conflict, the greater vision will emerge with more strength and will ultimately prevail.

As an example, with regard to conflict between the two big power blocs (A and B), dealing with it merely on its outer material level (i.e., the horizontal line) means being preoccupied in thinking only of arms versus disarmament, war versus enforced peace — without resolving the basic conflict.

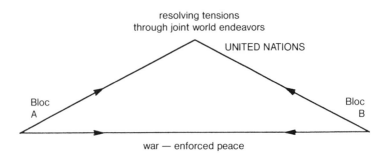

resolving tensions
through joint world endeavors

UNITED NATIONS

Bloc
A

Bloc
B

war — enforced peace

The cry for peace on this level is no more than a fear cry to escape war. Meditation can bring in the higher vision needed to focus a *spiritual cry* in a demand for the fuller life of all. Such vision could imply, for example, finding a common human goal so inspiring that both might be able to meet on more creative levels, thus transmuting aggressive emotions and fear.

Gandhi, when asked by a Quaker about his view of the religious tensions in his country, indicated that the only way to have them not destroy each other is to have them cooperate toward a common social goal.

Perhaps one could say that *meditation* is the vertical dimension of *mediation*. The "way out" often proves to be the "way up."

Meditation for the United Nations. The UN was founded on the basis of the belief that our only future is a united future. In the global age which is upon us, the need for a global management of world affairs demands to be met, and in this respect the UN has already accomplished much of great value. The conflicts of interest between power blocs, however, threaten to destroy the UN and its vision, and hence the great need for those who think more inclusively to hold in the light the original purpose of the UN. This means, in fact, to meditate on it and on the underlying principle of cooperation and to strengthen and refine the thoughtform in which the UN as an entity expresses itself.

Such groups as "Campaign for UN Reform," several UN Associations, and "Friends of the UN" are addressing this need. The positive thought and meditation of millions of people who hold the idea of the UN close to heart is invaluable to counterbalance the doubts and scepticism of those who are at present imprisoned in predominantly national, selfish thinking. In a paper, titled *The Inner Life of the United Nations*[7], I have stressed this need in greater detail, pointing also to the evolutionary reasons for strengthening the idea of the UN.

Meditation Group for the New Age. Since 1960 a worldwide project of "unanimous and simultaneous" meditation is carried forward under the above name by people in many countries. (Guidelines are available in seven languages.) Participants seek to think through and "anchor" in the human consciousness some of the higher laws and principles that should govern our life in the coming era, i.e.: the law of right human relations; the principle of goodwill; the law of group endeavor; the principle of unanimity; the law of spiritual approach; the principle of essential divinity.

Instructions and practical outlines for meditation are given in three one-year courses, written in western, psychological, and easily understandable language. The laws and principles mentioned above are taken as themes for meditation.

"Peace" in the view of this group is a *result* of bringing about right human relationships, and for these to be created *goodwill* is the essential principle by which it can be done. The sequence: (1) goodwill, leading to (2) the establishing of right human relations, leading to (3) peace, offers a sound psychological and creative approach for action. Goodwill has been called *the active principle of peace*. Inquiries about this meditation project can be addressed to: MGNA, P.O. Box 566, Ojai, CA 93023, USA; and Sundial House, Nevill Court, Tunbridge Wells, Kent TN4 8NJ, England. Correspondence addresses for Dutch, French, German, Italian and Spanish languages can be obtained there as well.

Triangles. This worldwide activity has been in existence since 1938. Groups of three people (not necessarily living in the same town or country) link up mentally with each other every day in a moment of quiet reflection, sending light and goodwill through their "triangle" into the world. They use *invocation* to spiritually empower this work. As most members are forming more than one triangle, a network of light and goodwill is spreading over the globe, creating a "lighted" and psychological atmosphere which will support all other constructive efforts of world service. (Inquiries: Triangles, 113 University Place, 11th Floor, New York, N.Y. 10003; or 3 Whitehall Court, Suite 54, London, England SW1A 2EF; or 1 rue de Varembe (3e) Case Postale 31, 1211 Geneva 20, Switzerland.)

Additional meditation activities could be listed but the above few may suffice to illustrate how meditation can be a way of inner action to bring the potency of higher spiritual energies and values to bear upon world progress. It is an inner way of adding support to all constructive forces.

Reaction against the light. Finally, there is one point which I would like to touch upon in connection with meditation. It will be clear that meditation is more than just a current vogue, more than a mere technique for feeling better. It is an undertaking of the "whole" person — and this has certain consequences which have to be faced. It will be found, for example, that the light one is trying to "bring down" may not always be received with gratitude, or appreciated by everyone. Even bringing new ideas which can potentially solve great problems may cause temporary resistance and antagonism in reactionary people as many world servers have found. This is not new; Christ already said that he did not come to bring peace, but the sword — that is, the sword of the spirit.

And this can be true also in another way, when the field of application is not an outer field of service, but our own individual lives. We can, and should apply to ourselves what we see in the light. We can, in meditation, gain totally new knowledge about ourselves; we may also see with totally new eyes parts of ourselves which are hindrances to growth. The light may reveal to us not only our true essence, but also our weaknesses. This might cause rebellion in us and even fear. We fear the consequence of really having to work at these limitations, of transmuting them within the light, and of overcoming selfishness. But this is exactly the creative work one can perform on oneself! It surely requires the courage to take risks and the persistence to follow through; these are the opposites of the love of comfort and safety. The latter can be a defense mechanism of those who fear growth. As Krishnamurti once said: "Comfort and safety are the graveyards of the soul."

Frank Haronian, in a paper titled *The Repression of the Sublime* [8] dealt very aptly with this fear of growth, the fear of the consequences of light. The sublime (which is the region of the higher unconscious) can be threatening to those who fear to live in accordance with it. Repression of one's "higher" nature may cause what Maslow interestingly called the "Jonah complex." [9] Jonah, in the Old Testament, received a prophetic vision, he had to give out a message to the people of Nineveh. But he was fearful and resistant, preferring to stay where he was. He denied the task and thus got into trouble! The Jonah complex, therefore, might well be the fate of those who prefer the comfort of letting things stand as they are to being true to their deeper selves.

The healthier reaction, however, is to work creatively with what is seen "in the light," trying to make it useful and applicable to one's field of service. This can give great inner joy. It is, in fact, participation in the great task of aiding evolution. It was Pierre Teilhard de Chardin who emphasized the fact that only now in the history of humanity can man begin to cooperate consciously with the forces of evolution. Man can consciously touch, and mentally recognize some aspects of the divine Plan and pattern; and then, in accordance with it, he can work creatively to manifest it. Ultimately, if there is a divine Plan for humanity, it will have to work out through humanity itself. And how could this be possible except through the use of our enlightened minds, loving hearts and firm wills? In this period of time, therefore, the processes of illumination and precipitation are of great significance. Through them we can aid in bringing to manifestation a more harmonious world, a more enlightened new age. Today, new qualities and new trends of life are only waiting to be precipitated.

For those who have their eyes open to the world problems of today, there is the impetus as well as the challenge to seek and precipitate the new ways and patterns of life.

Notes

1. Roberto Assagioli, M.D.: *Psychosynthesis,* 2nd Ed., Viking Press, N.Y. 1965

2. Abraham Maslow, *The Farther Reaches of Human Nature,* Viking Press, N.Y. 1971

3. Alice A. Bailey, *From Intellect to Intuition,* Lucis Publishing Co., N.Y. and Lucis Press Ltd., London

4. Michal J. Eastcott: *The Silent Path,* Rider, London.

5. Robert Leichtman, M.D. and Carl Japikse: *Active Meditation, The Western Tradition,* 1982, Ariel Pres, Columbus, OH.

6. Abraham Maslow: *Toward a Psychology of Being,* Van Nostrand, U.S.A., Canada, England, Australia, 1968

7. Jan van der Linden: *The Inner Life of the United Nations,* 1984, School for Esoteric Studies, 40 East 49th Street, Suite #1903, New York, N.Y. 10017 (free pamphlet).

8. Frank Haronian, Ph.D.: *The Repression of the Sublime,* 1972 Psychosynthesis Research Foundation (pamphlet available at The Institute of Psychosynthesis, 1 Cambridge Gate, Regents Parks, London NW1 4JN, England

9. Abraham Maslow: *The Farther Reaches of Human Nature,* 1971, Viking Press, N.Y.

Chapter 2
Communication Education — A Key to Peace

by Prachoomsuk Achava-Amrung
Professor Emeritus, Chulalongkorn University
Bangkok, Thailand

Background. A world educator, teaching in Thailand since 1940. Among her overriding concerns: Better understanding among people and nations, through clearer communication. Selected by her peers for leadership positions in many world organizations of peace and education, she is the current president of the International Association of Educators for World Peace (IAEWP), a UN nongovernmental organization. Specializations include economics of education, research methodology, education statistics, educational evaluation and assessment, and science education.

Her Article. The psychological barriers to efficient communication and the role a healthy social attitude plays in mutual international understanding are observed. Communication depends on two inseparable components. One entails the many technological tools of communication which have been greatly advanced. The other involves the will and learned ability to communicate well . . . a field which has been left far behind, developing slowly. This today is at the core of world peace issues. Social scientists should be responsible for the rapid progress needed to cope with the highly sophisticated scientific and technological equipment in use today. Samples of case analyses are briefly discussed.

If desirable values are to be cultivated, they must be cultivated purposefully and systematically . . . incubated through social interactions.

Communication Education — A Key to Peace

by Prachoomsuk Achava-Amrung

*C*ommunication education holds great promise to all citizens of the world. The countless benefits should be made public to accelerate the development and wise use of new communication methods . . . to coordinate the efforts of all responsible people in cultivating our values for desirable, compatible behavior around the world : . . so that a peaceful future can be guaranteed.

This article combines some ideas of retiring UN Assistant Secretary General Robert Muller and some of my own ideas on how to promote better understanding of serious world communication problems that need to be solved as soon as possible. A world of international understanding is the only world of peace, and communication is the means to understanding.

The term *communication* in its broadest scope encompasses many activities . . . the transmission of information; books, newspapers and other paper works; transportation; postal service and the like.

Communication education will be a growing concern in the future, since the Science Revolution of the world, begun three centuries ago, has been steadily transformed into the Information Revolution during the end of our century.

Robert Muller has pointed out how science and technology have brought great advancement of communication technology to our world, for example the long-distance telephone, the rapid transit system, and telecommunications via satellite. When President Anwar Sadat was assassinated during the military parade in Egypt that tragic afternoon in 1981, the news could be broadcast to TV sets throughout the world that same evening.

Problems with communication inter-relation, transmission of information and good understanding occurred, but not because of the lack of sophisticated equipment invented by science and technology. Social factors or non-technological aspects of communication were (and throughout much of the modern world are still) to blame.

Communication depends on two inseparable components . . . hardware and software. Hardware is such instruments as telegraph equipment, telephones, satellites, and computers, all of which have already been efficiently developed. Software includes not only computer programs and operating systems inside the hardware but also the values within us, such as human language, the will and capacity to communicate, cooperation, and the desire to make peaceful interaction. The development of these human values is still far behind.

This is among the most crucial problems of progressive communication. The declaration of 1983 as World Communication Year by the United Nations was an effort not only to improve communication hardware but also to make people, especially social scientists, pay more attention to communication problems caused by social factors.

In Ireland, people are forbidden to listen to American broadcasting because of a government policy to preserve Irish culture. This is one of many examples in the modern world of a wilful act to obstruct fluid world communication. In communication there should be the act of will to communicate. This should be an inherent part of one's emotional make-up, or *affective domain* in psychological terms. Without well developed affective domain for communication, the advancement of scientific and technological instruments cannot be of any use. In short, the advancement of science and technology alone cannot foster successful communication.

Chapter 2
Communi-
cation
Education,
a key to
peace

The development of the affective domain is the concern of educators as well as psychologists. One of the most important functions and responsibilities of these two particular disciplines is promoting effective communication. Following are some of the major nontechnological factors involved in doing so:

Language Learning and Teaching

All of us should learn at least two languages, our native language and a widely used language accepted as one of the international languages. At the United Nations five languages are commonly used . . . English, French, Spanish, Russian, and Chinese. (German was considered an international language until World War II.)

Language teaching should gear towards understanding for communication purposes. In April 1982, UNESCO held a conference on Sanskrit language in Nepal since the language is the root of many other Asian languages. It was found that the language was primarily used for describing thoughts and mysteries of nature moreso than for basic communicative purpose, which is quite different from western languages. At present there are still many people around the world who do not really understand such concepts as human rights and democracy. Although these terms have been widely used, when it comes to some serious consideration, their concepts have never been clearly defined. So it is not surprising that social and political behavior in many parts of the world deviates from what really should be, by UN values. Thanks to Dr. Mrs. Walai Na Pomphechara, Associate Professor of the Faculty of Arts, Chulalongkorn University. She initiated a program to publicize the knowledge of Human Rights of the United Nations to Thai common people. Walai and her staff compiled such knowledge in simple, everyday Thai language, instead of the original legal language. They also used posters and cartoons teaching the concept in various near and far rural areas. This type of social work should be highly recognized.

Attitude Development

Social sciences, especially education, should help people develop *neutral attitude.* They should help people eliminate their prejudices, illusions, obstinacy, and aggressiveness, which are the major causes of bias in communication. These factors often distort the real information and make people perceive only what they want to perceive or what interests them. Psychologists call this *selective perception.*

The development of neutral attitude here also extends to cover the elimination of discrimination in such areas as race, religion, language, culture, class and status. By providing education to people to eliminate the basic source of discrimination, it can help create a new society — a society that will be ready to communicate and willing to cooperate. Neutral attitude can help bring more progress to our families, our communities, our nations and our world. In short, we all could live more happily together.

Psychological Communication

The development of neutral attitude mentioned above is in fact for people who are receivers of the message. They need to have readiness and a nonprejudiced attitude in listening to and perceiving information. But those who send the message need to have and apply psychological communication so that what they transmit can be effectively perceived by others. They have to make their receivers comprehend, accept, believe, and be ready to cooperate whenever it is needed. This, of course, is not an easy task. It requires a system of learning and cultivating to become a good sender of messages.

The preservation of Thai national independence during the era of Western colonization can be attributed largely to their skill in bargaining with the invaders, who had more advanced weapons and were far more developed economically than Thailand. In Thai literature there can be found many examples of clever and efficient ways of negotiation. Sawitree uses her expert skill in talking her opponent into giving back her husband's life, for example.

There are also some recent examples of the psychological communication skill of Thai people. On December 28, 1972, four Black September radicals, fully armed with weapons, had sneaked into the Israeli Embassy in Bangkok and surrounded the place, demanding the release of 36 Arab prisoners. The vice prime minister, Field Marshall Prapart Charusathien, conducted a psychological operation near the embassy. After 18 hours of negotiation, all the terrorists agreed to disarm and boarded the Thai aircraft to return to Egypt, accompanied by General of the Air Force Thawee Chulasapaya and Admiral Chadchay Chunhawan for their assurance. Thailand could cope successfully with the situation without any bloodshed. Other countries, when invaded by terrorists, employ weapons to deal with the dreadful situation, generally resulting in bloodshed and failure.

History Learning

For more than 30 years, educators have concluded from their observations that learning history, especially the history of war and the mobilization of people of different nations, tends to be the major cause of rekindling the dissension of the past to the younger generations. It can prolong the feeling of anger indefinitely. Since World War II, WCOTP and UNESCO have tried to improve the learning and teaching of history in school. It is not an attempt to distort or change any events in the past but only to inform the facts without encouraging any responsive feelings toward those events, such as memories that make the learners angry and eager for revenge. Or those feelings that make the learners feel inferior and lose the dignity of their country, race and culture. These often are characteristics of under-developed societies, which is both unfortunate and inappropriate. Teachers of history therefore must serve an important role in getting us ready to communicate in a new kind of society.

apter 2
mmuni-
cation
cation,
key to
peace

Peace Values Cultivation

In education, affective domain (attitude) and cognitive domain (knowledge) have been found by science educators to be two independent human qualities.

To cultivate affective domain is one of the most difficult educational tasks. Educators in the past had considered affective domain to be a by-product of concomitant forms of learning. But now there is a realization that these values are of equal or greater importance to the knowledge objective, or cognitive development, in young people. If desirable values are to be cultivated, they must be cultivated purposefully and systematically.

There is an old saying in English that "Attitudes are caught rather than taught." Attitudes and values in the affective domain are naturally incubated through social interactions, environmental contacts and modelling effects. Direct experiences in real life provide the most efficient development of affective domain.

Nonformal educational systems can be very successful in forming desirable affective domain in students.

There is an upward trend in using out-of-classroom activities in promoting peace values and peaceful attitudes. Direct experiences and academic freedom of independent studies are the main principles in guiding these activities. Out-of-classroom activities that nurture desirable personal values include:

•Student clubs (such as history, language, sport, and science clubs)

•School fairs and exhibition

•Student government

•Student camp or field trips

•Girl guide, girl scout or boy scout activities

•Student services to communities

These activities are quite familiar, because it is a fashion to organize them everywhere.

Many traditional educators who emphasize knowledge over attitude development may doubt the value of out-of-classroom activities in which cognitive development is not stressed. The doubts are not justified, because the true value of these activities lies in the development of a wholesome attitude.

School attention should be turned to organizing these activities and putting more emphasis upon value development, especially peace-oriented values and attitudes. And, of course, they require close supervision by competent teachers and school personnel.

In conclusion, Communication Education is a wise approach in bringing a peaceful future to the world by creating better international understanding. A world of international understanding is a world of peace.

Chapter 2
Communi-
cation
ducation,
a key to
peace

25

Chapter 3
On the Move Toward Worldwide Communication

by Keith E. Clarke and Jon Chidley
British Telecom
United Kingdom

Background. The authors represent two basic aspects of modern telecommunications — computers to process information (Mr. Clarke) and telephone networks to disperse it (Dr. Chidley). Both gentlemen have written many articles on international standards for telecommunications. Their expertise is in electrical engineering and computer science (Mr. Clarke), and pure mathematics (Dr. Chidley).

Their article. The various aspects of telecommunications — computers, digital phones, fiberoptics and the ISDN (Integrated Services Digital Network) international standard — are leading toward smooth global information exchange ... people-to-people, people-to-computers, and computers-to-computers. But several obstacles, such as the slowness of the international standards process, are in the way. (While some terms in this article may not be totally familiar to all readers, most are explained or used in a context which makes their meaning clear.)

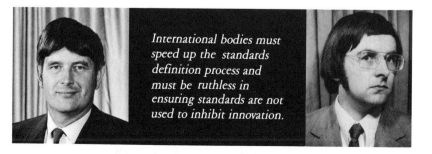

International bodies must speed up the standards definition process and must be ruthless in ensuring standards are not used to inhibit innovation.

On the Move Toward Worldwide Communication

By Keith Clarke and Jon Chidley

*T*he world is in the midst of a communication revolution led primarily by two trends in telecommunications — fiberoptics and international standards.

With fiberoptics and other technological innovations the trend is toward flexibility, further integration, and the ability to send oceans of information instantly. With the move toward increased standardization we will see the growth of telecommunication systems guided by international and global interests more than by national concerns as computers built, programmed and operating anywhere in the world may someday be able to communicate smoothly over fiberoptic telephone lines with any other computer in the world.

The most profound change in global communication is the quickening pace toward the use of optical fibers to replace copper wires. The UK, like other modern nations, is preparing for a complete overhaul of its communication networks — a conversion from the old analog equipment and copper wires to the new digital networks of fiberoptic cables. The new network, being introduced initially as an overlay, was scheduled for completion last year (1986). In the following two years it is planned to increase the capacity available to a level that will permit the total replacement of the existing analog network so that by 1990 the British Telecom trunk network will be 100 percent digital.

Why Fiberoptics?
Optical fibers are free from electromagnetic interference, small and, if well constructed, impervious to water. Taken together, these qualities mean that optical fiber cables can be installed at relatively

low cost in a variety of locations, such as sewers, canal beds, electricity pylons and lift shafts where the old-fashioned copper cables could not go.

Fiberoptics has other advantages:

•Light is a "cleaner" carrier than electricity, producing less noise.

•High voltage and heat, which are self-destructive elements of electrical wiring systems, are not part of the fiberoptic systems.

•Light spans more frequencies than electricity, which means more information packed into each transmission.

•Glass optical fibers are already cheaper than copper wire, and the price is still falling.

More "bits" of information are needed to send pictures than sounds. New techniques allow exploiting optical bandwidths with the sophistication currently applied to electrical and radio signals, and this will ensure an abundance of bit capacity at all levels of the global network. Overall, the development of fiberoptic networks and the optical devices designed to link up to them promise greater simplicity at lower costs.

The task of multiplexing and demultiplexing, for example (channeling many signals onto a single transmission path, and breaking them up again later), required complex circuits for electrical signals on copper wires, but for light transmission in glass lines multiplexers may become, in the words of one of our colleagues, "just like blocks of colored glass," and the most direct effect is likely to be further drops in transmission costs.

As optical fibers make large bit capacity substantially cheaper, the transmission of visual images and other large volumes of information becomes practical. We could see at the same time, reduced costs of computer terminals and computer link. The overall effect on the cost of telecommunication systems will be significant.

ISDN — Its Impact on the Evolving World Network

Perhaps no other industry uses more acronyms than the electronics industry in general, and the telecommunications industry in particular (simply to list the international organizations involved in some aspect or other of defining standards for the electronics industry can produce a wry smile — CCITT, CEPT, ECMA, CCIR, EBU, ISO, ILO, SEN/SENILEC) and one of the most popular acronyms of late is

ISDN, which stands for "Integrated Services Digital Network."

The ISDN is a set of standards now being developed by an international body (the CCITT, as a matter of fact) which hopes eventually to ensure compatibility among computer and telephone systems on an international basis.

As large organizations choose whether to acquire ISDN-compatible equipment and services, they will be considering three factors in addition to cost savings — compatibility with other companies, access to a variety of services, and more applications made possible by faster information transfer.

Compatibility. At present many of these companies use large, private networks, which depend on the fact that a large volume of information exchange occurs within companies. The trend is now picking up steam toward a substantial increase in the volume of

Fiberoptics and Standards

Our distant ancestors used crude vocalizations, clay tablets, and cave drawings to make their point. We today use telephones, computer display screens and televisions. Still, our basic modes of communication have remained the same down through the ages — speaking, writing and pictures.

One key to smooth worldwide communication will be getting our telephoned voices, our computerized data, and our video images all to blanket the globe in a smooth, dependable flow. We haven't long to wait; the stage is now being set. AT&T, British Telecom, and the other major national and international telecommunications companies are now stringing underground, undersea optical fibers around the world, linking continent to continent. Each fiberoptic cable can carry 1.7 billion bits of information per second, so that the entire Encyclopedia Britannica could be transmitted word for word, from one city to another, in two seconds.

Engineers can now break voices, data and video down into neat little "packets" of light bursts, so that it is no longer necessary to send voices on dedicated copper wires, computer data through dedicated modems, and TV broadcasts through dedicated metal cables or antennas. In the future all this

information exchanged electronically among companies as well. Electronic mail and message handling systems, Teletex and electronic funds transfer are likely to trigger a flood of intercompany information. ISDN promises to make the transition a smooth one.

More services. The term "Integrated Services Digital Network" conceals one of the main advantages to the customer, which is access to a variety of communication networks and services previously incompatible but now available through a single terminal or teleport, which is a box on the wall through which a customer can gain common access to the whole range of network services.

More applications. The higher bit rates available (more information per second) will facilitate a wide range of applications that are not economically feasible at present.

---

information will stream — as a series of energy packets — through glass optical fibers. You will be able to plug your telephone, TV and computer all into a single box on the wall — a direct link to a worldwide ocean of information.

Telecommunication standards are now being implemented at an international level to ensure a degree of compatibility among telecommunication companies and their burgeoning product lines.

Together these trends — fiberoptics, packet switching, and international standards — are pointing toward reliable, inexpensive communication everywhere in the world.

Third World Beneficiaries. As the global network emerges, poorest nations in the Third World may be at the greatest advantage. They can build fiberoptic networks almost from scratch, while industrialized countries face the tremendous task of replacing their extensive analog networks of twisted copper wires. Until that expensive undertaking can be completed, the richer countries are left to use a difficult hybrid of old copper networks interacting under serious limitations with the young, growing fiberoptic networks.

Chapter 3 n the move toward smooth worldwide communi- cation

— *Adapted from existing Earthview Press publications and from correspondence with several authors of this book.*

Some of the benefits made possible by these three factors of the ISDN are described below.

An Information Wonderland

Inexpensive Video Transmission. Slow scan TV equipment transmits still frames that change every 5 seconds from one location to another and can be used for security, traffic surveillance, distance

Some Issues Yet to be Resolved

If two people in the same household or two nations in the same world cannot or do not exchange ideas, information and feelings regularly, they gradually grow apart, and eventually become in some ways incompatible. While telecommunications technology seems destined to promote smooth worldwide communication in the coming years, a number of important issues have yet to be resolved.

Skills and attitudes. The most basic involves the concerns of Professor Amrung (Chapter Two): If two people do not speak the same language, or if they *do* speak the same language but lack the skills and attitudes involved in expressing themselves clearly and tactfully, technology cannot bridge the gap. People need to learn those skills and attitudes as a prerequisite to peace in their lives and in their world.

Who will regulate the information? As a world telecommunications network emerges, there will be political, social and economic issues to be resolved. For example, how and by whom should the oceans of information flowing throughout world society be regulated? Various nations, religions and organizations, and each individual, all might answer that question a bit differently. The free flow of information enjoyed by some modern countries (such as the USA) might pose a danger to more delicately balanced societies (say, in the communist bloc or in the Moslem world where society relies on regulated information for social stability and a reduced crime rate). It would be dangerous at this point in the development of humanity to assume that one approach to regulating information is better than another. We need to explore all current policies and observe the merits of each.

Meanwhile, perhaps the world network could develop in such a way that each individual, each organization and each nation or religion could tailor the information uniquely, within the

teaching, collaborative research and medical research. Entertainment-quality moving TV pictures require very high data rates beyond the range of the current ISDN standards, but that will no doubt improve in the future.

There are many applications where rapid access videotex frames

---

framework set by the higher levels.

That is similar to the approach taken today by most of the major telecommunications companies. They provide small networks (several hundred telephones and computer terminals hooked up to central computers) to companies, governments, hotels, schools, and other groups. Each of these networks can be tailored to the unique needs of the organization. Within that, each telephone and computer terminal can be further tailored to the specific needs of the individual who will be using it.

Carrying that philosophy to the global level — and carrying it carefully, with much discussion among today's diverse groups of people while it is happening — could provide the answer to the question, "How and by whom will world information be regulated?" Perhaps it will be regulated by people and groups at all levels, from personal to global . . . each person or group tailoring its own part of the system within the framework of the higher levels.

A comprehensive growth plan. Something still missing is a comprehensive plan to guide the growth of the emerging global communication network. Such a plan will require high-level, revolutionary ideas. For example, it might be decided to pattern a world network after the most advanced communication network ever known — the brain. An infant's brain is generously endowed with a rich surplus of neurons, and the entire package is "sculpted" according to what the baby sees and hears in the early years. The billions of unused neurons lie forever dormant. Perhaps the global network will be strung generously with a vast surplus of optical fibers in neatly patterned designs across the face of the globe, so that young, emerging nations, societies and social groups can use as much or as little of the network as they wish. The billions of unused lines could be activated later, as they are needed.

Chapter 3
'n the move
toward
smooth
worldwide
communi-
cation

— Adapted from existing Earthview Press publications and from correspondence with several authors of this book.

enhanced by high quality pictures would be valuable. These include estate and travel agencies, picture libraries, advertising, personnel identification, police and other security applications and signature verification. An additional bonus from the use of photographic techniques is the very low data entry costs for information providers and advertisers.

Advanced teletex terminals will be able to provide a "mixed mode" of operation in which facsimile images will be embedded in the text. This facilitates the display of company logos, letterheads, signatures and diagrams.

Text and Writing. Through ISDN transmission, pages of text are displayed in a fraction of a second so that when the customer is searching for data, pages can be changed very quickly. The effect is similar to that of flicking the pages of a book. This greatly speeds access to textual information particularly when it is arranged in alphabetical order.

If the reproduction of handwriting is required, the customer writes using a stylus on a digitized pad and the line thus formed is reproduced on the writer's screen and at the distant end simultaneously. Major applications include long-distance teaching and signature verification. The latter technique can be more reliable than existing methods since the computer will have available not only the final signature but also information on how it is formed.

A combined microphone and loudspeaker for simple voice communication between two meeting rooms can be augmented by graphics and text transmission: for example, a telewriting pad on which diagrams can be drawn with a stylus and reproduced in the other meeting room, VDUs enabling the transmission of text and fast facsimile. Image transmission might be by slow scan TV for remote diagnostics graduating into a full videoconferencing facility for the large customer.

Slow scan TV could be used in meetings to transmit still pictures or to inspect a piece of equipment for remote diagnosis of problems. Security monitoring, traffic surveillance, distance teaching and medical research are other applications.

Computer Applications. The sale and distribution of software to personal computers at home and in business, and to retail outlets, already takes place on either floppy disks or magnetic tapes moved physically. With the anticipated growth of personal computers in business and the use of professional-quality equipment in the home by "home-based knowledge workers," the rapid, error-free transmissions of longer programs will be required.

Manufacturing industries are adopting computer aided engineering (CAE) techniques to ensure the fast and economic introduction of many new products. Early schemes are often limited to a single site but the extension of the techniques within companies or among them will necessitate the transfer of large volumes of data.

Clearer Speech and Music. ISDN transmission facilitates high-quality speech, and this may itself be a saleable commodity for those requiring a premium-quality business service. Two lines, each carrying 64,000 "bits" of information per second, can provide stereo music, and this opens up the possibility of a high-quality sound "pay-per-listen" service comparable to the "pay-per-view" concept which is much discussed in the context of cable TV.

In many ways, the basic ISDN is best regarded as providing a more efficient and basically similar communication approach to that already existing in analog form.

Technical Hurdles Now Being Crossed

However, there are problems. The most basic is that the new equipment must interwork with the old over an extended period lasting for many years. An intermediate hybrid does expose problems that are more acute than either the purely analog or the purely digital situations. The obvious problem that can be minimized but not entirely overcome is that associated with transmission performance in this mixed environment.

But this problem of transition is only a temporary obstacle facing the development of a growing digital network that will link more and more people, organizations and nations for instantaneous exchange of ideas and information, anywhere in the world.

Obstacles to World Standards

Perhaps a more serious obstacle to the ISDN and a world communication network is a leeriness of standardization. There are some who see standards, even when presented as "recommendations," as restrictive. They are suspicious of bodies such as CCITT which they still see as "trade unions" of monopolistic-minded administrations. Certainly it is easy to highlight some real problems associated with the standards-making process. One can point out that the organizations consist of hierarchies of committees often five layers deep which meet, say, twice a year and at the higher levels work through translators. A recommendation which takes two

CCITT study periods (8 years) to complete may have had value for telephone administrations introducing equipment with a 30-year lifespan but is of little use to a TV manufacturer supplying the consumer market where products have a life of about six years.

Perhaps the most damaging argument against standards is the allegation that the standardization process can be used to inhibit innovation. If a nation or company presents a novel idea that carries them to the forefront of their competitive industry, their lead can easily be destroyed if standards are developed that are incompatible with their original innovation, thus putting all competitors back to the starting line.

But Standards Are Prevailing . . .

However there is another viewpoint. Seventeen years ago one of the authors was given the task of obtaining terminals to enable engineers to use the six computer time-sharing bureaus that had then just started operations in the UK. To the delight of the users, and to the considerable interest of computer designers of the day, it was discovered that a substantial majority of the services could be accessed from a single terminal. It had not occurred to computer designers, in the UK at least, that they could and should be designing to accommodate access from terminals other than those supplied by their company. The salesmen of the computer bureaus, who in those days usually provided the terminals on a rental basis, were perturbed because they had not considered the commercial implications of terminals maintained by their company being used by competing bureaus.

Two factors had contributed to the happy (from the user's point of view) situation. The first was the widespread popularity of the Teletype Corporation's Model 33 keyboard terminal. The other was the international standardization work that led to the definition of international code ISO7. Today, the basic issues remain identical although there has been an enormous increase in the number of technical parameters in the past 17 years. The fact that in many circumstances terminals can interconnect owes much to the painstaking work of the international standards bodies.

. . . At Least in Telecommunications

We can telephone all parts of the world and establish usable speech circuits but we cannot drive a vehicle around the world without encountering standardization problems associated with the position of the controls. Nor can we carry an electrical appliance, whether fitted with a plug or not, and use it on various continents.

The introduction of a liberalized telecommunications environment in the UK and other countries has highlighted rather than diminished the importance of standards. Some standards are a prerequisite if a customer with a choice of networks and multiple sources of equipment is to benefit from maximum interconnectivity. This is illustrated by cable TV in the UK which is being introduced on a geographically and technically fragmented basis but with the hope that it will contribute to the general communications infrastructure. Chances are limited unless the fragments can be made compatible.

The UK Department of Trade and Industry set up a body charged with making recommendations on standards (the Technical Working Group) and this found itself relying heavily on the basic groundwork laid by the international standards bodies.

Conclusions

We would draw several conclusions from all this. The role played by the international standards bodies is growing enormously as systems become more complex. They must speed up the standards definition process and must be ruthless in ensuring that it is not used to inhibit innovation. This may well imply departing from the tradition of consensus. Popular standards established by manufacturer dominance cannot and should not be ignored and should be offered an appropriate place in the standards scene.

With standards still evolving, how can decisions be made now as to what sort of equipment to purchase? That depends on the nature of what is being bought. For small investments on a customer's premises, where the anticipated life is four or five years, it is probably reasonable to buy the most cost-effective solution to the problem in hand whether or not this conforms fully to anticipated standards.

For telephone companies and others investing hundreds of millions of pounds or dollars in a national network, the importance of accurately intercepting standards that will have long validity is more important than ever. Telecommunications managers investing millions in computer and communications equipment on behalf of their company will increasingly be faced with difficult dilemmas.

Chapter 3
the move
toward
smooth
worldwide
communi-
cation

An interesting debate about standardization has emerged from the user and supplier communities concerned with the ISDN. On the one hand there are those who are advocating minimum standardization, a basic network terminating point and transparent channels to allow the maximum flexibility in equipment design which could perhaps result in customers being locked into a particular type of equipment. The other view seeks the higher levels of standardization which will permit the greatest compatibility within the network between differing types and makes of equipment. There needs to be a reconciliation between these viewpoints. Readers of this book who are also telecommunications users should take every opportunity to make their views known.

The standards bodies themselves have become aware of the importance of a wider input of users' views, and the International Telecommunications Union has instituted a series of conferences called "USERCOM." the first was held in 1985, in conjunction with the International Telecommunications Users' Group. Next is due in 1987.

Further information on the interaction between customers and telephone companies can be found in papers by author Clarke and others in the Proceedings of the Usercom Conference held in Munich, 17-19 September, 1985. Copies of these papers can be obtained from the International Telecommunications Union in Geneva and the International Telecommunications Users' Group.

Further information on the ISDN can be found in the Proceedings of several conferences organized by Online Conferences Limited.

A few passages have been borrowed with permission from the journal "Computer Communications" Vol 8 No 6 (December 1985) © Butterworth & Co (Publishers) Ltd 1985.

PART TWO:
WHO SHOULD REGULATE
WHAT?

*T*he most important question of this century may prove to be, "Who should regulate what?" This is the principal issue dividing the superpowers, one advocating fair regulation by a knowledgeable central government, the other favoring freedom for the people to decide. These opposite approaches to the regulation question are at the root of mistrust between the two nuclear blocs . . . and if anything would have triggered the unthinkable in the four decades following World War II, that probably would have.

Misconceived regulation may be the principal cause of unrest at *all* levels of society — the so-called "power struggles" in the business world, the tension generated as children test their parents' or teachers' authority in an endless quest for boundaries, border disputes between nations, the occasional flare-up between church and state in Christian democracies over such issues as abortion . . . the list is probably endless. It seems that whenever two or more people or groups get together there is bound to be some degree of tension until it is agreed-upon (whether in writing, or in oral consent, or intuitively sensed) who should regulate what.

Regulation plays such a prominent role in our moment-to-moment, day-to-day, era-to-era lives that we have come up with a wide assortment of terms for it — management, governance, administration, direction, supervision, oversight, ministration, disposition, officiation, directorship, leadership . . . and having all these different terms for essentially the same process does not make it any easier to decide who should decide or regulate what. The authors of Part Two combine many years of experience to provide some valuable answers.

Regulating ourselves. We look first at methods we can use to manage our own affairs. Archie Bahm, an authority on world religions, describes an age-old method people still use today to seek personal peace and contentment by regulating their own desires (which seem to be the culprits largely responsible for our frustration and unhappiness).

Levels of authority. Proceeding to higher levels of regulation, economist and Nobel laureate Jan Tinbergen shows the need for a hierarchy of authority from the personal level to the global level, and suggests a rule of thumb for deciding what particular level should act in a particular situation.

Regulating from space. Caesar Voute explores the role of space technology in helping to manage the affairs of earth. He is an author and professor at an international institute for aerospace studies.

World governance. Retired diplomat John Fobes observes the next big step toward world order — devising a framework of the world situation, its problems and their solutions.

Revitalizing the United Nations. Marc Nerfin and Hanna Newcombe, each well known among peace researchers, offer two different but compatible views on methods to streamline the world body that is having such a difficult time trying to manage world affairs.

Chapter 4
Personal Peace — The Need for Self-Control

by Archie J. Bahm
Professor Emeritus, Philosophy
Albuquerque, NM, USA

Background. A prolific author and foremost authority on religion and philosophy. Among his most noted books: *The World's Living Religions* (Dell). Founder of the Peace Union, an organization involved in monitoring, cataloguing, and integrating the efforts of international peace groups. Recently retired from a career in university education.

His article. Many years of deep research into the rich values of the world's religions have shown the author the means by which personal and social peace have been attained down through the ages. One principle has emerged, shining, which has been at the very core of Oriental values for 15 centuries to help make society peaceful. Although introduced to the Western world by the Christian, Moslem and Jewish religions, the principle of nondesire has somehow, to the misfortune of the industrialized world, become misplaced and tarnished in the shuffle of progress. For the sake of peace it must be found and polished to its original luster.

The principle of nondesire, like the other truly great, fundamental principles of science and religion, is perfectly clear and completely true in its simple, self-evident formulation.

Personal Peace — The Need for Self-Control

By Archie J. Bahm

While the most successful policies and practices for achieving personal peace should result from advances in contemporary psychology and psychiatry, and while too many doctrines formulated in the ignorance of ancient times persist as vicious religious fanaticisms instilling personal fears and triggering suicidal wars ... many ideas of long ago stand as timeless spiritual monuments, even today unsurpassed in their benefits and in their indispensibility in our quest for personal peace.

Granted that treatments for certain complex psychiatric diseases benefit from advances in psychochemical services not available long ago ... nevertheless some ancient capsules of wisdom on the fundamentals of human nature include psychological principles that still must be practiced by anyone who succeeds in achieving personal peace.

While acknowledging the wisdom of Lao Tsu,[1] Krishna,[2] Confucius,[3] Jesus,[4] Mohammed and the other great prophets, I select for this article instead the wisdom or "enlightenment" (bodhi or buddha) of Sidartha Gotama, c. 567-487 B.C., prince of the Shakya kingdom,[5] to exemplify ancient wisdom available today for those in search of personal peace.

Don't Desire the Unattainable

The teachings of Gotama, the Buddha, center about a single psychological principle which we all accept, once we understand it: "Desire for what will not be attained ends in frustration. Therefore to avoid frustration avoid desiring what will not be attained." The principle is both self-evident and verifiable in everyone's life. We need merely recall our own experiences of suffering frustration to recognize how true the principle is in explaining much of our own misery ... a childhood desire for a friend's toy, an adolescent desire for instant maturity and the respect that comes with it, an adult longing for a friend's spouse, envy of other people's lives ... examples are many.

The principle of nondesire, like the other truly great, fundamental principles of science and religion, is perfectly clear and completely true in its simple, self-evident formulation. So obvious questions arise ... such as why do people continue to be unhappy?

First of all, Gotama notes another psychological principle persistently operating in human nature. In actual practice, we all want more than we are going to get, at least a little more. Therefore everyone suffers, at least a little bit. This principle has been formalized in English translation as "The First Noble Truth: All is suffering." Unfortunately additional explanations intending to exemplify suffering of particular kinds — in birth, illness and death, for example — often obscure the fundamental universality of these principles.

How Can You Know?

There is a second question, always encountered then and now. "How can you know whether or not your desire is going to be satisfied or frustrated?" Even though we all learn from experience something about which kinds of desires can or cannot be satisfied, we also all have many desires whose outcomes are unpredictable.

Gotama, raised as an orthodox Hindu, was aware of the traditional view that, "Since desire is the cause of frustration, to avoid frustration avoid all desire." Traditional practices of yoga were all designed to eliminate desires completely. The final goal of life, moksha or mukti, can be achieved only by complete elimination of desire.

Chapter 4
Personal
Peace, the
need for
self-
control
But Gotama was aware of the paradoxical predicament that the desire to eliminate desires must itself be eliminated. He thus pursued many varieties of yogic austerities for seven years. His sudden insight (enlightenment, bodhi or buddha) that only unsatisfiable desires end in frustration and that therefore only unsatisfiable desires should be eliminated, contradicted the orthodox view so radically that he believed that his fellow peace-seekers would regard him as a crackpot. But having precommitted himself to share any findings with his fellows, he finally went to them and confessed. When the self-evident

truthfulness of his insight was recognized, he aroused some interest and soon found other monks (peace-seekers) following him.

How did he answer the question, "How can I know?" By asking another question involving a repetition of his first principle: "Do you want to know more than you can know? If so, then you are adding to your to-be-frustrated desires." Why, when you cannot be sure about whether your desire will be satisfied or frustrated, do you want to have more such assurance than you can have? If you avoid desiring more assurance than you can have, you will avoid at least frustrating this desire.

The Middle Way

His answer involves what has been called "the middle way," the way between avoiding excessive desire for the unattainable and avoiding the desire to avoid such excessive desire. Sound complicated? It's really not. It turns out to involve a willingness to accept things as they come without wanting them to be different than they are when they do come. This "middle way" has also been called, in translation, the Fourth Noble Truth."

Gotama illustrated the need for such willful acceptance by an example troubling people then and now: Is there or is there not a next life?

His answer:

"If you desire a next life and there is a next life, you will not be frustrated. If you desire no next life and there is no next life, you will not be frustrated. But if you desire no next life and there is a next life, you will be frustrated. And if you desire a next life and there is no next life, you will be frustrated. (So, if you desire either way, there is a 50-50 chance you will be frustrated.) What is important is not whether there is or is not a next life but whether you are willing to take which ever way it comes."

Although Gotama responded to questions regarding all disputed issues by interpreting them as examples involving excessive desire and refused to take sides on the issues themselves, his followers persisted in regarding their issues as important. The long history of Buddhist philosophy includes many towers of sectarian falsehood erected on an original foundation of truth. Even his earliest followers unintentionally distorted much of the significance of his "middle way" which was intended as a universal principle applicable to all desires, and thus to all kinds of desires.

Gurus, called upon to explain how it applied to all kinds of desires, found it convenient to resort to a traditional fingerable (eight-fingered) scheme regarding beliefs, attitudes, language, conduct, employment conscientiousness, self-regard, and meditation. Each area was embellished with additional examples, and the list of goodies was illustrated by examples from local mores and found useful in promoting moral education. The powerful appeal of interpreting life as purposeful led to interpreting the eight areas as "The Eight-Fold Path" to be taken stepwise, ending in "concentration," preparatory to moksha, and involving four additional more subtle steps, the fourth of which involved another four still-more-subtle stages. In this directional trafficking, much of the significance of the original "middle way" was lost . . . even its name was replaced. Many now remember "The Fourth Noble Truth" only as "The Eight-Fold Path."

Untangling the Misconceptions

Our concern here is not with the tangled history of misconceptions of Gotama's insight by hosts of authors regarding themselves as Buddhists, but with the availability of his principle for achieving personal peace today:

"If you want what you do not have, you are unhappy.
If you want what you are not going to get, you are going to be more unhappy.
Therefore, if you desire to be happy, desire to have what you have (your desire is already satisfied), and desire to have what you are going to have (you will have more satisfied desires)."

If you recognize the existence of another principle — to live is to desire, and you just cannot stop desiring even if you try — then, according to Gotama's principle, you would accept the desires that you have as a part of what you have.

This includes being willing to accept a degree of unhappiness. Being unhappy about your unhappiness simply makes you more unhappy. So recognizing that (according to the First Noble Truth), you are going to be at least somewhat unhappy simply because you are a desiring being and thereby desire more, at least a little more, than you have or are going to get.

Chapter 4
Personal
Peace, the
need for
self-
control

The goal of life is not perfect peace (complete desirelessness can be achieved only in death) but in as much peace as is possible. To want more peace than you are going to get is itself a cause of additional unpeacefulness. But if you believe that the chances of increasing peacefulness are greater when you put forth effort to achieve it, then this belief and desire are part of the way things are ... and your acceptance of them, and any prospects for failure as well as success, itself involves a kind or degree of peacefulness.

Notes:

The author extracted ideas for this article from several of his previous works:

1. "The intelligent man accepts what is as it is." *Tao The King by Lao Tzu*, p. 12. New York: Frederick Ungar Publishing Co., 1948.

2. "The wise worry about neither life nor death." *The Bhagavad Gita, or The Wisdom of Krishna*, p. 19. Bombay: Somaiya Publications, 1970.

3. "Treat each other person as you would be treated if you were that person." *The World's Living Religions*, p. 182. New York: Dell Publishing Co., 1964; Carbondale: Southern Illinois University Press, 1971. See also, The Heart of Confucius. New York/Tokyo: Walker/Weatherhill, 1960.

4. "Love casteth out fear." *The World's Living Religions*, p. 259.

5. *Philosophy of the Buddha*. New York: Harper and Brothers, 1958. Also, The World's Living Religions, pp. 98-104.

Chapter 5
Wise Management for a More Humane World

by Jan Tinbergen
Nobel Laureate, Economics
The Hague, The Netherlands

Background. Shared (with Ragnar Frisch) the first Nobel prize in
economics (1969). Many said he was worthy of the Nobel peace prize
as well. With intuition, research and a mathematical background, he
pioneered numerous theories, models, and principles on the
economic growth and behavior of nations, all based on an underlying
compassion, optimism, and love for humanity. Located intellectually
as well as geographically between the socialist and capitalist worlds,
he advocates a healthy compromise between centralized and
decentralized management.

His article. For the solution of all problems that humanity has to
face, a hierarchy of regulation is needed — from personal and local,
via national, to continental and world authorities. For each problem,
a level of decision-making exists that is optimal. This level should be
1) the lowest possible, but 2) high enough that the interests of all
affected by the decision are represented fairly. Most decisions can be
made at a low level (personal or local). The high-level decisions
deserve our utmost attention in this crucial era.

*We are used to giving top priority to
choosing the type of social system we want
to live in. That must change. Nuclear
weapons and a deteriorating global
ecosystem force us now to adjust our
priorities, or no human society may be
left to inherit a better social system.*

Wise Management for a More Humane World

by Jan Tinbergen

The decision structure of our planet is a very complicated structure, shaped by numerous forces which have operated during longer or shorter periods of history. Decisions are taken at all levels, from the family or company level, upwards to municipalities, provinces or cantons, and the state or national level.

At each of these levels we find numerous institutions. Municipalities may decide on schools for elementary and secondary education, but the state on universities or schools for higher vocational education. State-level ministries generally decide on problems of agriculture, transportation, and taxes, and formulate regulations on schooling. Some nations are *federations* of states, for instance the USA ("United States of America"), or the USSR ("Union of Socialist Soviet Republics"). This means that above the state level there is a *federal level*. The central banks in the USA are also organized at that level in the Federal Reserve System.

In the course of history many nations have come into existence, particularly during the *decolonization* process of the 1950s when some 120 new nations have come into existence. They are all members now of the United Nations. Among the 159 members there are very *large* ones, such as China, with about a billion inhabitants, or India with half a billion. There are also small nations, such as some Caribbean islands, or Surinam, or Luxemburg, with a few hundred thousand inhabitants.

What history has left us does not look very appropriate from a *managerial point of view* and it may be worthwhile to ask ourselves whether better patterns can be suggested. All the 159 members consider themselves to be *sovereign* nations and are very proud of being sovereign. For the solution of many problems sovereignty does no harm, but for other — important — problems it is less appropriate. Consequently, for the solution of these problems a number of countries have signed treaties, such as the Warsaw Pact (WP), and formed organizations such as the European Community (EC), or the Council of Mutual Economic Assistance (CMEA) or "Comecon."

New Problems

In the course of history the world has been faced with many changing problems. Population has increased at a quickening rate, especially in the last few decades, industries have expanded and new types of industries have developed as a response to large numbers of scientific discoveries or technical inventions. Conflicts have led to wars and the areas involved grew. So the war from 1914 to 1918 was called a World War; and the war Hitler started in 1939 became World War II, implying the name World War I for that of 1914-18. The world's political face was shaped by the October 1917 revolution, which resulted in the Soviet Union. Technical development continued and some results are discussed below.

Already in the 19th Century international trade was an important phenomenon, linking the world's nations. After World War II the need was felt to establish institutions to assist national governments in their decisions on trade policy and the General Agreement on Tariffs and Trade (GATT) was established, with its secretariat in Geneva. Similarly, and in fact earlier still, two institutions in the financial sphere, had been created — the International Monetary Fund (IMF) and the International Bank for Reconstruction and Development (IBRD), later called World Bank (WB), both located in Washington, D.C. These three institutions are mentioned to illustrate that, for some important fields, nations cooperated to solve some important common problems and so took decisions to higher than national levels. National governments came to understand and accept that some elements of sovereignty had to be shifted upwards to the international institutions.

Chapter 5
Wise manage-
ment for
a more
humane
world

And now, further changes have created problems whose solutions also require supranational (or world-level) decisions and their implementation. Population and industrial growth have begun to pollute the environment and to threaten the world's forests and arable land surface. Chemical industry and motor transport, by the gases they emit, have caused acid rain; population increase has led to the cutting of trees and the reduction of forest surface. The environmental problems are fairly new problems, the consequences of mismanagement (failure to stop the emission of toxic gases, or to stop cutting forests). They affect not only the country in which an inadequate policy is followed, but also other countries, sometimes the whole world.

The United Nations, at its 1972 Stockholm meeting, established a new institution, the United Nations Environment Program (UNEP), with its secretariat in Nairobi, Kenya. This institution collects and distributes large quantities of useful information and recommends appropriate policy measures to national governments.

The Basis of Regulation

Regulation is sometimes mistaken for an urge to dominate, or a thirst for power. It is an unfortunate mistake. Regulation is a vital, healthy process that promotes order. Domination and such are crusty remnants of our distant past — a time when powerful human urges and desires in a lawless setting made intimidation and threats both a tool of acquisition and a necessary means of protecting one's possessions and oneself.

Today these urges and desires have been diluted throughout most of humanity by thousands of years of improved communication, religion, broadened knowledge, steady character development, and other polishing forces of civilization . . . so that such things as tyranny and bullying often appear ugly and out of place in today's world.

Assuming with optimism that these unsightly remnants are gradually disappearing, let's explore the nature of sensible regulation.

There are probably as many ways to describe or define regulation as there are names for it. Seminars, articles and books outline the four styles of leadership, the seven principles of management, the eight steps to effective administration . . . the actual numbers and terms depending on the outlook of the people involved.

If you tossed all these ideas into a pot and boiled them down, you would probably wind up with two basic ingredients of sensible regulation — monitoring activities and making changes when necessary . . . only when necessary.

Implementation of Decisions

In order to reduce the threat to human environment a large number of decisions must be made by governments, of the types mentioned:

•Stop or reduce toxic gas emissions by motor cars and factories,

•Stop the cutting of trees,

•Stop storing intoxicated materials,

•Stop polluting rivers and canals,

Monitoring does not necessarily imply a constant vigil.
•We might monitor environmental degradation, weather patterns and the growth of civilization on the planet's surface with an occasional series of photographs from a satellite orbiting the earth.
•Monitoring a child at play might require an occasional glance.
•Monitoring employees in a company might involve an occasional report by each employee on the status of his or her projects.

Making changes is easy, but making the appropriate changes at an appropriate time is a bit more challenging:
•When to restrain the rapid growth of societies and industries to protect the oceans, atmosphere and rain forests . . .
•When to call an exploring child back within easy earshot . . .

•When to interrupt an enthusiastic employee whose project is moving ahead quickly but is starting to veer off-course . . .

These are difficult situations to judge. Excessive restraint can stifle enthusiasm and innovation. Excessive liberties can lead to chaos and crisis.

A key to effective regulation is deciding how closely to monitor activity, when to make changes, and what changes to make. These questions seem to be present at all levels of our lives, whether it involves parents in a household, teachers in the classroom, managers in a corporation, government in our city or nation, or the United Nations in a tense, modern world.

— Adapted from existing Earthview Press publications.

Chapter 5
Wise manage-
ment for
a more
humane
world

51

Emissions by motor cars can be reduced, for example, by furthering electric traffic or by building a "catalyzer" into cars. Similarly, factories can be improved by installing instruments to purify the emissions.

For these ideas to become helpful the decisions or recommendations must be *implemented* . . . but there are obstacles in the way. For example, in several of the situations mentioned, the current behavior often has a harsher effect on citizens of neighboring nations, than on those of the polluting nation, so the willingness to take these measures may be weak, and the measures may not be taken at all. Such is often the case with "acid rain" and polluted waterways. So the environmental supranational authority must have the *power* to have the optimal policies implemented. Today this power is not in

Minimal Regulation Can Work

How do we decide how tightly or how loosely to regulate? Perhaps we can generalize: The more knowledgeable, responsible and dedicated a person or group is, the less he, she or it needs to be regulated.

Any group — be it a family, a club, a company, a community, a nation or humanity at large — thrives when all the members are knowledgeable, responsible and dedicated to the group.

Knowledge is gained from practical experience, training and education. It includes knowledge of a person's role in the group, how that role fits into the overall workings of the group, and how the group as a whole fits into its broad surroundings and higher-level groups.

A sense of responsibility comes when the group has well-defined values, standards and guidelines that are generally compatible with those of other groups the member belongs to, and when the member accepts them as his or her own.

Dedication comes when people care about each other as people, watching out for each other's sensitivities and needs while interacting.

If everyone in a group were knowledgeable, responsible and dedicated, there would be little need for regulation. As it is, every group has members who for one reason or another are short of one or two of the needed qualities. Without exception,

the hands of UNEP. A reform is needed which creates an environmental police and an environmental court.

Some of the United Nations institutions, for instance IMF and WB, do have power (in this case *financial* power) to impose their decisions on the receiving countries concerned. Most of the United Nations institutions don't have that power, however. This is certainly not an example of optimal management.

Manage the World Like a Well-Run Nation . . . or Family

In order to understand better how our planet — the world at large — can be optimally managed, it is useful to consider how optimal management is operating at lower levels. In a well-run nation we find, as already observed, several levels of decision making, from very

every one of us has been short on knowledge or responsiblity or dedication at different times in our lives . . . in the various groups we have belonged to.

For that reason, certain people are selected to help regulate groups at all levels of humanity, to help keep order. Whether their title is boss, foreman, parent, president, or whatever, they help maintain order with their managerial skills.

The two main skills of a sensible regulator are 1) the ability and determination to help the group members become knowledgeable, responsible and dedicated, and 2) a flexibility to monitor and change as much or as little as necessary in any given situation.

In a company, for example, a sensible department manager closely supervises new, inexperienced employees who feel uncertain in their new positions. The manager provides the direction they want and need. As the newcomers become more knowledgeable, responsible and dedicated, the manager gradually backs off until the employees become self-regulating. If their dedication slips later on, perhaps for personal reasons, the manager is there to help and support.

The same basic idea can be applied to relationships between parents and children, government and society, club officers and members . . . and even perhaps to a world body like the UN and the various nations, religions, transnational corporations and other large social systems in today's world.

— *Adapted from existing Earthview Press publications.*

low ones — the individual level — to increasingly higher. There is a family level, perhaps an extended family level; there are levels of voluntary associations or political parties, and within a party even there may be levels.

Geographically the quarter where a family lives, the municipality and several geographical units of increasing size may have a decision level.

The various levels often are part of a hierarchy. We may have government authorities in a hierarchy, but also associations and political parties know their hierarchies. And last but not least, the company or production process in which we are employed has its hierarchy, from the work floor (production workers), via the supervising and the administrative workers to management and coordination workers. Individuals and committees at each level make decisions on a large number of problems.

In a well-run nation the hierarchy of authorities is characterized by the geographical peculiarity that the total area of the nation for which the highest level is responsible is subdivided into smaller areas for which the next lower level of authorities is responsible and that· this pattern may repeat itself until the lowest level is reached. The optimal management is the distribution of tasks (that is, decision making) which maximizes welfare of the population as a whole. I submit that two rules define the optimum:

•Rule 1: Decisions should be made at the lowest possible level.

•Rule 2: The level of decision-making on any problem should be chosen as to be responsible for all those (and *only* those) who are affected by the decision.

Rule 1 implies that decisions are made by those who are closest to those affected by the decisions. It means that a maximum of participation or codetermination prevails. It should be admitted that the assumption is added that those affected by a measure are simultaneously those best informed about the solution of the problem, hence the best experts.

Rule 2 warrants that everybody whose welfare is dependent on the solution of the problem is represented in the decision-making authority. The decision should not affect the welfare of people not represented at the decision-making level of authority.

Examples:

Decisions of local impact are those on local transportation, such as the course of local tram, bus, trolleybus or underground routes, or the places where traffic lights have to be placed. These decisions can be made at the city level. As soon as a problem comes up that also affects other cities, for instance the color of traffic lights for "go" and "stop," the interests of the world as a whole are at stake. The decision must be an international one. It is an inconvenience that in some Anglosaxon countries road traffic is keeping left. Sweden was kind enough to switch from left to right.

Another illustration is the example already discussed of schooling: where to build a school and who should appoint teachers may be decided by local authorities for elementary and secondary education, but not for universities. Some general rules about the programs of elementary and secondary schools are better made a state task, however.

Increasing and Intensifying Links Among Nations

Under "New Problems" we discussed some examples of international cooperation in trade and financial policies. In the last 40 years the interrelationships among countries have been multiplying and intensifying. This implies that for their optimal solution more and more problems require decisions at higher than national levels, because national decisions increasingly also affect the welfare of citizens of other countries.

Energy, raw materials, and food often have to come from more distant sources than before, and competition in markets of industrial products has become more intensive. Market agreements on energy, raw materials and food are in the interest of most countries, but are completely dependent on voluntary negotiations. UN institutions such as the UN Conference on Trade and Development (UNCTAD), the UN Industrial Development Organization (UNIDO), the Food and Agricultural Organizaton (FAO) and the International Fund for Agricultural Development (IFAD) lack the power to implement participation with their recommendations.

A very special new link is formed by the oceans, whose resources have been found to be much more abundant than was thought a century ago. So in a series of negotiations taking nine years, a new Law of the Sea has been agreed upon, providing machinery to let all countries share in these riches. These consist of oil and of manganese nodules found at the bottom of the deepest parts of the oceans. Unfortunately, after agreement had been reached with the previous governments of the rich countries, the new conservative governments of the USA, the UK and the FRG refuse to ratify the treaty. We must hope that those countries will change governments.

More Shifting of Sovereignty to Supranational Agencies

In view of all the changes in human environment and new
technological trends, it seems appropriate to start a fundamental
enquiry into the optimal management of our planet. The preceding
sections point out that several world institutions, in order to attain
their optimal operation, need the power to enforce the
implementation of their decisions.

Unfortunately we cannot assume that national governments will act
voluntarily, given the exaggerated importance they attach to
sovereignty. This attitude of many governments seems to rest on a
misunderstanding, namely the idea that sovereignty enables a nation
to keep its situation under control. In reality, a nation's situation
remains dependent on other nations' acts. It is often better that all
nations concerned discuss the problems at stake and find a method of
joint decision-making. In the various examples discussed this means
that *parts of each nation's sovereignty must be shifted to higher
levels.*

For the sake of peace we need to answer two serious questions:

1) What is the precise way in which decisions can be made jointly for
optimal results?

2) Specifically what types and groups of problems to be covered, now
and in the future, should be part of the study to be undertaken?
Earlier in this article we listed a considerable number of problem
groups — shrinking forests, loss of arable land, acid rain, and so
forth.

We should not be astonished if in the future more problems have to
be added to our list. In order best to serve humanity's welfare we
should be open to new ideas.

Why an Openminded Approach?

We must remain openminded in a rapidly changing world. The great
thinkers of the past, on whose views socialism, capitalist democracy
and other modern socio-economic systems are based, could not
foresee some of the fundamental changes in the productive forces
now available and the environment in which we must live. For the
market economies Adam Smith was the leading thinker and for the
centrally planned economies it was Karl Marx.

•They could not foresee the discovery of nuclear energy, a consequence of Einstein's theory of relativity.

•They could not foresee the development of the chemical industries, consequences of a large number of chemical discoveries ranging from medicines and preservatives to detergents and pesticides.

•They could not foresee the resulting destruction and pollution of the environment that would become such a threat to our lives and future.

Theories on socio-economic systems have to be adapted to these new discoveries and changing conditions. In particular the use of nuclear energy for military purposes creates totally new problems. But also environmental policies are a new species of policies because of our tremendous growing impact on the ecosystem. Adapting political ideologies and policies to the new realities shaped by scientific innovation and its side-effects will require a new sense of openmindedness in national and international politics. Karl Marx applied the scientific approach to society's development. It is in this spirit that the adaptation of Marxian theories to the new realities be undertaken in a scientific way. We, who are responsible for the scientific adaptation, have to do this ourselves; the answer cannot be found in scientific publications of more than a century ago.

One example of the scientific foundation of environmental policies was discussed earlier — that anti-pollution policies cannot be sovereign national policies, for the reasons set out.

Another example is security policy. Nuclear weapons in the quantities now available imply that their use means suicide to the aggressive nation which uses them. They cannot therefore be actually used . . . a government can only threaten to use them. This means that nuclear weapons are different from conventional arms. If they cannot be used, possible threats cannot be carried out. After this non-execution of a threat has occurred, the threat will gradually lose its impact and in the end become non-credible. The only threat that remains will then be the accidental use of nuclear weapons. This can better be avoided by a cooperative policy of the superpowers. Again sovereign policies will have to be replaced by common policies.

The same applies to a defense against a missile attack, specifically President Reagan's Strategic Defense Initiative (SDI). As long as both superpowers try to find a technology of defense against missile attacks independently of each other, hence in a sovereign way, the danger of the opponent reaching first-strike capability exists. Also this search for a technology of defense against missiles must not be a sovereign policy, but a common policy.

Reforms of the United Nations and the Attitudes Required

From the preceding analysis it will be clear that optimal management of our planet requires a number of reforms of the United Nations family of institutions; in addition, such reforms will only be possible if the attitudes of most governments change.

Reforms of the United Nations might include changing some existing institutions or adding new institutions. Two overall reforms badly needed are a fairer way of representing member nations and the introduction of the authority for the UN to implement its decisions. Better representation means that large countries have more votes than small countries. Also, countries which contribute more to the institution must also have more votes, at least for now. This differentiation may gradually be reduced as has occurred at the national level during the past 100 years. A century ago in some nations, citizens paying more taxes had more votes than citizens not paying taxes; but in modern democracies all citizens (over a certain age) are entitled to vote.

So, large nations and large contributors to the UN deserve more authority in the decision-making process in the UN, particularly in the General Assembly and in the Assemblies of many institutions (ILO, UNCTAD, UNIDO, etc.). In the IMF and WB, however, relatively more influence of the low-income countries is desirable.

Perhaps the General Assembly would be more efficient if only large countries and federations of smaller countries were represented. These federations would have their own assemblies. This would reduce the number of UN members and so improve the efficacy of decision-making.

Even more important than reforming the representation of member nations, is giving more power to the UN as a whole to implement its decisions. This will require a transfer of elements of national sovereignty to United Nations institutions, the point made several times in the preceding text, and it is probably the most important step humanity must take in the coming years on the road to world peace.

A new institution I want to propose is a World Treasury (WT) or World Ministry of Finance. Its use may be illustrated by looking at the organization of well-organized nations. Among their central financial institutions we find the Central Bank, an Investment Bank and a Treasury. At the world level the future central bank may be a reformed IMF, and the Investment Bank already exists: it is the World Bank. In well-run nations the Treasury is the most important of the three institutions, but at the world level it does not exist. Not only would a Treasury collect taxes in a more equitable way than is done now, but it could also finance — through its capital budget — out of the current revenue some of the development investments and so avoid the complications of financing these out of loans. Loans have the difficulty that an interest rate has to be agreed upon, and that debts may grow too much.

A reformed UN is only a partial solution to the problem of how best to regulate the planet. In closing let us discuss another vital concern: What changes in attitude are necessary. So far, the shift of sovereignty from nations to multinational institutions appears only to a limited extent. The most noticeable shift involves the two main military alliances, the North Altlantic Treaty Organization (NATO) and the Warsaw Pact (WP), which now carry much of the decision-making power once held by their members — at least in matters of defense.

But this is not the sort of shift we are concerned with. What we discussed earlier is a shift to one world organization, the United Nations, in which adversaries are not pitted against each other, but are enjoined under compatible values against mutual problems and obstacles.

And that constitutes the important change in attitude needed. We are used to giving top priority to choosing the type of social system we want to live in. That must change.

Nuclear weapons force us now to give priority to a world security system, because without security there may be no human society left to inherit a better social system.

A deteriorating global ecosystem forces us now to give equal priority to a clean environment, since without a clean environment no human society may be left to inherit a better social system.

Chapter 5
Wise manage-
ment for
a more
humane
world

Chapter 6
Using Space to Help Regulate the Earth

by Caesar Voute
Professor, International Institute for Aerospace Survey and Earth
Sciences (ITC)
Enschede, The Netherlands

Background. International authority on the use of aerospace
technology to regulate certain broad, earthbound activities (such as
weather, environmental degradation, and the growth of social
systems) more effectively and more humanely. Lectures and advises
various UN bodies and workshops. Has written over 200 papers on
geology, technology in society, military and peaceful uses of space,
and remote sensing techniques. Since 1951, ITC has trained over
7,000 technicians from over 160 nations (80 percent from the Third
World).

His article. Like other technologies, space science has the capacity to
magnify all aspects of our nature — the violent side as well as the
peace-loving . . . the destructive side as well as the creative and
productive. It is up to us to decide what type of relationship we want
with space and, in so doing, largely determine our future. This article
provides ideas on how space technology can best be used for peace
and development.

*We face a juxtaposition of two separate,
seemingly opposite requirements: the
interests of humanity on one hand, and
optimal opportunities for the individual
on the other. Together, space technology
and telecommunications can bridge the
levels of human life — from personal to
global.*

Using Space To Help Regulate the Earth

by Caesar Voute

*O*ur space venture started less than half a human lifetime ago. Though achievements have been spectacular in that brief period, we fail to see the full promise of the space age. Little consideration is given to the fact that the unique features of the space environment provide us with opportunities to perform new functions, hitherto impossible and never even dreamed about. Yet the common attitude remains in all sections of society — governments and individuals, regulators, experts and scholars — to look upon space technology as a means to carry out traditional tasks and functions faster and better.

One of many examples of this "space illiteracy" (in the words of African scholar Joseph Pius Ben Muga Ouma) is mapping and mineral prospection, activities with a written history of at least three millenia. Here, earth observations from space are mainly used for consolidating old mapping and inventory concepts ("what is where") with the improvements in efficiency and quality of information. It is time to define new ways and means of managing the earth using the unique potential of space in a cohesive and comprehensive manner. There are two objectives:

•To build up confidence among nations, reducing the dangers of confrontation and distrust, and

•To promote cooperative efforts directed towards harmonious socio-economic development.

Achieving these goals will rebalance society, resources and environment, and will achieve improved opportunities for the individual to realize social and cultural aspirations guided by ethical or spiritual norms in equilibrium with the needs of society.

Experience teaches us that conflicts are often due to destabilizing processes provoked by changes within societies and nations, or in the relations between nations. Insensitivity to the cultural environment, in particular, can be a source of turbulence and conflict as in the case of Iran vs. the USA, or Afghanistan vs. the USSR. It is therefore of fundamental importance to search and find measures of promoting development with a minimum of destabilization, and in addition to define nonviolent ways to solve conflicts so as to reach acceptable levels of development. In such an overall concept space technology and its applications have an important role to play because they can perform innovative functions which, moreover, by their very nature are regional and global rather than national or local.

Managing Earth from Space

Space science, space technology and space applications can — and should — fulfill many functions for the benefit of humanity. In order to assess the state of the art and to determine what steps should be taken to reap the expected advantages, a special United Nations conference (UNISPACE 82) was convened in Vienna (Austria) in August 1982. (See the accompanying article in this chapter.)

Around the same time an international roundtable of scholars, scientists and specialists was assembled to provide independent input to the UNISPACE 82 conference. These experts, representing the natural sciences, social sciences, law, international affairs, diplomacy and high levels of administration, addressed such questions as:

•Should we (humanity) militarize space?

•How can we most wisely regulate satellite remote sensing and the flow of information?

•How can we gauge and prepare for the impact of the new technology on society?

•Should a well-meaning central authority assume all responsibilities for action, or should the individuals be motivated to act at the local level?

These and other questions are inherent in the context of the true meaning of "development."

Chapter 6
Using
space to
help
regulate
the earth

A Holistic Approach

My only regrets are that the roundtable limited its considerations to a large number of separate issues, however important they are, without tackling the potential of space as a holistic concept, and that insufficient attention was given to the specific ethical problems of the space age. In this respect it reflects the piecemeal way in which space technology and its applications have been developed since the launching of Sputnik a quarter-century ago.

A different approach, until now rarely followed, would be to analyze the potential of space in terms of the various possible orbits (altitude, position, etc.) in relation to spacecraft payloads and functions. It is then possible to distinguish groups of orbits, each well suited for a number of functions, like communications and direct broadcasting, navigation and positioning, meteorology, oceanography and land observations, area surveillance and regional or local monitoring. Likewise, an optimization of payload selection is possible with due regard to tasks to be performed and appropriate orbits.

Earth observations from space constitute potentially an important instrument for the management of natural resources and human society. They cover various activities, such as:

•surveying and mapping,

•inventory of resources,

•observation of slowly or rapidly changing phenomena.

An important application, yet to be developed, for which space technology is eminently suited, is the monitoring of routine processes with a series of satellite pictures, based on a thorough understanding of the nature of these routines and the factors influencing them. The objective of monitoring these routines is to trigger action if deviations observed are surpassing a set threshold. Monitoring, therefore, includes the establishment of criteria (which are often partly politically determined) and presumes that the will (and authority) for action does exist. Monitoring of moderately and highly dynamic processes in Nature and of human outdoor activities will soon be feasible with operational, high-resolution satellite remote sensing systems and rapid delivery of data at low cost.

What factors are involved in making satellite monitoring an other aspects of space technology operational? They include:

•design of space and ground segments in terms of hardware and software,

•purpose of the applications and choice of the methodology in terms of efficiency, cost effectiveness and social acceptability,

•management structure of the facilities concerned and of the organizations serviced by the various applications,

•socioeconomic and sociocultural functions of the information produced or transmitted by the space-supported systems, and the related political objectives in terms of development of natural and human resources and the transformation of society.

Satellite communications are another important application of space technology to human affairs, where the information content and the purpose for transmission or broadcasting are more important than the technical facilities used for transmission or direct broadcasting and reception.

Satellite communications are fully operational through international networks and through growing national networks connecting important urban centers. They also hold high promise for integrated rural development. Direct broadcasting via satellites, in addition to providing an expansion of existing mass media services, also constitutes a promising area for distant learning systems and, in combination with satellite remote sensing, for rural extension services. It is moreover being used to promote culture, the awareness and the sense of responsibility among citizens, and for religious teaching.

All told, there exist several areas of potential or proven space applications which could be of benefit to the world in general and developing countries in particular, such as:

•space manufacture,

•space medicine,

•navigation systems for ships and airplanes,

•geodetic precision positioning,

•emergency communications for maritime search and rescue operations,

•telecommunications and direct broadcasting,

•earth observations applied to oceanography, meterology, inventory and management of resources,

•monitoring of the environment,

Chapter 6
Using
space to
help
regulate
the earth

•disaster prediction, prevention and mitigation,

•ship routing, and

•off-shore industries.

Thus, viewed in a broad, cohesive and comprehensive manner, space technology can go a long way in contributing significantly to a more rational and responsible management of matters on earth, thereby reducing existing or perceived incompatibilities in the distribution of power, the fulfillment of needs and the availability of resources. This in itself would already constitute an important step towards conflict resolution and the promotion of peace, since incompatibilities in society or between societies are at the root of all human conflicts.

In short, space holds vast potential for the betterment of life on earth. However, underlying all the many promises is an unshakable reality:

World cooperation must be a central element in a program for detente. The aim should be to develop patterns of cooperation in which competition is regarded in increasing the effectiveness (nationally) of using common means and facilities. Interdependence now more than ever before should take the place of detente and coexistence.

Our plan of action must bring together many separate and seemingly opposing concepts — law of humanity, planetary law, freedom, interdependence, common ancestry, innate unity of all humanity, balance between Nature and humanity.

We face a juxtaposition of two separate, seemingly opposite requirements: the interests of humanity and global management on one hand, and equal rights and optimal opportunities for the individual on the other. The first involves action at a planetary scale, the second activity with a human dimension. Or, paradoxical as it may seem, the new technology base embodied in space technology, informatics and "telematics" (the combination of telecommunication and informatics) has the potential to bridge the levels of human life — from personal to global.

Space technology, using satellites orbiting the earth, is bound to be global in nature. The investments in R&D, industrial production, initial and recurrent costs are very high and often beyond the capacity of single nations. International cooperation is of great advantage to all concerned, if not a prerequisite, and facilitates managing the earth. At the same time we have to find ways and means to restructure society — preserving human dignity without abandoning the benefits of advanced technology.

The ideal situation will provide global centralization in space with a decentralized setting on Earth. The space systems (satellites, computers, software, etc.) could be developed to precise, uniform standards and values, while the ground systems could pick, choose and tailor the information from above to fit national, local and personal equipment, objectives, laws, routines and customs.

Or, technically speaking, capital-intensive and highly complex equipment could be incorporated in the spacecraft payloads, funded and managed in common, and could produce cheap and user-friendly equipment for use on the ground in modes decentralized almost at will, permitting applications at levels down to local communities or even the individual, coupled, if desired, with semi-central control functions by national, regional or multinational bodies.

Considering differences on earth, we must develop side by side a number of different political, socio-economic, educational and science and technology models, each valid for a certain region of cultural environment. For the Third World, in particular, it will be necessary to develop endogenous alternatives in all areas mentioned based on socio-cultural and socio-economic considerations with due regard to indigenous standards and values.

The industrialized nations, from their side, have to develop alternative scenarios and strategies designed to meet the need for a whole range of technologies. They furthermore have to assist the developing countries in promoting collective and national self-reliance, for instance through the depackaging of technology in order to provide for greater flexibility and user-friendliness of ground operations.

One often overlooked fact should be stressed in particular. Humanity has a rich cultural history and a tradition of many centuries of religious and humanistic thinking and development of philosophical, ethical, legal and social value systems. The challenge of using outer space for the benefit of all humanity involves more than intellectual capacities, science and technology. Responding to moral issues is at least as important, the basic question being, "What human development could and should result from the conquest of space?"

Chapter 6
Using
space to
help
regulate
the earth

A second, equally essential question is, "Space for whom?"

Unless we strive earnestly to find satisfactory answers to these two questions, ambition and knowledge without wisdom may tempt us into formulating poorly thought-out space policies and into adopting equally poorly conceived measures for their implementation, without ascertaining the short term and long term impacts on society and on international and interpersonal relations.

Where We Stand Today

In closing, let's look briefly at some of the space technology plans being adopted by the developed world to see if they are heading in the directions outlined here.

•What about the proposals of the US National Commission on

The Cosmic Challenge

Space has always had a special fascination for people, ever since the first intelligent being looked up into the sky. Our ancestors worshipped the sun as the life-giver even before science had shown it to be so, and the moon has had an aura of romance around it for centuries. In our collective psyche, space has always meant freedom, romance, the challenging unknown and — for some — "heaven."

Now, after millennia of looking upward and outward from the earth, we have acquired the ability to do the reverse also: to look at our home planet from a vantage point in space. What we see is immensely beautiful and very revealing: a planet whose life processes are inextricably interdependent, where life depends on the delicate and unique balance between humanity and Nature. What is not visible is equally revealing: we cannot discern different countries and separate people. Space has given us a new perspective on the universe, our solar system and our own planet. Can it also give us a new perspective on ourselves?

— UNISPACE 82 Report, paras 1 & 2 (United Nations, 1982).

•The human population explosion means that, for the first time, earth is overrun by one species which has the capacity, but so far has refused the responsibility, for putting its habitat in

Space, "Pioneering the Space Frontier — An Exciting Vision of Our Next Fifty Years in Space" (22 May, 1986)? **No.**

•Or the report of the Earth System Science Commission, NASA's Advisory Council (26 June, 1986)? **No.**

•Or, for that matter, the Long-Term Space Policy of the European Space Agency decided upon 31 January 1985 by the European minsiters? **No.**

The only plan that points toward what I would consider to be healthy world growth is a set of space policy proposals published by the Federal Republic of Germany (24 June 1986). This plan is based

---

order.
   •The atom bomb irrevocably symbolizes the power we now have of destroying ourselves and, with us, life on earth.
   •We have become a "global village . . . ."
   •We have made our first moves to explore and use outer space.

Together, these phenomena speak of power and vulnerability . . . We can choose to act so that outer space becomes a further dimension of our destructive capacity, or an added dimension to the growth potential of the human race.

We can choose to transform outer space into a new arena for our conflicts on earth . . . extending our fears and distrust into outer space. There are recent warnings about space laser weapons, killer satellites and space platforms fuelled by military interests. Taking this road we would project into space human self-destruction. We would contaminate outer space with moral pollution and exercise human folly on a cosmic scale.

The other road (the road toward wise use of space) is more difficult, challenging, and requires an immense intellectual and managerial effort . . . .

— UNISPACE 82, Statement by Soedjatmoko, Rector, United Nations University, read by Edward J. Ploman, Vice-Rector Global Learning Division, United Nations University, on 10 August 1982 at the General Debate, Second United Nations Conference on the Exploration and Peaceful Uses of Outer Space — UNISPACE 82, Vienna (Austria) 9-21 August, 1982.

Chapter 6
Using
space to
help
regulate
the earth

on an integrated concept with due consideration for the social, cultural, and ethical dimensions of diverse cultures. It was prepared by a group of 27 persons including representatives from the academic world, industry, administration, the labor unions and members of parliament.

When it comes time for nations to sit down and formulate a plan for the future of space technology, the policy proposed in the Federal Republic of Germany may well provide the model.

Chapter 7
The Next Step Toward World Order

by John Fobes
Adjunct Professor, Political Science
Asheville, NC, USA

Background. From his UN Secretariat appointment in 1945 to his
role as deputy director-general of Unesco (1971-77), he has been a US
diplomat, aid adminstrator and international official based in New
York, Washington, London, Paris and New Delhi. Current
memberships include Club of Rome (executive committee), World
Futures Studies Federation, United Nations Association, Society for
International Development, International Studies Association,
Americans for the Universality of Unesco (founder-president).

His article. The regulators of a social system must reflect the
diversities of the system to be of service to it. In a world as diverse as
ours, envisioning a system of world governance is no easy feat. In fact
it is impossible without a comprehensive, acceptable framework or
model of the world situation, its problems and their solutions.
Developing such a framework is the next big step toward world order.
Who will develop it? What can you do?

*How can a new world system reflect the
complexity of the natural and manmade
environments instead of trying vainly to
control and limit those environments with
outmoded mechanisms?*

The Next Step Toward World Order

by John E. Fobes

We often equate social order with government, and so it follows that we would equate world order with world government. In reality, order at all levels of society — from local to global — is created and maintained by a broad spectrum of institutions, only one of which is government.

It is a complex spectrum, and it is likely to grow moreso. Not only has the number of so-called sovereign states (and their governments) tripled in 40 years, the number of intergovernmental and international nongovernmental organizations (the IGOs and INGOs) has grown almost more impressively (from 49 IGOs and 170 INGOs on the eve of World War II, to more than 300 IGOs and 10,000 INGOs today). Forty years ago there was no International Telecommunications Satellite Organization or United Nations Environment Program. Since 1946, also, the Specialized Agencies of the UN have encouraged formation of a host of international professional, civic, trade and other citizens voluntary associations related to health, agriculture, the arts, communications, and a host of other fields of human endeavor. New technologies, especially electronic communication, have spurred the number and velocity of transactions among these diversified actors.

That so many individuals and groups want "to get into the act" is both hopeful and chaotic. It is hopeful insofar as these actors are driven largely by responsibility, compassion and cooperation, so that we can expect the emerging "global society" will eventually develop institutions and customs of caring, nurturance, preservation, and collaboration.

Meanwhile we have a world of incredible diversity to contend with, and trying to envision systems of governance for such a world is no easy feat. According to Ashby's "law of requisite variety," the regulators or governors of a system must reflect the variety of that system in order to be of service to it. One consequence of this is that survivor communities and societies must adopt measures to assure that information and knowledge flow freely, that maximum access to such information is available, and that opportunities for participation are magnified (which implies decentralization).

From a distance, however, the world seems to be hesitating, even recoiling, from taking the next steps to develop appropriate world governance. The world seems to be saying,

"Yes, we know that this is one planet, one humanity. But it seems too difficult to move from the present unsatisfactory, fragmented world order to a better system."

So, where and what is the solution? Examining the scene closely, one finds that at local levels there is almost a boiling over of creative activity, trying of new solutions, grasping for new behaviors. We see in these trends a more vigorous assertion of individual dignity and rights ... and we see hope.

It is time to be radical in our consideration of governance at the planetary level if that governance is to be appropriate to our time. The 1970s were marked by a series of UN global issues conferences. These conferences have sensitized opinion to some extent, but they hardly questioned the fundamentals of structures, of relationships and of forms of representation (and who should be represented). They told of growing complexity but relied on traditional solutions and controls.

How can a new world system reflect the complexity of the natural and manmade environments (including the "ecology of knowledge") instead of trying vainly to control and limit those environments with outmoded mechanisms?

Chapter 7
The next
step
toward
world
order

To reform and renew the agencies of world order and prepare for the 21st Century, we must have our visions based on a revival of values and hope. If we are to be realistic, we must evolve plans for the UN system of agencies capable of supporting world order. We need to aim for short-, medium-, and long-term reforms simultaneously.

In all three levels of action, it should be recognized that national governments, constrained by growing domestic problems and by short-term thinking, will need ideas and leadership from the extra-governmental communities. Those communities — civic, professional, scientific, religious, academic, artistic — should not only help governments but push and cajole them when necessary into action to affect changes at the global level.

These citizens voluntary organizations can also be commissioned to undertake more projects on behalf of the international agencies and to participate in the councils which exercise program oversight.

Immediate Reforms

Today there is a general complaint over lack of coordination among the growing number of international agencies and programs. This criticism has been used to oppose the creation of new services and institutions of multilateral cooperation. Yet it can be argued that the present global systems of governance are, like that of national governments, too traditional, simple and rigid, lacking the requisite variety and flexibility needed to deal with the complexities of the planet.

We need creative solutions to this growing problem of coordination. One might imagine, for example, a corps of individuals and a set of public review bodies whose function it is to provide information exchange and program mediation services among the world institutions. Such individuals and review commissions could develop a capacity to sift, interpret and present information and evaluations to all actors and to each part of the complex world system. The aim would be to build a reasonable congruence, and occasional synergy, among those parts.

Such a coordination system would require that we start now to prepare the new cadre of facilitators-evaluators-information interpreters and transmitters for the 21st Century. They will require both formal training and periods of practical experience. This could be regarded as an investment in the future, a future which will undoubtedly be even more complex than today. One could envisage also a supportive network of centers around the world where the records of progress (and set-backs) toward global order would be maintained and constantly culled and re-interpreted.

Medium- and Long-Term Reforms — Starting the Transformation

Governments tend to focus on immediate reforms in the procedures of the international agencies. Because of this short-sightedness, fundamental adjustments may not be politically acceptable today. Situations may well arise during the next decade, however, when circumstances will persuade enough governments to accept revisions in the basic documents of multilateral cooperation.

Breakdowns in international financial systems, mounting terrorism, climatic changes resulting from atmospheric pollution and increase in international migrations are some of the "systems breaks" which will demand adjustments in the institutions and procedures of cooperation. An inventory or already existing reforms may prove useful.

While the immediate reforms are being installed and studies of long-term adjustments are encouraged, the more fundamental process of re-thinking needs to begin.

One of the difficulties of reaching agreement on priorities and action in the UN system is the lack of an agreed framework for describing the world situation — its problems its possibilities. With such a framework (the "problematique") we could expect a progressive future for world governance. But in adopting a framework, we must remain thoughtful and flexible, farsighted, and open to alternatives. There is a danger of too great a concentration on what seems feasible in the short run or on those ideas and projects of immediate attraction or benefit to the discussants. It may help to exercise imagination and a planetary view by first considering, in very broad terms, what world order arrangements would be desirable for the grandchildren of those living today, that is, about 100 years from now.

The ideas, the vision, the inspiration will most likely come from those who combine the following:

•awareness of past experiences,

•a broad comprehension,

•a most generous motivation,

•a will to put prodigious efforts into the rebuilding.

Chapter 7
The next
step
toward
world
order

These will be men and women who are even now linking up with others of like minds across borders. They are initiating informal networks or groups, beginning to work with and animate selected transnational non-governmental organizations (or creating new ones where necessary). They are looking for those individuals within governments and intergovernmental organizations who are sensitive to the need for change.

Perhaps there could also be a continuing open "world seminar" to regularly publish and amend an outline statement of the main elements of the ongoing world situation as seen from different regional and cultural perspectives. Even though such a framework would be subject to constant adjustment, the process of its creation would exercise an integrative, stabilizing influence. Those involved in any aspect of planetary governance — and they are likely to be growing in number and diversity — would be able to locate their part in such governance on the "map" and better grasp their relationships to others in the service of humanity.

What Can We Do Now?

Local groups are right to ask, "But what do WE here do tomorrow?" I offer four suggestions:

•Do more of what you have already started to do to prepare the children and the young people for a revised UN system. Help the schools and the teachers and encourage the students to learn about the present system, to imagine its improvement and to devise alternative futures.

•Link up locally with other civic and professional groups who share interest in world order.

•Make contact with other active and concerned local groups in your country and abroad for information sharing and encouragement.

•Put pressure on the national headquarters of your associations to pay more attention to the entire UN system and to be more radical in their thinking about the future.

Today, more individuals and groups, world-around, are working to improve human conditions and institutions. We need not wait for dramatic breakdowns to shake the comfortable complacency of the privileged centers of traditional power before planting the seeds and establishing the networks which will gradually transform the institutions of survival and world order. In fact social, economic, scientific and technological forces are already transcending and transforming the patterns and maps of the past, nationally and globally.

Breakdowns there will be, but we only need a small minority which does not succumb to the helplessness and hopelessness of crumbling civilizations. The results of the work of such a minority — the emergence of new orders which they had been working to create, often informally and "underground" or parallel — will be revealed by the crises.

Chapter 8
Five Changes for the United Nations

by Marc Nerfin
President, International Foundation for Development Alternatives
Nyon, Switzerland

Background. A world citizen born, like Jean-Jacques Rousseau, in the city-state of Geneva. Has travelled to over 70 countries, living in Tunisia, Ethiopia, USA, Mexico, and his native Switzerland. Speaks French, English, and Spanish. Vice president of Inter Press Service, Third World News Agency, since 1980. Author and editor of many works on the UN and the Third World . . . and the directions in which they should proceed for world stability and peace.

His article. Global relations are too serious an affair to be left solely to governments and transnational corporations. The author proposes a restructured world body which represents 1) the national governments, 2) the world's economic interests, and 3) the 5 billion people of the planet. He presents dozens of compelling questions about a UN and a world in crisis, and the answers are implicit in the asking.

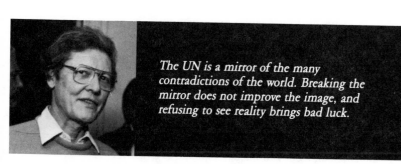

The UN is a mirror of the many contradictions of the world. Breaking the mirror does not improve the image, and refusing to see reality brings bad luck.

Five Changes for the United Nations

by Marc Nerfin

The world as seen in 1945 from San Francisco or Lake Success during the birth of the United Nations was essentially white, western and Christian. Its basic paradigms were Newtonian. Profound changes have occurred since then.

The most striking change is the geopolitical transformation of a largely colonized world into a polity of 159 sovereign member states of the United Nations — that is, the emergence of the Third World, both in numbers (now 127 countries) and in organization (the nonaligned movement, founded 30 years ago in Bandung; the Group of 77, founded 20 years ago at UNCTAD I; and a number of regional and other South-South groups).

One should also ponder over the rise of Japan and Western Europe, and the challenge they pose to the hegemony of the two superpowers which grew out of the 1939-1945 war.

And one should attempt to gauge the real significance of the demographic explosion (two out of three of our fellow human beings today were not yet born when the UN was created).

Today, largely as a result of the "great awakening" of the Third World, but also because we can now view our planet from outer space, humankind is recapturing its wholeness. No one can any longer ignore the existence of the cultures, in the widest sense, of Africa, pre-Columbian Americas, Arabia, Asia and the Pacific.

Snapshot of a World in Crisis

We are confronted with serious challenges:

•The immediate holocaust of hunger and dispossession in a growing segment of humanity, not only in Africa, with the persisting crisis of underdevelopment and maldevelopment everywhere — that is, the growing fracture of every society in two . . . those who are, and the excluded.

•The possible holocaust of the nuclear winter,

•The current crisis in the world economy and in international
relations (USA-USSR, Afghanistan, Central America, Kampuchea,
Iraq-Iran).

Under such circumstances we must come to understand better the
nature of this general crisis, whose multiple aspects, causes and
consequences — positive and negative — include:

The economic and financial crisis. The inadequate and extrovert
nature of most growth processes and its links with the persisting
unequal exchange, both within and between countries, and the
resulting poverty; the origins and consequences of the debt, its
relative importance for the world system and for the debtor countries,
its servicing as reverse transfer both from South to North and from
poor to rich, the use of the borrowed resources (outward-oriented
production capacity, arms purchase, elite consumption, speculation,
private investment abroad, corruption versus need-satisfaction-
oriented investments, import substitution), the evolution of the rate
of interest, the US responsibility (dollar value and real debt burden),
the role of the capital market (autonomy from both national interests
and productive processes), the rate of profit of the banking system;
protectionism and Third World deteriorating terms of trade;

The environmental crisis. The implications of the withering away
of the resource base (deforestation, desertification); the
externalization of costs to neighbors (e.g. the acid rains oiriginating
from US, UK or Czechoslovakia); urban decay; new risks as
exemplified by the Mexico explosion or Bhopal; the outer limits of
the biosphere (ozone layer, climatic changes, etc.); the hegemony of
short-term rentability; the social causes (the combination of poverty
and affluence, that is injustice) of ecological deterioration;

The social crisis. The growth and irreversibility of unemployment;
the challenges to the welfare state; the marginalization of the urban
poor in the South; the "new poor" in the North; the small farmer as
an endangered species all over the globe; the migrations from South
to North; the tide of xenophobia and racism; persisting gender
oppression; growing feelings of powerlessness and alienation among
people and societies;

The cultural crisis. The homogenization of societies; the role of the
mass media (propaganda, malinformation, advertisement, standard
consumption values and patterns); westernization of the elites of the
South; ethnocentrism and lack of recognition of the Other's values;

the identity crisis; the loss of both roots and purpose; the poor understanding of the ethnic resurgence;

The ideological crisis. Fundamentalism and integrism — be they capitalist, marxist or religious — their roots and utilization; the shaking Western modernization paradigms — that is, to use different terms, the moral crisis and the spiritual crisis;

The political crisis. The rise of the authoritarian state in the Third World, and the fragility of the reborn democracies of South America; the risks of "friendly fascism" in the US; the failure of the Soviet system (which did not "catch up", except, perhaps, in weaponry) and the lack of success of the internal reform movements; the pervasiveness of bureaucracies (public and private) everywhere; the negation of human rights;

The security crisis. The impact of bipolarization and hegemonic policies: East-West rather than South-North approaches; invasions (Afghanistan and Grenada); destabilization; terrorism, private and statist; militarization of economies and societies; the scramble for resources and the diversion of resources from the satisfaction of human needs; the ever-open questions of Palestine and Southern Africa; the local wars made possible by arms exports; and, above all, the nuclear risk;

The Third World differentiation crisis. The 1973/74 missed historical chance for genuine South-South cooperation; relations between oil exporting, newly industrialized, and poorest countries; the contradictions within the Non-aligned movement, and the lack of leadership after the deaths of Nehru, Nasser, Tito, Boumedienne; the inability to establish permanent secretariats in either the Non-aligned movement or the Group of 77;

The theoretical crisis. The wave of neo-conservatism as an acid test for past development theories; state/market relations in both East and West; the relevance of international discussions for national development strategies and practices; the limited impact of alternative models;

The development cooperation crisis. The reasons for dwindling expectations and resources; the cooperation "fatigue"; the shift from aid to Third World development to aid to Northern exports; the role of food aid; the crisis of multilateral channels.

This list is not complete, but it is long enough to suggest that we are not in a mere "cyclical" economic crisis. As a matter of fact, and without any doomsday suicidal complacency, we are probably in the midst of a mutation crisis.

The two questions we face are, Will we survive? and, if so, Under what conditions of a new age on this planet?

The United Nations Under Attack

These crises affect our lives and our social systems in all spaces, from personal and local, to national and global. Likewise, the solutions lie in the efforts of virtually all people and groups. In the global space the only available instrument is the United Nations system, which is embroiled in a crisis of its own at the present time.

What exactly constitutes the crisis of the UN? That depends on whose perception you view:

•The International Organizations unit in the US State Department and committed Third World representatives or former representatives,

•Western journalists and the opinions they inform and influence one way or another,

•UN desk staff and senior civil servants in Western capitals and conventional ministries in Third World countries,

•Nonaligned countries and client countries,

•Countries withdrawing (USA from Unesco or Poland from ILO) and countries sometimes threatened with exclusion,

•UN civil servants of all grades and citizens who "in UN believe."

There are probably as many perceptions of the crisis as there are those who perceive it. The crisis is thus ill-defined, and it would be prudent for anyone entering this debate, to recognize that his/her views are likely to be partial in both senses of the word.

In recent years the main criticism levelled against the UN has come from the USA— the Reagan administration, some of its supporters (for instance the Heritage Foundation) and some of the US media. Why the attack by the UN?

The declining hegemony. The US used to control the deliberative organs of the system, but its capacity to influence the votes of gevrnments as such or of individual delegates has decreased as Third World solidarity, including its expression through group voting, has increased. Furthermore, its control over the execution of decisions (through key staff and the power of the purse), while still very much part of daily reality, appears to be somewhat receding;

Resistance economic regulation or restructuring. Third World efforts towards restructuring world economic relations (the New International Economic Order, the Charter of Economic Rights and Duties of States) or their embryonic regulation (the Convention on the Law of the Sea, the codes of conduct on transfers of technologies, activities of transnational corporations, marketing of drugs or baby food) and the concomitant emergence of the idea of development accountability all somewhat reduce the omnipotence of free enterprise. US companies, which are subject to some regulation at home, however, oppose its introduction in the other spaces where they operate;

The role of ideology. The new self-assertiveness of the US, the desire to overcome the moral crisis linked with the Vietnam war, its strategic superiority, the general feeling of being the leader of the world, all these — not to mention obscure but terrifying Armageddon analogies — are translated into ideological postures such as those of the Heritage Foundation, which believes the US no longer needs the UN since "it no longer serves US national interests."

Western Europeans for the most part seem to have accepted the US case without much discussion. The frustrations over the incapacity of the UN to solve major pending problems — be they political (Palestine or South Africa) or economic (the restructuring of world economic relations) — are often transformed into rhetorical statements and symbolic votes.

It is impossible not to note the lopsided nature of the media discussion of the UN crisis: there was much talk, for instance, about the "crisis of UNCTAD," which reflects better the aspirations of the South, and none about the IMF, which acts as the sheriff of the Western banking system. There is much noise about the crisis of Unesco, but none about, for example, IAEA, ICAO, ITU, WIPO or WMO*, which are necessary to the North. Seen from this angle, the "UN crisis" is largely a Northern expression of a felt challenge to the old order and a reflection of the North's unwillingness to accept that change is necessary.

---

*These acronyms, which may not be familiar to everybody, stand for the International Atomic Energy Agency, the International Civil Aviation Organization, the International Telecommunication Union, the World Intellectual Property Organization and the World Meteorological Organization, respectively.

Weakened by Internal Problems

This does not imply that there are no internal problems. On the contrary, there are many, reflecting the aging of the institution as well as the difficulties in adapting to new situations. Among the internal factors of the crisis, the following call for particular scrutiny:

The proliferation of agencies, programs . . . The need to restructure the system as a whole was advocated as far back as 1969 by the Jackson Report and 1975 by the Dag Hammarskjold Report, What Now: Another Development, and by the Ad hoc Committee on Restructuring. Instead, attempts were made to address new problems through the establishment of new agencies, thus making even more difficult a system-wide and systemic approach to development cooperation;

The proliferation of diplomatic meetings. If anything, these are draining the limited resources of Third World and smaller industrialized countries rather than helping them. This may explain at least some of the problems in the quality of representation and the style of deliberation (lengthy, repetitive speeches, lack of real discussion);

The proliferation of bureaucratic reports. Their volume has reached proportions which exceed the managing or decision-making capacity of any government or delegation; the general decline in UN studies is more serious still, since they are intended for wider audiences;

The whole problematique of the Secretariat and its staffing. The problem is not one of sheer numbers since the UN bureaucracy, which deals — and rightly so — with almost every aspect of the peace and development problematique, remains rather modest compared to, for instance, that of the European Communities or to most national administrations and many local ones. The real questions are about the methods of recruiting and election (including for the highest positions), duration of tenure, working conditions, efficiency, competence, integrity and independence of the Secretariat. There is, however, no evidence that the Third World is more responsible for the present unsatisfactory state of affairs than, say, the permanent members of the Security Council;

The question of the costs. This is a result of the previous deficiencies and, again, the question is not that of the total cost which is very small in global terms, whatever yardstick one uses, but rather that of the effectiveness of the operation, the deployment of resources, and, perhaps above all its financing.

Poor public relations. The UN system's relations with the media and other opinion-formers and with the scientific community affect principally those countries which have a stake in a better performance of the organization, e.g. the Third World and those smaller powers in the North which have no pretense at world leadership and need a strong international organization.

Now we must launch a serious drive towards streamlining and strengthening the UN system.

Regulating with Tied Hands

The UN is primarily an instrument of governments, and this may be seen not only as its original sin but also as its major shortcoming. It can function properly only when there is a measure of agreement among governments, and anyhow it has only the political power they delegate to it. Thus, the UN is in many respects a mirror of the contradictions of the world; and, as folk wisdom always knew, breaking the mirror does not improve the image and refusing to see reality brings bad luck.

As a mirror, the UN cannot be held responsible for the failure of the superpowers to live up to the commitments to peace they accepted when signing the Charter; it cannot be held responsible for their lack of willingness to limit armaments, for their military interventions or for the arms exports, without which the "local wars" which have never stopped in the Third World since 1945 could not have taken place to such an extent.

Similarly, the UN cannot be held responsible for the failure to set up a proper development cooperation mechanism or even a coherent approach to genuine development, since it could not and still cannot go much beyond what governments (so-called "donors" and "recipients" alike) want or will tolerate.

What Exactly is the UN?

There is something which could be called a UN entity, which always had a measure of autonomy, and may thus be seen as constituting "the UN." This entity is made up of three distinct but interrelated layers:

1. Governments in their capitals — that is, when there is a UN policy (which is not the normal case) the small group of policy makers and senior civil servants who define the government position in the UN assemblies;

2. The permanent delegations (only a study based on insights would reveal the relative autonomy of delegations, but it is well known, for instance, that except for major or well organized powers, influence, in New York or elsewhere, depends more on the quality of the delegation than on the weight of the country); and

3. The Secretariat, which, whatever its essential collective and individual dependence on its governmental masters, enjoys a certain freedom of initiative.

These three constituents of the "UN entity" are living in a kind of symbiosis through contacts between delegates and Secretariat (quasi-permanent with resident missions, less frequent but no less regular with visiting delegations) as well as through personnel movements among them: what proportion of new staff members, especially at the decision-making levels, come from the UN desk in the capitals and from permanent delegations?

The very idea of an international organization implies that there is something which cannot be reduced to the sum of governmental decisions; there has always been a cadre of truly international civil servants, supported by enlightened national ones, who place a global vision above narrow national interests, competition and rivalries, and act at the service of the world at large. The capacity of such forerunners of a future world to influence the course of events is obviously determined by their imagination and independence. We shall try to assess the UN performance from this perspective of relative autonomy.

Assessing Its Value

The UN has a moral role. Even in its "operational activities," the UN is no substitute for governmental action, but the extent to which it has influenced, positively or negatively, peace and development, and in the latter field, theory and practice, should be assessed, as well as its role as the vehicle of the first sense of global awareness ever to occur on this planet. An agenda for evaluation may in this light, cover such topics as:

1. The avoidance of war (e.g. the role of Secretary-General U Thant in the 1962 "missile crisis" in Cuba); the peace-keeping operations in West Asia and elsewhere; the experience of the "blue helmets;" the Congo operation; education for peace and the promotion of disarmament;

2. The process of Third World decolonization;

3. The limitations, achievements and potential of the commission on human rights;

4. The role of the UN system in such strictly global affairs as the common heritage of humanity (especially in the Law of the Sea but also with reference to outer space and "intellectual property"), as well as in expanding knowledge (including statistical) of this planet and its inhabitants;

5. The role of the UN system in postal services (UPU), civil aviation (ICAO), maritime transport (IMO), telecommunications (ITU), or meteorology (WMO);

6. The development of international law and the place of the International Court of Justice;

7. The role of the Committee for Development Planning, ECOSOC, the Secretariat and others in the elaboration of the three International Development Strategies; the relevance of these strategies to both national development and international cooperation; their usefulness in socializing the development debate and fostering the cooperation movement; their limitations reflecting the prevailing development ideology and the vested interests at stake;

8. The contribution of the sectoral agencies, funds, programs, etc., to the strengthening of the autonomous capacity of societies to develop, meet their needs and master technologies, for example, FAO and the World Food Council as far as food is concerned, WHO for health, Unesco for education, science and cultural understanding, Habitat for housing and human settlements, ILO for labor protection, UNIDO for industry, UNEP for environment, etc.;

9. The role of ECOSOC, UNCTAD, the regional commissions and their institutes, such as ILPES or IDEP, as well as UNITAR, UNRISD, and perhaps UNU, in clarifying and enriching development theory;

10. The role of UNCTAD in facilitating and moralizing North-South trade and in providing a forum for discussion on the restructuring of the world economy; of the Regional Commissions in support of regional cooperation; and of the Centre on Transnational Corporations in providing information and analysis on global economic power;

11. The results of the "operational activities" of the system, those of UNDP, UNICEF, IFAD, WFP, UNFPA, HCR, UNDRO,UNWRA, etc. on the one hand, as well as those of the Bretton Woods institutions,

the IMF and the IBRD, on the other. This should include an analysis of the relevance of the implicit models of development informing such activities, the nature of the interaction between suppliers and users of resources, the level and quality of transfers, and the proportion of such transfers which have really contributed to the autonomous capacity to develop, as well as, in the case of relief agencies, the quality, relevance and timeliness of their interventions;

12. The influence of the Joint Inspection Unit through monitoring the functioning of the system; were its analyses properly studied and its conclusions acted upon?

13. The influence of the major World Conferences, since Stockholm in 1972 (environment, population, food, human settlements, desertification, water, science and technology, agrarian reform and rural development, new and renewable sources of energy and, as far as actors are concerned, women) in bringing to the fore the emerging themes of the development problematique, in offering new approaches to old themes and generally, because they reached far beyond the space of governments, contributing to a new global awareness; similarly, the role and significance of the many thematic "days," "years" or "decades;"

14. Finally, but of great relevance for the next century, the use by the United Nations University of its autonomy (somewhat unique in the UN system) to tackle the fundamental questions of the future through linking up, with forward-looking scientists, the wise among us, and the new social actors.

Among the general criteria against which to evaluate such activities, one should take into account the contribution of the UN system to the exchange of experiences and the generation and dissemination of new ideas, as well as the countless personal contacts it has facilitated among men and women from all regions and many cultures.

In the final analysis, the basic question is simple: could the world as we know it today be possible without the United Nations? The answer is equally simple: no.

There has been no world war since the founding of the organization. Third World decolonization has been virtually completed. Small and otherwise powerless countries now have a tribune. Development cooperation, however problematic, has started. The feeling that we belong to this only one earth is spreading.

The UN is the first attempt in history at global organization, the first step toward establishing values and standards accepted by all. It is the first tool ever for global dialogue, understanding, conflict resolution and cooperation. They bear a terrible responsibility, those who weaken the United Nations by refusing the rules of the game, outside which there is only the law of the jungle — a law of poverty, war and death.

On the contrary, the UN needs strengthening. This can be achieved only through rethinking, restructuring, and upgrading. Forty years of experience — of achievements, mistakes, shortcomings, failures, successes, and new perceptions of the world and humankind — are there to learn from. We are better equipped than in 1945 to make the UN a more effective tool for peace and development.

Steps Toward a New World Organization

The aggiornamento, or modernization of the UN will not come from governments alone. However "realistic" the proposals, governments as such will not act collectively if not pushed. One cannot be limited by too narrow a concern for what governments may now find "feasible" since change, if it is to come, will result only from a movement of opinion.

Such a movement is possible. For perhaps the most important fact about the United Nations is the result of an opinion survey carried out in May 1985 in the US, the UK, Japan, the Federal Republic of Germany and France. The message from the five hard-core industrial countries is crystal-clear:

1. Whenever people do have an opinion about the United Nations, the majority (except in Japan) considers it is doing a good job;

2. An even larger majority, in all five countries, does not believe, as some American integrists claim, that the world would be better off without the UN; and

3. Except in the US (where this is the position of half of those expressing an opinion), at least six out of ten people do not think that the Third World has too much influence on the UN.

In understanding the UN, people are ahead of governments, just as there have always been people and movements ahead of governments for decolonization, for peace, for human rights, for women's liberation, for the environment, and for consumers' self-defense.

UN Restructuring

This offers to the UN a line of action to consider when it ponders its future: get closer to the people. Here are five questions which, one way or another, appear relevant to the future of the United Nations and its aggiornamento in that direction.

Which functions? The UN may not have the power to change the world, but it can certainly do more than record speeches and ineffective resolutions on peace and development while reflecting the status quo. As the only global instrument, that is, strictly speaking, as the only instrument of the human species as such, and if it is to smooth the transition from the old order(s) to the new, more humane, order(s) which survival requires, is not its primary role to be open? . . .

•Open to new realities, notably the multifaceted emergence of the Third World, within and without the nation states;

•open to new aspirations, notably the people's expressed need for liberation from the threat of nuclear omnicide, from hunger and other forms of maldevelopment, and for mastering their lives;

•open to new paradigms, notably those concerning security, development, relations between societies, human beings and genders, as well as between the species and the environment of which it is part and parcel?

As the only instrument of the human species as such, could the UN do more and better, in a universal, independent and pluralistic manner, to

•monitor both nature and societies, through the collection, analysis and dissemination of all relevant information;

•facilitate the sharing of experiences and ideas;

•promote mutual understanding and education, through dialogue and negotiation among countries, cultures, and societies;

•formulate alternative policy options for the steering of the world society in transition?

Better decision-making. The voting system in the UN General Assembly is based on the principle of "one country, one vote," but the Security Council has a politically-weighted voting system, and the

Bretton Woods institutions (and UNDP) an economically-weighted one, and whatever the noises about "automatic majorities," the UN by and large still operates under the control of the big powers of the North.

Would it be possible to overcome such an outdated pattern without moving from one hegemony (real) to another one (possible)? Could an arbitration or reconciliation system be worked out?

Could the fact that, say, Brazil, India or Nigeria, and the US, the USSR or China, have a larger global responsibility than Vanuatu, Dominica, or the Seychelles, be reconciled with the fundamental right of every polity, whatever its size, to have a proper say in planetary affairs, that is in matters concerning its survival?

Could a new system, reflecting both the general and the different responsibilities of different countries in different matters be imagined? Could, for instance, the voting system of IFAD or that of the International Sea-Bed Authority be a precedent for other operational agencies?

Could the post-war Unesco system be revisited, rehabilitated and perhaps extended to other agencies? Its Executive Board was then composed of competent persons serving in their personal capacity "on behalf of the Conference as a whole and not as representatives of their government." Only in 1954 were members of the Board made to represent their governments — as a result of a 1952 proposal by the US government, which today complains about "statism."

Greater financial autonomy. Resources at the disposal of the UN system are not commensurate with the magnitude of the needs of development cooperation. How could these resources be increased and become more automatic?

What scope is there for reducing administrative expenditure in favor of development cooperation expenditure (but who ever complained about the administrative budget of the World Bank, which is fully automatic, being financed by the difference between the interests paid to lenders on the market and interests paid by borrowers, that is Third World countries)?

Can a levy on the use of the global commons and a tax on military expenditures be collected by the UN and affected to development cooperation?

The US share in the regular budget of most UN agencies is 25 per cent, and more in most voluntary programs. This is in agreement with the principle of the capacity to pay embodied in most national tax systems. This also gives the US an excessive leverage on UN activities, either indirectly through staffing or directly through the power of the purse. Can the scale of assessment be modified and the share of any one country be limited to, say, 10 per cent of the total, without decreasing the total income?

Are there effective ways to delink the payment of dues from influence on the actual functioning of the organization?

An independent secretariat. Article 100 of the Charter provides that the Secretariat "shall not seek or receive instructions from any government" and that "each Member of the United Nations undertakes to respect the exclusively international character of the responsibilities of the Secretary-General and the staff and not seek to influence them."

Possibly no other article of the Charter has been more widely ignored than this crucial one. The superpowers have been and remain particularly guilty in this respect, from the dismissal of staff members during the McCarthy era in the USA to the exploitation of USSR (or USA) staff positions by the KGB (or the CIA). More generally, this provision has been virtually nullified by the routine submission of appointments to governmental clearance, probably the major weakness of the Secretariat.

True enough, Article 100 expresses the liberal naivety of the founding fathers, who sought to fashion the institution in their image. Even without "instructions," members of the Secretariat, belonging as they do to different cultures (political, ideological, etc.), cannot but reflect them "in the discharge of their responsibilities."

Yet, could the independence of the Secretariat be improved?

How could a Secretariat, of largely American-British-French parentage (as recently as 10 years ago, members were still primarily drawn from these three countries), become a truly pluralistic image of the diversity of world societies and polities?

Could the best traditions of its servants, both past and present, become the model rather than the exception? Could the example of a Dag Hammarskjold inspire all Secretariat members, from the most modest to the top?

Do the answers, or at least some of them, reside in different selection procedures; in the enforcement of criteria based exclusively on efficiency, competence, integrity and commitment; and in the delegation of appointment decisions to independent committees of people who themselves have strictly and consistently and over a long time met such criteria? Would the limitation of the terms of tenure restrict bureaucratization? Would the institution of a staff college help? Could the experience of religious orders or revolutionary parties in the selection, apprenticeship and development of their cadre, be of relevance? What mechanisms of social accountability for Secretariat members could be set up?

How could member states be made to respect their commitment to respect the independence of the Secretariat?

In sum, how could the margin of autonomy of the Secretariat component of "the UN entity" be widened? How could the Secretariat become the melting pot of a new cadre of men and women exclusively devoted to the world community at large and to its emancipation? There is perhaps no more important question for the future of the UN.

More voice to the people. States and governments, important as they are and will continue to be, do not reflect the richness of societies. Even when democratically elected, governments represent at best the majority of a society, not the whole of it, and UN continuity suffers from shifting majorities, as exemplified by the fate of the Convention on the Law of the Sea. There are other social actors. Some represent the economic powers, such as, in the global space, the transnational corporations or the international banking system. They are part of the problem, and they must also be part of the solution. People in their diversity (and contradictions) express themselves through other actors: religious movements, peace movements, consumer movements, ethnic movements, trade unions . . . Can the UN accommodate these actors?

This would require a radical alternative to past and current thinking and practices.

The question is not to "mobilize the opinion" (a catch phrase which one will hear in almost every UN speech, including those of the Secretary-General): the people are quite able to "mobilize" themselves, if necessary. The question is not whether to tinker with the bureaucratic arrangements for the so-called "non-governmental organizatons" in "consultative status" with the UN and its specialized agencies. The question is whether the UN will be able to perceive that its real constituency lies beyond governments. The challenge is to seize the opportunity of the modern crisis to re-think and re-establish the UN's relations with the people and their associations.

Consider a three-Chamber UN, one representing the countries of the world, each represented by its respective government. This first system could be called the Prince Chamber.

The economic powers of the world could form the second system, or Merchant Chamber. These powers would include bodies from all levels of world economy — transnational, multinational, national or local, belonging to the private, state or social sectors, since at the same time we need them and need to regulate their activities — which is better done with them.

Last, and perhaps most important, the people and their associations could be the third system, or Citizen Chamber. With as many women as men, the Citizen Chamber would, through some mechanism ensuring adequate representativity, speak for the people and their associations. At the very least, this would make it possible for citizens to hold Princes and Merchants accountable for the consequences of the exercise of power.

Can one think, perhaps along the lines of the European Parliament or through some arrangement with the Inter Parliamentary Union, of giving a space in the UN assemblies to the current political minorities, since they may well be tomorrow's majorities?

Are there more immediate ways to open up the UN system to the people? What could the third system itself do? What mechanisms can be devised and established which would make the UN, as it is now and as it may unfold, at least accountable to the people?

Whatever the depth of the crisis and the predicament looming upon us, there is no excuse for despondency. On the contrary. If "crisis" means moment of decision, which it did in Greek, our ability to make the right decisions depends on our capacity not to lose sight of the underlying hopes.

Through these first 40 years of the United Nations, scientific, technological, conceptual, practical and political advances have been many and significant. There have been many positive changes in our understanding of nature and society, and the experiences accumulated offer a prodigious capital to choose from and build on. Our task is now to sketch a vision of a more humane world and to explore ways to approach it.

Democracy has had its setbacks. They continue. But dictatorships have not been able to resist people's pressure, in Greece, Portugal or Spain nor, more recently, in Argentina, Brazil, Uruguay or the Philippines. In Western Europe and in North America, the people's response to and sense of solidarity with those starving in Africa has been overwhelming. Everywhere, over the last 40 years, people have been ahead of governments.

Finally, perhaps, one major reason for hope and confidence is the very youth of humankind. More than half of those living today are less than 25 years old, and the children of today are going to be in charge tomorrow.

At the same time, this places an unavoidable responsibility upon the adults of today, the artisans of the present world order, to keep the option of life open and to manage the transition to a world in which people can truly live. The first responsibility in this respect is to invent and explore new institutional paths to make the UN the instrument we need. For the UN is much more than 159 member states: it is a project which, as the only embryo of a planetary organization, belongs to all of us, members of the human species living on this only one earth.

Chapter 9
Revamping the UN Voting Structure

by Hanna Newcombe
Co-Director, Canadian Peace Research Institute — Dundas
Dundas, ON, Canada

Background. Widely known and honored by peace organizations for her peace efforts, the high pitch of which started in the 1960s when she joined the United Nations Association, the Society of Friends (Quakers), and the Voice of Women. In the same period, she along with her husband Alan helped found the Canadian Peace Research Institute and started the Canadian Peace Research and Education Association. Her research work has centered around UN restructuring.

Her article. In a more moderate proposal for UN reform, the author takes a detailed look at weighted voting formulas as an alternative to the current one-nation, one-vote system now at work in the General Assembly. One of the biggest obstacles to UN effectiveness is the unwillingness of nations to compromise their autonomy. The value of weighted voting would be its acceptability to world leaders. This article lists all modern nations by their voting tendencies on world issues.

The superpowers prefer to prevent any strengthening of a United Nations which they do not control.

Revamping the UN Voting Structure

by Hanna Newcombe

*T*he formal power structure in the UN, as outlined in the Charter, is based on these principles:

•In the General Assembly, the voting power of all member states is equal. Substantive resolutions require two-thirds majority for adoption, procedural resolutions a simple majority.

•In the Security Council, as reformed in 1965, the majority required to adopt an important resolution is 9 of 15, but the 5 "great powers" (USA, USSR, China, UK and France) have to concur. If any one of them votes against a resolution (that is, vetoes it) the resolution cannot be adopted.

•Other UN bodies have rules of their own.

The formal structure represents one-to-one equality of nations in the General Assembly — one nation, one vote — but a division into great and lesser powers in the Security Council (stronger nations have bigger votes). The result is a very basic — and somewhat crude by modern standards — political structure for world regulation. There seems to be an uneasy compromise here between equality and power.

Digging beneath the stiff, rather awkwardly compromised power structure we find the real politics of the General Assembly. What counts in the living undercurrents is how nations align to each other on the various roll-call votes taken, what alliances or coalitions (permanent or fleeting) they form . . . in other words, the informal bloc structure.

To some extent, the voting blocs parallel the caucusing groups, which regularly consult together . . . but not entirely.

These blocs (see Table 1) can be compared to world political parties operating in the General Assembly. The actual outcome of votes on resolutions depends on this informal structure, superimposed on the formal, one-nation, one-vote structure. Forecasts can be made by counting the nations that will probably support a given resolution, to see if the number exceeds two-thirds of the membership; and counting the nations in opposition, to see if they have "the blocking third" that will prevent adoption.

Several questions arise:

•How fair is the one-nation, one-vote approach?

•Is it fair that small nations like Fiji, populous nations like India, and rich nations like Japan all have equal weight while voting?

•If we were going to redesign the General Assembly voting scheme, what factors should be taken into account when determining which nations have how much weight in their votes — population, wealth, energy usage, dues paid to the UN, etc.?

•Should a nation have the same weight in all votes, regardless of the subject under discussion?

These questions and others will be answered in this article, but first let's take a closer look at the informal General Assembly structure.

Before 1974

The blocs that existed in General Assembly roll-call voting have been mapped. The structure evolves over time, with certain well-marked transitions along the way. One such transition took place in 1960, when the new French African bloc was added. From 1960 to 1973 there were 8 blocs, arranged as follows:

Bloc	Main Nation
Soviet	USSR
Afro-Asian	India
Pro-West Afro-Asian	Lebanon
French African	Dahomey/Benin
Latin American	Brazil
Scandinavian	Sweden
Western	USA
Imperial	South Africa

Soviet Bloc
Bulgaria
Byelorussian SSR
Czechoslovakia
Democratic Kampuchea
German Democratic Rep.
Hungary
Lao People's Democratic
  Republic
Mongolia
Poland
Ukrainian SSR
USSR
Vietnam

Afro-Asian Bloc
Algeria
Angola
Bahamas
Barbados
Benin
Bhutan
Botswana
Burma
Cameroon
Cape Verde
C.A.R.
Chad
Comoros
Congo
Cuba
Cyprus
Djibuti
Dominica
Egypt
Ethiopia
Equatorial Guinea
Gabon
Gambia
Ghana
Greece
Guinea
India
Iraq
Jamaica
Kenya
Kuwait
Lebanon
Lesotho
Libya
Madagascar
Mali
Malta
Mauritius

Mozambique
Nicaragua (Sandinista)
Nigeria
Pakistan
Romania
Samoa
Sao Tome & Principe
Senegal
Seychelles
Sierra Leone
Solomon Islands
Somalia
Sri Lanka
Sudan
Swaziland
Syria
Togo
Trinidad
Uganda
Vanuatu
Yemen
Yugoslavia
Zimbabwe

Scandinavian Bloc
Australia
Austria
Canada
Denmark
Finland
Iceland
Ireland
New Zealand
Norway
Portugal
Sweden

Central American Bloc
Antigua
Belize
Colombia
Costa Rica
El Salvador
Grenada
Guatemala
Haiti
Honduras
Israel
Malawi
Nicaragua (pre-Sandinista)
Paraguay
St. Christopher and Nevis
Saint Lucia
Saint Vincent

Uruguay
Venezuela

Western Bloc
Belgium
France
Germany, Federal Rep.
Italy
Japan
Luxembourg
Netherlands
Spain
United Kingdom
USA

ASEAN Bloc
Indonesia
Liberia
Malaysia
Maldives
Niger
Philippines
Singapore
Surinam
Thailand
Upper Volta
Zaire

Chinese Bloc
Albania
Burundi
China
Guinea-Bissau
Guyana
Rwanda
South Yemen
Tanzania
Zambia

South American Bloc
Argentina
Bolivia
Brazil
Chile
Dominican Rep.
Ecuador
Fiji
Ivory Coast
Mexico
Nepal
Panama
Papua-New Guinea
Peru

Table 1 — Bloc Membership

Total Member States: 145
Not Voting: 5 — Total Nations: 140

98

After 1974

In 1974, a new alignment began to emerge, with some of the blocs remaining intact, but others changing. Essentially, these are the changes, which were valid into the late 70s when these analyses ended.

Bloc	Main Nation
Soviet	USSR
Chinese	China
Afro-Asian	India
South American	Brazil
Moslem	Saudi Arabia
Southeast Asian	Indonesia
Scandinavian	Sweden
Central American	Nicaragua*
Western	USA

*pre-Sandinista Nicaragua, before Somoza was overthrown.

The old, pre-1974, pro-West Afro-Asian and French African blocs reapportioned themselves among the new Chinese, Afro-Asian, Moslem, and Southeast Asian blocs. The old Latin American bloc split into the South American and Central American wings, rather far removed from each other along the political spectrum. And the old Imperial bloc has disappeared, with the changeover in Portugal and the habitual nonparticipation in votes by South Africa.

Some reasons for these changes from 1960 to the 1980s might be:

•The 1973 Arab-Israeli War,

•The oil embargo and oil price rise that followed,

•The revolution in Portugal in 1974 and subsequent liberation of Portuguese African colonies,

•The call for a New International Economic Order, based on a new unity of the developing countries,

•The end of the Vietnam War in 1975,

•The rapprochement between the USA and China,

•The entry of China into the UN in 1971.

While the names of the blocs imply geographic locations, they are really political, with the geographic designations not always appropriate. For example, Israel votes with Central America and Cuba with Afro-Asia, and Albania with China. (See Table 1.)

Weighted Voting

Now if nations had numbers of votes proportional to their populations, or to the UN assessments they pay, or a combination, or some other "weighted voting formula," these bloc alignments would still be the same, but counting the majorities would be different. The balance would swing much harder when a large nation like populous India or rich Japan changed sides, than if a tiny nation like Fiji did. The same informal power sturcture, superimposed on a different set of formal rules, would produce different results.

Calculations show that the results would usually not shift any more than to cause some 10 percent of the outcomes to be reversed (resolutions previously adopted now being rejected, or vice versa). With many weighted voting schemes, the change would be far less than that.

Is a change of 10 percent a drastic one? That depends on how controversial the issues are. Sensitive issues like nuclear weapons proliferation in the North, the right to survive in the Third World, and deforestation of rain forests, might be affected significantly by a 10 percent change.

What Changes Could Be Made in the General Assembly?

Assuming that the one-nation, one-vote scheme in the General Assembly is less than ideal in a world of vast international diversity in GNP, population and other factors, let's look at some alternative schemes.

After analyzing numerous voting formulas based on population and various socio-economic factors such as GNP, UN tax assessment, energy consumption, and health and education expenditures, we at the Peace Research Institute have emerged with 24 different formulas. Of these, we will look at nine typical formulas for this article:

1. One nation, one vote (the existing formula).

2. Proportional to population.

3. Clark and Sohn — 30 votes each to the four largest (most populous) nations, 15 each to the next 8 largest, 6 each to the next

20 largest, 4 each to the next 30 largest, 2 each to the next 34, 1 each to the rest.

4. Square root of population.

5. Population and energy consumption, proportional, 1:1 ratio.

6. Population and GNP, proportional, 1:1 ratio.

7. Population and health-and-education index, 1:1 ratio.

8. Square root of UN assessment.

9. Proportional to GNP.

My personal favorite is the seventh on the list — a composite of population and the health-and-education index.

These or other, similar formulas might be employed by the UN General Assembly while voting on different issues . . . the idea being that there seems to be no single formula that is acceptable in all situations to all nations, all people, and all social groups. Theoretically, these diverse fragments of humanity could use this set of weighted voting formulas as a tool for compromise on issues in question. We seem today to be a long way from the point where all nations can arrive at a fair, stable consensus on issues via the UN. This set of weighted formulas could be an important step in that direction.

By proposing these particular weighted voting formulas we are moved by two considerations — one, the desire for fair representation, and two, the wish to be realistic, to reflect existing economic influences accurately. These two considerations — fairness and economics — are not identical, but neither are they contradictory. For example:

•It is "fair" to give a nation with more people more votes at the UN, because we believe in the democratic right of representation by population.

•It is also "fair," in a different sense, to give more votes to nations which contribute more of the UN budget. This is some kind of "shareholders' justice."

•If we want to reflect economic influence, we would probably weight votes according to GNP or some other, more accurate and practical economic indicators.

We do not want to get involved in giving nations more votes for military power, not in a peace-keeping organization like the UN.

Now, weighting by economic influence gives very different results to weighting by population (according to democratic fairness considerations), but very similar results if we weight by UN assessment (according to shareholders' justice). Also, we can achieve any number of compromises by using two factors, one for democratic fairness considerations and one for economic influence considerations.

Energy can be a useful economic factor because it is a physically measurable quantity without the theoretical problems posed by a GNP aggregation. (Economists are uncertain about what GNP actually measures, especially in different types of economies.) But energy consumption (and perhaps GNP as well, at least in the countries that already consume excessive resources by world standards) is not something we want to encourage by rewarding it with extra votes (just as we balked at rewarding military power). So for reasons of giving incentives for "good behavior," we introduce health and education expenditures as a factor.

We are now ready to see how these proposed voting formulas would affect the outcome of votes in the General Assembly's informal bloc structure. This is done by calculating the bloc vote percentages, which are illustrated in Table 2.

Calculating the vote percentages is a simple procedure. We just total the voting weights of all nations in a given bloc, using the bloc memberships (Table 1) as a guide ... and this sum becomes the voting weight of the bloc.

Then we compare that sum to the total of all voting blocs to determine the percentage of each particular bloc.

Conclusions

Studies of possible methods of weighted voting, such as these, elucidate the possibilities of reform. The chief purpose of such a reform, in conjunction with others, would be to strengthen the UN to enable it to carry out its primary duties with regard to maintaining world peace, and with regard to helping solve certain other global problems.

Elucidating the possibilities, and the effects they would have, is one thing. Quite another matter is implementing such reforms in the real world. The feature of the weighted voting formulas which is

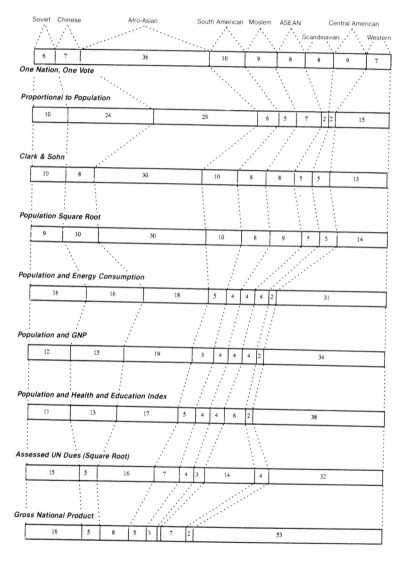

Table showing voting blocs and weighted voting schemes:

Scheme	Soviet	Chinese	Afro-Asian	South American	Moslem	ASEAN	Scandinavian	Central American	Western
One Nation, One Vote	6	7	36	10	9	8	8	9	7
Proportional to Population	10	24	29	6	5	7	2	2	15
Clark & Sohn	10	8	30	10	8	8	5	5	13
Population Square Root	9	10	30	10	8	9	5	5	14
Population and Energy Consumption	16	16	18	5	4	4	4	2	31
Population and GNP	12	15	19	6	4	4	4	2	34
Population and Health and Education Index	11	13	17	5	4	4	6	2	38
Assessed UN Dues (Square Root)	15	5	16	7	4	3	14	4	32
Gross National Product	16	5	8	5	3	7	2		53

What bloc gets what proportion of control under which voting scheme?
Nine weighted voting schemes:

Nine voting blocs in the current United Nations

Table 2

important for such an estimation is not so much its fairness or its ability to reflect influence accurately, but its acceptability to top decision-makers. The acceptability would have to be based on a series of compromises, since it appears from the above results that different blocs would find different formulas in their own best interests.

The results show the reason why discussion of weighted voting is not popular at the UN today. The nation-blocs which form the usual majorities tend to do quite well under the 1-nation 1-vote formula used at present. The blocs that would benefit by weighted voting, oddly enough, are the Chinese, Soviet, and Western, which do not command a majority.

Until recently the superpower leaders themselves have opposed weighted voting, even though they would seemingly benefit by it. There have been unfortunate reasons for their opposition:

•They preferred getting their crucial resolutions through by soliciting the votes of other nations through threats and promises; that is, what would be called "side-payments" in game theory.

•They could always ignore resolutions adopted which they did not like.

•They preferred to prevent any stengthening of a United Nations which they did not control.

Now the USA is insisting on weighted voting according to contributions to the UN budget, threatening to leave the UN unless this is done. This type of weighted voting would favor the Western bloc, especially the USA.

PART THREE: TRANSFORMATION

We as individuals and as nations are steered along our paths by our values — such things as moral beliefs, goals, dependencies, routines and rituals. There is nothing more personal and more sacred to most of us than our values. When it comes time to leave the path we must first adjust our value systems ... and that is not always an easy task. Sometimes, depending on the severity of the crisis, it involves a major transformation. Alcoholics and drug addicts often replace their chemical reliance with a deep spiritual devotion. Workers whose jobs are replaced by new machines may develop a contempt for machines before they finally adjust their values and learn new job skills.

Nations, religions, and other human institutions run into similar crises, especially in today's changing world. The Moslem world is forced to deal with modernization, freedom-loving Western nations with the growing need for planning and regulation, the socialist world with the human needs for freedom and incentive, all industrialized nations with a deteriorating environment, and on and on.

Peace among nations requires peace between the sexes. First, psychologists Chellis Glendinning and Ofer Zur observe the need to fine-tune the age-old masculine and feminine value systems ... to call a permanent truce to the "battle of the sexes."

How transformation occurs. Next, senior social scientist Willis Harman takes an in-depth look at exactly how individuals and nations go about transforming their belief systems.

World values. Professional peace researcher Hanna Newcombe explores a rich cross-section of values formulated in recent decades by some of the world's great social thinkers . . . values available to us when our transformations begin.

From nationalism to globalism. Globalist Gerald Mische looks at the difficult transformation our species is undergoing from a world of sovereign nations to a collection of interdependent systems.

A new age of world socialism. Economist Jozsef Bognar looks at world socialism, which is now entering its second stage — decentralization and growing economic vitality.

Global spirituality. Author Patricia Mische observes from a spiritual perspective the global transformation now underway.

Chapter 10
Men/Women, War/Peace: A Systems Approach

by Ofer Zur
Psychologist and Faculty,
California Institute
of Integral Studies
San Francisco, CA, USA

Chellis Glendinning
Psychologist and Director,
Waking Up In
the Nuclear Age
San Francisco, USA

Background. Deliver joint lectures on the relationship between gender and war, exploring myths of battle and the psychological effects of looming holocaust. Glendinning, co-founder of "despair and empowerment work" (psychological approaches to becoming active in a tenuous world), has written *Waking Up in the Nuclear Age* (William Morrow, 1987) and a variety of articles and book chapters. Zur, a former Israeli military officer and oceanographer turned social and clinical psychologist, is known for his controversial research on gender and war, and is currently developing a graduate program in peace/war and global studies.

Their article. How can men and women participate in the rites of passage into more complete human beings and a more complete world order? The battle of the sexes and war among nations seem to be deeply interrelated. The splits that divide us must be mended collectively as we move toward a new age of peace.

In these times both sexes need protection, and the talents of both sexes are needed to protect our endangered planet.

photo by Nick Allen

Men/Women, War/Peace: A Systems Approach

by Chellis Glendinning and Ofer Zur

*B*aby is born!" This was the cable the Manhattan Project sent to President Truman to report the first atom bomb test.

The revealing Bikini bathing suit was named for the Pacific islands where nuclear testing took place.

We say: "All's fair in love and war."

Men tell "war stories" about their "conquests over" women.

Connections between gender and war-making lie deep within the modern psyche.

Most of us are acquainted with the age-old battle between the sexes, which is based on a perception of rigid polarization of women and men. This polarization is also the main quality defining warfare.

While in everyday life men and women are split off from each other and from crucial aspects of themselves, war is the ultimate splitting of human from human. War also separates the population along sex lines, and in that respect it resembles childbirth. In war, women are traditionally excluded from the military; in birthing, men were until recently excluded from the birthrooms. Also, to make nuclear war possible, our society splits the most fundamental material of existence — the atom — and so, as Albert Einstein predicted, "we drift toward unparalleled catastrophe." The nuclear threat brings urgency to the way we view warmaking, and the double-edged pain of sexism brings urgency to the way we view women and men. For survival, healing the splits is required. (Glendinning, 1987)

The authors of this chapter bring humility to this task. We also bring hope. Our subject is the role of gender in warmaking and its potential impact on peacemaking. It is how, in the Nuclear Age, women and men can become participants in rites of passage towards the creation of more whole human beings and a more whole world order. As psychologists interested in social change, we take a systems approach. We attempt to understand our subject by identifying its many facets, their interrelationships, and the totality they form.

A False Belief: Men Fight, Women Love

To begin, if we look at observable actions and interactions of men and women, we see that in wartime men are mobilized toward the front line and perceived as the warriors, aggressors and protectors. Women stay home. They are seen as the peace-loving, the passive, the protected. Consistent with this split is a myth, or collectively held belief, that war is a male institution that holds no appeal to women. Men assume the role of "the warrior," while to women falls the role of "the beautiful soul" (Zur, 1985).

Myths, as portrayed in literature, film, fairy tales, science, and everyday language and imagery, compel respect not necessarily for their truth, but because those who believe in them need them. Myths lay the basis for a society's perception of itself and its members' sense of identity. They also reflect a set of attitudes that, in the words of Joseph Campbell (1980), are "behavior perpetuators." Myths about war perpetuate warfare and as such, merit our special attention, especially in the face of nuclear holocaust (Harman, 1984; Zur, 1986A). Myths that men favor war while women are inherently peaceful reflect a dangerous and, as the reader will see, untrue split that keeps us from addressing the issues of gender imbalance and warfare with a fuller understanding.

It was personal experience that inspired Zur's research on aspects of the relationship between men, women and war. From a recent paper:

"In the 1973 War in the Middle East I served as a Lieutenant in a trained paratroopers' unit. We were kept at the rear, far from action, for the first part of the war. To my surprise, I found that most of the seasoned paratroopers in my unit devised any possible strategy to secure service at the front. When I questioned their motives, I discovered that their desire to return home to their wives and sweethearts with a glorious or grisly war story outweighed the fear of injury and high probability of death. I realized the incredible power of the women waiting at home on the soldiers at the front. Ultimately, it became obvious to me that the noncombatants, the protected, are an invisible but potent force at the front (Zur, 1986A)."

A similar systems approach has been used by psychologists who study and intervene in cases of girls sexually abused by their fathers. Aggressor, victim and passive bystander each play a part. Without assigning blame to the girl-victim or the mother-bystander, diffusing responsibility of the abuser or denying the hierarchical power structure of the family, these therapists also explore the role of the mother who keeps her passive position, often denying reality for years.

When this systems approach is carried over to the context of war, we see that the role of the protector does not exist in a vacuum. A protector implies a protected person, and both of them rely on real and/or projected threats from the outside for role definition and identity formation (Stiehm, 1982).

In the case of nations, the protector is the military, an institution from which women are traditionally excluded. Men in political positions are the ones who usually define threats to the nation, who may in their own perceived interest exaggerate its potency, and whose exaggeration may provoke additional threats, further endangering both themselves and their protectees. Also, those who are protected often use the threat to test the protector and to enhance a real sense of personal safety.

Boys Play to Win, Girls Play to Play

The relationship among men, warriorship and war is complex. Regardless of innate differences between males and females, boys are socialized differently from girls. Qualities like assertiveness, courage to take physical risks, aggressiveness and lack of demonstrated emotions are encouraged so that men are set up to become "all they can be" — soldiers.

Differences are also initiated at a level deeper than socialization. Recent works by Nancy Chodorow (1978), Carol Gilligan (1982) and

Dorothy Dinnerstein (1976) suggest that child-rearing structures in our culture produce differing perceptions of survival in male and female children — and therefore differing personalities. These theories stress the impact of nuclear families wherein mothers are the primary caretakers and fathers the primary breadwinners, unavailable emotionally or physically to the child.

According to Chodorow's theory, in order to develop a healthy gender identity, the male child must make a dramatic break with his primary love object and the person he depends on for physical and psychological survival — the mother. The problem begins when no adult male is present on a daily basis to turn to. Male development, then, is based on rejection of the female and everything associated with her, and then striving to relate to and identify with a distant, separate figure who lives in a world of rationality and rules (Chodorow, 1978).

In her studies of male and female moral development Gilligan (1982) demonstrates these same insights from the point of view of social perception. In this culture a male's sense of morality is based on impersonal and hierarchical definitions of what is right, and these are identified as the correct and most highly evolved ones.

Boys' games further illuminate this development. Games like basketball, football, racing and poker emphasize competing to win — to separate oneself out — and competing within the boundaries of set rules. If the rules don't succeed at containing the game, change the rules. If changes can't be negotiated or don't work, win by might.

Unlike boys, girls do not have to rupture with the primary love object and caretaker in order to develop a healthy gender identity. They can maintain the bond with Mother throughout their lives. A female sense of personal survival, then, is based on connection, relationship and communication. Women grow to have a fluid sense of boundaries and develop a relational sense of self. No attempt is made to separate oneself out, individuate or establish ego boundaries (Chodorow, 1978).

Gilligan carries these insights into the social realm. She finds that when judged by accepted male standards of moral development, females score "deficient." Yet she shows that females are indeed not deficient, but rather live by a different sense of morality. Women of all ages and backgrounds live in a world of relationship and social relativity, a world where awareness of the connection between people gives rise to a sense of responsibility for one another; where belief in communication is the primary mode of conflict resolution (Gilligan,

1982).

Lawrence Kohlberg (1969) observes that traditional girls' games like hopscotch, jump rope and jacks are turn-taking games in which competition is indirect and one person's winning does not depend on another's losing. Plus, when a quarrel breaks out — and, says Glendinning, I remember this from my childhood — girls tend to end the game rather than battle it out. As Gilligan (1982) claims, they subordinate "the continuation of the game to the continuation of the relationship."

Women's Role in Warmaking: Supporters and Victims

Unlike the role of men during war, which is clear and apparent, the full role of women has not always been acknowledged. While men are at the front line, women are the protected at home, but they are also the soldiers at the home front. They are the Rosie-the-Riveters working in wartime industry; the Florence Nightingales healing the wounded; the worried mothers, proud sweethearts and acclaimed widows. They take care of all other noncombatants, and they participate in many operations of defense. Fulfilling these roles is an inherent and necessary part of the war effort. It is what enables the soldiers to carry out their complementary roles.

In recent research Zur (1986B) revealed that indeed women support warmaking, but for different reasons than men. While men favor war for abstract reasons — for defense of "freedom" and to protect allies with whom one has formal treaties — women support war when an appeal is made based on empathy for oppressed and vulnerable human beings. They also relate more easily to the dynamics of group cohesion and intensification of community during war as it is consistent with their psychological makeup. For example, women responded more favorably than men to such Likert-type items as:

• Aiding an attacked ally justifies war.

• One of the benefits of war is that it intensifies connections among civilians.

• Any country that violates the rights of innocent children should be invaded.

One of Zur's conclusions: women are not just the passive "beautiful souls" our myths describe them to be. They participate in war activities in numerous capacities, and they cooperate, support warmaking, and collude in it, albeit in different ways and for different reasons than men.

Women's relationship to war, however, is more complex. They are also its victims. On the other side of the proud mothers and enthusiastic workers lie the women who, as a class, never make the actual decision to wage war, but whose loss of father, husband, brother, son and lover always means devastating personal grief. For many women, this loss of relation and loved one also spells economic hardship for the rest of their lives. Second, women are the target of dehumanization in wartime pornography. Degrading pinups that reduce women to sexual objects are the constant companion of the troops in their barracks, planes and submarines. Dancing, singing women entertain soldiers at the front. Third, the vicious and violent rape of women is a universal and accepted part of men's violence in warring (Brownmiller, 1976). Finally, women are the victims of modern warfare in that the battlefields, which used to be far from the kitchens and marketplaces of society, are now anywhere that a long-range missile and its nuclear warhead can reach. Today all the world, and all the human beings in it, are the battlefield too.

The question then arises: How can women be both active supporters — nurses, typists and proud mothers, making war in an interactive dynamic with male warriors — and also victims of the universal dehumanization, rape and intimidation that men enact in war?

Another question arises: How can men be both heroic soldiers, fighting for homeland, family and the women back home, and also bullies committing insensitive and violent acts against women?

The Systems Approach

The contradictions inherent in these questions bring us to search for a bigger perspective. At this point a systems approach is required that includes not just observable actions and interaction of different sectors of society or the myths that determine and give meaning to behavior patterns. We need a system that includes the overall psychological, cultural and social context that surrounds and often determines those actions, interactions and myths.

We live in a society that is founded upon myths and institutions that value and carry forth what has been defined as the "male principle," without benefit of the balancing effect of "feminine" values. Barbara Zanotti (1979) describes this society:

"Patriarchy is a system of dualisms: mind over body, thinking over feeling, heaven over earth, spirit over flesh — dualisms in which women are identified with the negative side. Patriarchy is a system of values developed through male experience: competition, hierarchy, aggression, bureaucracy, alienation from the earth, denial of emotion, generational shortsightedness, the objectification of the other."

Within the context of this kind of society, women are too often the

Men and Women — Poles Apart?

Men and women . . . the differences that unite us in love, divide us in society. We're obviously built differently, we are conceived from different chromosomes and hormones, and recent studies seem to indicate that we also think, behave, communicate, and view life differently.

But how different are we . . . really? If all men moved to the northern hemisphere of our planet, and all women moved to the southern hemisphere, would all masculine aspects of humanity now be at the top, all feminine aspects at the bottom?

Not at all. Actually, everyone is a composite of male and female qualities . . . so in a sexually segregated situation there would still be a worldwide mixture of masculine and feminine qualities. Let's go a step further and put the most masculine men at the north pole and the most feminine women at the south pole. Along the equator would be those frustrated individuals with the physical characteristics of one gender but the compulsions of the other — "women trapped in men's bodies," and vice versa. Everyone else would be distributed along the latitudes according to how masculine or feminine they are in physical appearance, behavior, and hormonal make-up.

A psychological study would probably show men in the far northern communities to be heavy in masculine traits — rational, active, direct, gifted with spatial skills (math and science), intelligent, project-oriented, out in the world, and competitive. Women in the southernmost communities would be ultrafeminine — sensitive, emotional, passive, intuitive, creative, gifted with verbal skills, mysterious, people-oriented, internal, home-oriented, and cooperative.

A demographic study would probably show that the communities at the poles and along the equator had the smallest populations; the sexual extremes seem to make up only a small proportion of humanity. Along the middle latitudes would be scattered most of the people — those with a comfortable balance of feminine and masculine aspects. Men of these midnorthern latitudes might have a sensitive, people-

unwitting — or witting — expressions of the narrow categorization of them as servers to men's goals, in anything. They are the nurses, mothers, typists and wives not just for warmaking, but for all endeavors. And they are prepared for these roles by a system — by

oriented side to polish up their masculine nature. Women of the midsouthern latitudes might have a rational, competitive side to round out their feminine aspects.

Now imagine that this segregated world can suddenly become integrated. People move where they wish, find partners, and settle. New social systems grow. But let's assume that this integration occurs with one very important fact underlying the whole process: Humanity is a joint venture of men and women; every system, subsystem and unit within it can be complete and in top form only when the masculine and feminine aspects are in a comfortable balance.

So, some people select mates who can balance out their strong male or female qualities. Other individuals learn to nurture and develop within themselves their opposite gender traits to become more complete individuals, and then unite with a member of the opposite sex who has done the same. It is this latter relationship — two people striving for wholeness within self — that seems to be the most stable. It is based on traits such as love, trust, respect and growth rather than neediness and dependency.

As the higher social systems develop — communities, companies, states, nations, and so on — all develop with a balance of male and female traits . . . unlike most cultures of the present world. Today most cultures foster and respect the masculine side because of its predominant role and domineering nature. Lately women around the world have been developing their masculine side in order to compete with men in a man's world. The women's movement has fueled this trend. At the same time, men are being asked to be more sensitive and more in tune with their feelings and their homes.

Women have pioneered this development out of necessity, also to gain the respect that the feminine aspect deserves but has not received lately. It is time for men to join with women in the vital move toward integration of our species — not behind them, not in front, but side by side. The world will find peace only when the sexes have found peace through integration.

— *Information provided by Regina Macy,*
counselor and psychotherapist

the interactions they experience as infants, by their socialization, and by the roles made available to them. In other words, by psychology, economics, culture, social opportunity (or lack of it), and by force.

When war is declared, the need for community cohesion is

Opposites Attract

Girl attracts boy. Boy pursues. Girl resists. Boy persists. Probably the most widespread conflict in human history, and for many people no doubt the most fun. Flirting and romance, subject of vast volumes of literature down through the ages, seems to be driven by two basic urges — the feminine urge to attract and tempt, and the masculine urge to conquer and dominate.

These urges that can excite us in love, often divide us in society. They spice up the inner workings of our social groups, but indiscriminate spice often ruins the entire meal. Flirting and romance in inappropriate places at inappropriate times with inappropriate people can generate friction and conflicts in our schools, clubs, companies . . . in any social systems where males and females interact.

Besides discretion, the secret to peace between the genders is to maintain respect for and knowledge of the opposite sex. Here are some of the things modern psychologists are learning about masculine and feminine aspects.

Children's games. Boys tend to play competitive games outdoors in large groups. The games are often long-lasting and involve a lot of skill. Disputes break out fairly often, but boys seem to enjoy resolving conflicts as much as playing the game. Boys are preoccupied by game rules, referring to them frequently to work out disputes. While playing, boys learn competitiveness, independence, and organizational skills that will be helpful later in life in coordinating the activities of large, diverse groups. Meanwhile, girls like to play indoors, usually in small, intimate groups. The games are less competitive, more cooperative, and when disputes break out the girls usually end the game rather than threaten the relationships. Girls are more flexible than boys; they are more likely to bend the rules and adopt any changes that will result in greater fairness and less pain all around. Girls learn to cooperate smoothly while nurturing and preserving interpersonal relationships. They become open-minded.

magnified. The female personality that our society encourages presupposes women to the often invisible, "helping" roles that maintain the fabric of society in wartime. Plus, these roles often place women in positions where they are vulnerable, dependent, and easily

Law and morality. Women generally have a more difficult time than men making moral decisions because they consider many variables. They analyze a situation, looking for the "right" option — the one that will cause the least conflict and pain. Men seem to prefer making hastier, more rational decisions. They eliminate many variables by creating legal and moral boundaries and rules. To make the "right" decision they simply consult the rulebooks. They want quick, neat justice . . . even if it sometimes causes pain to individuals and puts a strain on relationships. Women want to nurture healthy relationships, even if it requires more time, more creativity, and a bending of rules to come up with the "right" solution.

Communication. Women tend to express their feelings openly. Men generally do not. Girls while away hour after teenage hour exchanging their feelings and analyzing relationships over the phone or in hushed, excited conversations. Boys talk about cars, girls, sports, studies . . . virtually anything but their feelings. Boys and girls each think that the other gender's subjects of discussion are trivial.

Interpersonal fears. If men and women were to make separate lists of the social conditions they fear most, women might have a sense of separation and isolation near the top of their list, along with being held in suspicion or being rejected by others for being too successful and competitive. Men might have among their greatest fears feeling entrapped or betrayed, humiliated by deceit, and smothered in a clingy relationship. Coming together intimidates men, while moving apart intimidates women . . . a situation reminiscent of the combined forces of the sun's gravity and our planet's centrifugal force — one trying to pull our solar system together while the other tries to pull it apart. If either force were to prevail, the system would be destroyed, but when working together they keep our sun and Earth in comfortable harmony.

A peaceful world will require the efforts and skills of both genders working together in comfortable harmony, in mutual respect and understanding.

— *Adapted from existing Earthview Press publications and from reference material (Gilligan) cited in Chapter 10*

victimized.

Our systems approach must recognize that men, too, are the unwitting — or witting — expressions of narrow categorizations of them. They are the soldiers, experts, leaders and protectors, locked into the feeling and behavior available to such roles. Men are prepared for them, again, by psychology, economics, culture, social opportunity (and lack of it), and by force.

Since the declaration of war always involves a series of splits into us-them, men-women, soldiers-civilians, godly-ungodly, the male finds it a mode consistent with his personality. When a young man enters the military, despite the grueling and authoritarian nature of basic training, he can find it a unique haven, psychologically speaking. While provided with food, shelter, entertainment and medical care, he can learn in an all-male setting what it is to be a man. The exclusion and degradation of women and female values is not accidental here. They are crucial parts of this system of "building men."

We may view warmaking and its escalation as a result of the patriarchal emphasis on competition, power-over and conquest. We may also view it as a result of the patriarchy's narrow categorization of human beings through rigid sex roles. In this kind of system, the loss of full human development for both women and men, may result in frustration, resentment, anger, grief, powerlessness, conflict, violence and lack of vision.

Ironically, in the context of this system, making war also provides the opportunity for women and men to become more whole human beings. Working in industry, business and the military, women have the chance to become physically and mentally more assertive, take risks and be independent. Likewise, men can experience an enlarging of their boundaries. They can touch each other, care for one another, and see their personal survival linked to communication, trust, and group cohesion. In light of these insights, we then wonder: Is war the best vehicle for offering psychic wholeness to human being? Or, as Betty Reardon (1985) asks: Is peace even possible as long as patriarchal societies that split male from female dominate the globe?

Looking at this predicament from a pragmatic point of view, we could say that the very phenomena which the modern world needs to complement current values are those that women, as a class, know most about. In the Nuclear Age all human beings need, desperately, to remember our connection with one another — whether that be viewed as material connection through economic or ecological reality, or psychic connection through spiritual reality. We need to communicate our needs, our fears, our desires and our dreams. We need to subordinate the continuation of the game to the continuation of the relationship.

The absence of these "feminine" qualities and phenomena in the public forum has led to the excesses of our era. Were these same qualities to be reintroduced into our lives — not just in girls' games and at home, but at all levels of society — human survival would be more likely than it is today.

A rite of passage into the Nuclear Age for women, then, involves acknowledging, valuing and manifesting women's special concern for connection, relationship and communication on a societal level. To accomplish this, ironically, women must learn to selectively break the bonds of connection that they constantly seek. They must individuate enough, separate enough, develop ego boundaries enough, to bring their concern into the world.

Men encounter a different set of tasks. For them the problem is not that there is anything inherently wrong with the qualities and phenomena that have been cordoned off and called "male." Separateness, ego development and rationality are essential characteristics of human life and are crucial for the kind of thinking we must use if we are to survive, but in many societies they dominate and are not subject to the healthy balancing and complementary effect of those characteristics we call "female."

What we are called upon to do in the Nuclear Age is to undertake a rearrangement of psychological, cultural and social forces so that the male-dominated system by which we live does not arrive at its destined end point — a win-lose game leading to a lose-lose conclusion of nuclear weapons — but rather becomes more balanced and life-affirming. A rite of passage into this Age for men has to do with making this kind of transition. As for women, it involves acknowledging and validating what resources are already present: the will to individuate, the passion of the warrior, the desire to protect; but what is new is that this rite of passage cannot be complete until these qualities are manifested and honored in the context of connection and relationship.

As Shepherd Bliss (1985) has said, at this junction of history the value of men "shedding their armour" and "tending their wounds" is undeniable. With this tending comes an acceptance of the nurturing, reflective aspects of the male self, as well as direct, unprojected experience of the impulse behind violence against fellow living beings. Male involvement in child rearing and care also breaks the cycle of patriarchal development, offering the male adult the opportunity to explore nurturance and connection. Plus, it gives both boy and girl children the chance to relate to and identify with the male, and to grow into more whole human beings.

At this point we are well aware that "male" cultural configurations stand challenged by the nuclear reality. While the ultimate bomb may have been the technological device that destroyed Hiroshima, the ultimate "sex bomb" was Rita Hayworth, a decal-picture of her body glued to that bomb as it was dropped from the belly of the Enola Gay, a plane named for the commander's mother. In these times it becomes clear that militarism and sexism emanate from the same system of thought and that this system must change. The old myth of the male warrior-hero no longer works. There is no more triumph in winning. There is no more separating oneself out, and no more putting down women in the process. As Mark Gerzon (1983) has written: "The frontiersman now becomes the healer, the soldier becomes the mediator; the breadwinner becomes the companion; the expert becomes the nurturer."

As we embark upon these rites of passage, women and men join together to reduce the world's nuclear arsenal; to ask questions about our myth of war and peace, women and men; and to accomplish change — not just in policy, but on all levels of our human being. In these times both sexes need protection, and the talents of both sexes are needed to protect our endangered planet. Working together we stand at the fragile edge of a vision — a world made up of more whole women and men no longer engaged in the battle of the sexes.

Notes

Bliss, S. (1985). "Men, wounding and war." Paper presented at Self, Society and Nuclear Conflict conference. University of California, San Francisco/Langley Porter Psychiatric Institute, October 19-20, 1985, in San Francisco, Calif.

Brownmiller, S. (1976). *Against our will: men, women and rape*. New York: Bantam Books.

Campbell, J. (1980). *Myths to live by*. New York: Bantam Books.

Chodorow, N. (1978). *The reproduction of mothering: psychoanalysis and the sociology of gender*. Berkeley, Calif.: University of California Press.

Dinnerstein, D. (1976). *The mermaid and the minotaur*. New York: Harper Calaphon Books.

Gerzon, M. (1983). *A choice of heroes*. New York: Houghton Miflin.

Glendinning, C. (1987). *Waking up in the nuclear age.* New York: William Morrow and Company.

Gilligan, C. (1982). *In a different voice: psychological theory and women's development.* Cambridge, Mass.: Harvard University Press.

Harman, W. (1984). "Peace on earth: The impossible dream become possible." Journal of human psychology 24 (3) pp. 77-92.

Kohlberg, L. (1969). "Stage and sequence: The cognitive-development approach to socialization." In D.A. Goslin (Ed.), Handbook of socialization theory and research. Chicago: Rand McNally.

Lorenz, K. (1966). *On aggression.* New York: Bantam Books.

Reardon, B. (1985). *Sexism and the war system.* New York: Teachers College press.

Stiehm, J. (1982). "The protected, the protector, the defender." Women's studies international forum 5, pp. 367-76.

Zanotti, B. (1979). "Militarism and violence: A feminist perspective." Paper presented at Riverside Church Disarmament Conference, New York.

Zur, O. (1985). "Men, women and war." Paper presented at the Western Psychological Association annual conference, April, San Jose, Calif.

Zur, O. (1986A). "The myths of war: Analysis of the most common beliefs of the nature of warfare." Paper presented at the California State Psychological Association annual conference, March, San Francisco, Calif.

Zur, O. (1986B). "Men, women and war: A new scale of attitudes towards war." Under editorial review.

Chapter 11

Peace, Beliefs, and Legitimacy

by Willis Harman
President, Institute of Noetic Sciences
San Francisco, USA

Background. Has had the rare privilege of exploring the national and world future as a full-time career for 16 years as founder of and senior social scientist at the Futures Research Group at Stanford Research Institute (SRI). Professor of engineering-economic systems at Stanford University. Member of the board of regents, University of California. Author of many articles on electrical and systems engineering, futures research, social policy and analysis, and the current transformation of society.

His article. The most profound changes in history come about not when a few leaders make big decisions, but when vast numbers of people change their minds a little bit. How does this transformation occur, and what sorts of changes will it involve in the coming decades? The article takes a "noetic" approach, which implies expanding the knowledge of the nature and potentials of the mind, and applying that knowledge toward a healthy future for people and our planet.

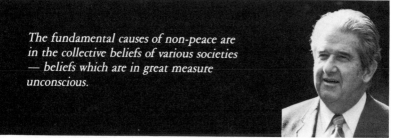

The fundamental causes of non-peace are in the collective beliefs of various societies — beliefs which are in great measure unconscious.

Peace, Beliefs, and Legitimacy

by Willis W. Harman

*E*ach of us has an "inner map" of reality which influences how we perceive the world about us; our perceptions in turn tend to reinforce the "inner map". When two persons with different "inner maps" try to communicate, let alone to live together, the consequences can be disastrous.

A society or nation, too, tends to have a dominant picture of reality that is tacitly understood by its members or citizens. That internalized picture shapes the perceptions of other nations and international situations. Those perceptions, which have been influenced in the first place by the internalized picture, tend then to reinforce it. Breaking this vicious circle is a key to the problem of achieving peace in the world.

Beliefs and Perceptions

We humans have an awesome ability to deceive ourselves. Once we have settled on one perception of "reality," all evidence to the contrary tends to become invisible. All hints that our picture might be wrong or even seriously incomplete are warded off. For instance:

• Anthropolgists find that individuals who are raised in different tribal cultures literally perceive different realities — and each one finds that his or her experience bears out the tribe's traditional view.

• Shivering, hypnotized subjects who have accepted the suggestion that they are in a cold chamber at sub-zero temperatures may not be convinced otherwise by being shown a thermometer registering room temperature.

The annals of history and of psychotherapy are full of examples of "resistance" and "denial" — classical ways of warding off evidence that challenges the person's "inner map" of reality.

We do not necessarily perceive the world in a way that would be most in our real self interest. For example:

•The paranoid sees the environment in a way that causes much self anguish, and rational argument or even contradictory experience may fail to change that perception.

•The business executive whose stressful existence has brought about cardiovascular disease will often continue his self-destructive behavior patterns rather than perceive his work in a more comfortable, less stressful way.

•It does not serve us well to perceive the world in such a way that there is no viable alternative to the perilous nuclear weapons impasse, yet that is the all-too-common perception.

This picture of "reality" that we protect so carefully can be changed . . . sometimes by a mere suggestion.

•In the well-known placebo effect, the suggestion that an inert substance is a powerful medicine results in its acquiring an apparent efficacy to heal.

•A hypnotized subject striking an imaginary "solid wall" (present only in the suggestion of the hypnotist) comes away with a bruised fist!

•Thousands of professional and business persons during the last couple of years have discovered, in "firewalking" workshops, that if they shift their minds into a different state of perceiving reality, they can walk barefoot over burning coals without harming their feet.

It does not come easily, of course, to recognize that the view of reality which we have held most of our lives, and which is also held by most of those around us, is a parochial view that has been shaped by all the suggestions we have absorbed along the way — just as the perceived world of the hypnotized subject has been shaped by the suggestions he or she has accepted from the hypnotist. In fact, this is such an unpalatable recognition that it appears a vast number of persons would risk the destruction of civilization rather than risk fundamentally changing their perceptions of the world.

It is time now to change our perception to one in which the goal of world peace seems far more possible. How do we make such a profound change in attitude, from a pessimistic sense of world destiny to an optimistic one? Perhaps the same way it is done at the personal level. This analogy is what might be called a "fundamental lesson of psychotherapy." Many, many people have undergone a

fundamental reorganization of their "inner maps of reality."
Typically, this change was brought about by life's crises. Sometimes it
was characterized by trauma and breakdown, by a bout with drug
addiction or with alcoholism, or by attempted suicide; sometimes the
passage was aided by formal psychotherapy or a spontaneous spiritual
awakening. However diverse their individual experiences, person after
person has learned the same basic lesson: No matter how insoluble
and overwhelming may seem the problems faced — emotional,
financial, in relationships, at work, or in the family — perceived
another way, they are all solvable and, furthermore, all the resources
necessary for their solution were available all along!

No one could have persuaded the person, before his or her dramatic
transformation, that such a conclusion was possible. Similarly,
rational arguments alone may fail to convince that a change in our
"inner maps" could make the global problems appear solvable. And
yet that may be the case.

The Fundamental Causes of Non-Peace

It is characteristic of the process of human change that we will
typically hide from ourselves that which we most need to know (and
at a conscious level may think we want to know). This comes out with
particular clarity in the so-called "Twelve Steps" of Alcoholics
Anonymous' program for personal change. The first two of these
steps are:

1. We admitted that we were powerless over alcohol — that our lives
had become unmanageable.

2. We came to believe that a power greater than ourselves could
restore us to sanity.

The awareness represented by the first step is typically very strongly
resisted. It is a fearful thing to recognize that one's life has become
unmanageable; however, the cure cannot proceed without this
admission. The inner awareness associated with the second step is
resisted as well. In a way, this step challenges the person's claim that
"I don't know what to do." There is a part of the mind that does
know — a part that ordinarily is not directly accessible to conscious
awareness.

We are suggesting that something like this may apply in a collective
sense with regard to global problems. The "first step" is to recognize
that global society has indeed become unmanageable. We may expect
that step to be strongly resisted, as in the case of the alcoholic. The

"second step" is to recognize the deeper-level resources that can come into play when a society is inspired by an adequate vision.

Let us return to the individual whose life is full of conflict — who, indeed, may be carrying on a "war" with his/her spouse, work, with life in general, with self. It is not obvious to that person, but long experience amply demonstrates a basic truth: The fundamental cause of non-peace is to be found in the individual's unconscious beliefs. Those beliefs shape the person's perceived "reality" within which lie the origins of the individual's non-peace. Change those beliefs and the conflict changes form or disappears.

"Buying Into" a Dangerous Value System

The idea that collectively held beliefs create world conditions for non-peace is much less widely appreciated than the relationship betwen individual beliefs and personal problems. Consider the implications if we were to be persuaded that *the fundamental causes of non-peace on the planet are to be found mainly in the collective beliefs of the various societies — beliefs which are partly consciously held, but are in great measure unconscious.*

It is by no means apparent that this is the case. In fact, on first reading, the above statement may seem not only wrong but nonsensical. We are used to seeking explanations of the state of global nonpeace in national competitions; in the ambitions and frustrations of leaders in those countries; in the flaws of past treaties; in religious and ideological conflicts. No doubt these explanations are partially accurate. But underlying them, as a more fundamental breeding ground of non-peace, are the largely collective beliefs and value systems that so subtly create barriers, separations, tensions, and collisions. These values are difficult even to become aware of, and certainly to challenge, mainly because the people around us in our own society tend to share the same values and tacitly to take them for granted. We are all subject to the same "cultural hypnosis" and experience a common "reality."

Consider, for example, what beliefs and priorities are implied by the (so-called) "defense policies" of the United States and the Soviet Union, and by the fact that the separate goals of the two superpowers are for each so compelling that no alternative can be found to massive nuclear confrontation. (It may help, in attempting to view this afresh, if you picture yourself to be a cultural anthropologist coming in from another civilization, say from another planet!) Imagine, too, the beliefs implied by the enormously expensive and unprecedented worldwide arms race in "conventional" weapons which is assumed to be unavoidable — regrettable as it is that the diversion of effort and resources into arms is thwarting satisfaction of the most basic human needs in many of the poorer countries.

What can one infer from the fact that Western capitalist society, which exerts such a powerful influence over the rest of the world, lauds consumption of goods and services — approvingly referring to citizens as "consumers" — even though frugality would clearly be preferable from the standpoints of resource depletion and environmental impact? Far-reaching decisions are based on economic criteria and the short-term financial bottom line, even when the social and ecological consequences of those decisions are disastrous. (One aspect of this is a formalized disregard for the welfare of future generations — overuse and depletion of agricultural lands, profligate consumption of fossil fuels, discounting the future, all justified by "sound economic logic".)

The competitive and materialistically acquisitive drives observed in persons' economic behavior are considered "normal"; however, the currently prevailing scientific understandings tend to deny or explain away the noblest of human motivations because altruism, love, and spiritual yearnings are "unscientific" concepts. These examples but hint at the underlying irrationalities which an objective observer might deduce from our collective behavior. To such an observer, the solutions to our problems would lie quite apparently in a change of beliefs.

Now, could we change our deeply held beliefs rapidly enough to delegitimate both war and preparation for war? As I mentioned earlier, there is a strong resistance to such change, which shows up in psychotherapy. Still it is vital that we overcome this resistance when our values threaten our well-being. We are influenced to overcome this resistance in a number of ways. Life trauma makes it necessary, some overpowering transcendental experience stimulates it, some close and trusted friend prompts it through having made a similar change. Some of those conditions are being met these days in the lives of a great many individuals in the US, national traumas such as Vietnam, Watergate, and Nicaragua provide the stimulus for personal life traumas.

It is important to note a distinction between two degrees of change of mind. One is the change that would be required to achieve the permanent liberation of humankind from serious conflict through replacement of hate by love, and of self-centered competition by altruism and cooperation. The other is a much more limited goal. It is sufficient change of mind to bring about the total delegitimation of war, including the abolition of nuclear weapons, and the international sharing of sovereignty in some sort of peacekeeping function similar to that outlined in the UN Charter. The former, more profound change of mind may well be the long-term evolutionary destiny of humankind, but for the time being it may appeal only to a limited group of people. The latter makes much less demand on the individual. Given modern communication techonolgies, it could potentially be achieved well within a generation.

Challenging "Legitimate" but Dangerous Value Systems

One of the key beliefs in an individual's total belief system is that regarding one's ability to affect one's own destiny. As this sense of personal empowerment strengthens, so does the sense of being able to affect the legitimacy rules of one's society . . . and one's world.

Something like this was happening in the US during the 1960s, when a host of social movements came into being or took new form from older movements of the 1920s and 1930s; there was a women's movement, an extension of the women's suffrage movement into claims of other rights beyond the vote; an environmental movement growing out of the old conservation movements; and so on. One heard a good deal about "radicalization": Certain demonstrations and other activities were carried on, not so much to win a tactical objective as to bring about a "radicalization" of minds, a lessening of the hold of the accepted belief system of the culture.

This radicalization or change of perception was primarily in two directions — outward and inward. One of these involved altering one's perceptions with regard to what were claimed to be oppressive, regimenting, depersonalizing, alienating, stupefying, stultifying characteristics of modern social institutions. Deliberate confrontations with authorities were provoked, for instance, to invoke the "mind-changing" quality of such confrontation. The other direction of radicalization was that associated with the sudden interest in yoga, meditation, Eastern philosophical-religious systems, transpersonal psychologies, psychedelic chemicals, and the like. This involved changing self-perception, specifically in recognizing one's essential spiritual nature.

By the mid-1980s this had all changed somewhat. The ecological movement, peace movement and women's movement are now clearly recognized to be different faces of a single wave of transformative change. While there is some student involvement, the issues have come to have appeal for many more mature citizens as well. The term "radicalization" is seldom used, and "changing consciousness" has taken its place.

With this change in consciousness:

•We perceive how the whole pattern, the underlying paradigm, of Western industrial society (both forms: capitalist and communist) leads inexorably to the kinds of problems and global dilemmas we now face.

•We realize that the dilemmas have their satisfactory resolution only through change in the dominant paradigm.

•We recognize that we unwittingly "buy into" belief systems in which the Earth exists to be exploited, "premodern" cultures are inferior, women have a subordinate role, nuclear weapons bring "security," profligate consumption is "good for the economy," etc., etc.; and that a major step is taken when realization comes that the things our society takes for granted are not necessarily true — that it is not necessary to "buy into" beliefs.

• We realize that all institutions in society, no matter how powerful, obtain their legitimacy from the perceptions of people — and hence that people have the power to change institutions by challenging the legitimacy of prevailing institutional behaviors.

•And most specifically, we recognize that people have the power to challenge the legitimacy and glorification of war as an instrument of policy, for any nation.

The really fundamental changes in human history — such as the ending of the Roman era or of the Middle Ages — have come about not through the arbitrary decisions of a few leaders, but because *vast numbers of people changed their minds*, just a little. *People* give the legitimacy to all institutions, and on occasion in history people have awakened and remembered that they also have the power to withdraw legitimacy. In the past, legitimacy has been withdrawn from slavery; imperialism and the keeping of political colonies; cruel and unusual punishment; officially sanctioned torture; dueling; subjugation and mutilation of women; female infanticide. (Some of those things still happen, of course, but by and large they are not accepted nor viewed as legitimate.)

It may seem that delegitimating an institution as durable and as venerable as war is a step so large that it is hard to imagine. Yet like other major shifts in attitude throughout history, it can come about if the people of the world change their minds and demand it. We have noted earlier how, over the years since World War I, legitimacy has already been largely withdrawn from wars of aggression and territorial gain. The only kind of war that retains the cloak of legitimacy is that for which the preparation was in the name of "defense," and the initiation is non-deliberate. That is precisely the war that is most hazardous — the one which the world fearfully awaits.

Since World War II, war is no longer a contest between trained armies; it is the desolation of civilian populations. The legitimacy will be removed from war when people's consciousness changes enough, and their will to act is awakened.

The Profound Power of Inner Imagery

Challenging the legitimacy of our nations' dangerous value systems is not enough to bring peace, however. There is another concept essential to an overall peace strategy adequate to the challenge of a nuclear age. This is the underappreciated power of unconscious beliefs and the under-recognized potentiality of changing them.

Our beliefs shape our values and lead our actions. Both in research and in experience (for example in psychotherapy and management training), this statement is being found to be true in a way more profound than we have in the past tended to take into account. What we deeply believe and imagine to be true tends to become real. In general, people who are aware of the horror of the nuclear reality and the complexity of international affairs overwhelmingly do not believe that permanently sustainable peace is a feasible goal — certainly not one to be achieved in our generation. Yet that negative belief may itself be one of the greatest impediments to achieving peace. Thus a central task of any effective peace strategy is to try to change this prevailing negative affirmation to a positive one.

Modern studies of conscious and unconscious processes are unequivocal in their conclusion that what we affirm and program into our unconscious belief system, we tend in subtle ways to bring about. When we establish and affirm an intention or a goal, imagining that it is already so, the unconscious mind is programmed to achieve that goal even in ways which the conscious part of the mind does not plan or understand. There are many practical applications of this principle.

•Athletic coaches train athletes to image championship performance.

•Doctors train cancer patients to heal themselves by imaging the functioning of the immune system in ridding the body of the cancer.

•Business executives learn to affirm that desired goals are already achieved. This basic principle has long been a core idea in the esoteric, inner-core understandings in the world's spiritual traditions; the most familiar formulation in the Christian tradition is found in Mark 11:24: "Whatever you ask in prayer, believe that you receive it and you will."

To appreciate how this power of affirmation and inner imagery might be far greater than we at first imagine, consider again the lessons of hypnosis. Through the mysterious power of the accepted suggestion, we can be persuaded to perceive something that isn't there, or to fail to see something that is there; to experience limits that exist only in our unconscious beliefs, or to some extent at least, to transcend limits we ordinarily experience as real. We are all "culturally hypnotized" from infancy, having accepted the ubiquitous suggestions of our surrounding environment as to how we should perceive reality, and how we should perceive what is possible within that reality. Yet the farther we explore the mysteries of the deep mind, the more it becomes apparent that the limits we experience are chiefly, if not entirely, the limits imposed by our individual and collective belief systems.

No brief argument can convince on this point, and no demonstration can be found in the form of conventional scientific research. Yet the repeated testimony to this effect found in the esoteric understandings of the world's spiritual traditions give it a certain credibility. It is not clear that there are any limits to the human mind/spirit that do not in the end appear to be imposed by our beliefs. Conventional believing would insist that you cannot bruise your fist by striking an imaginary wall — yet change the internalized belief, and the hand gets bruised. Conventional believing would insist that if you walk through burning coals in your bare feet severe burns will result — yet change the internalized belief, and the feet are unharmed.

What, then, are the ultimate limits to the power of affirmation and imagery? They are not what conventional logic would suggest. For one thing, much evidence indicates that at some subterranean level minds are joined. (Thus, for example, it is a fairly common occurrence that a person "knows" when a distant loved one is in trouble. Or, two people who have lived together for years find the same thoughts spontaneously occurring in both minds.) But if that is true, then presumed limits that implicitly assume our separateness will not necessarily be found to hold — my affirmation may indeed affect things for someone else; my imaging may influence someone else's healing. In numerous other ways we are reminded that the "reality" we experience is a function of our particular cultural hypnosis (even when we reassure ourselves that it is, after all, "scientifically" verified). In the very practically focused affirmation workshops that have found increasing acceptance in the business world, persons are encouraged not to assume any limitations regarding their affirmations; since they don't know what ultimate limits are, believing in any limit insures that limit will be experienced.

A collective belief in the achievement of global peace will contribute toward the achievement of that goal, just as the collective disbelief is now thwarting it. However, for affirmation to work well we need to be as specific as possible. The coach does not teach the athlete to image receiving the gold medal at the judges' stand, but rather to image the specific athletic activity to be carried out. Similarly the affirmation of sustainable peace will be most effective if it is not a general "pray for peace" outlook, but rather affirmation of a rather specific, plausible scenario.

An "Existence Theorem" for a Strategy for Peace

Mathematicians sometimes put forth an "existence theorem" proving that, despite the fact that no solutions to a particular problem have been found, nevertheless in theory a solution exists. In that spirit, all of the preceding discussion could be thought of as leading up to an "existence theorem" that a strategy for achieving "operational peace" within a generation is a feasible goal.

This would not be a strategy for remote decision makers, but for *people*. Its feasibility, as we would freely admit, is not in any sense demonstrable through rigorous argument. And yet the at-first-incredible possibility that it could succeed is made more plausible through recognition of the potential power of the concepts mentioned earlier.

This feasibility argument rests on ten fundamental premises which are reasonably well substantiated, and which further research can undoubtedly make more so. These are:

1. The need for whole-system change. There is no solution to the nuclear weapons dilemma that does not involve fundamental change in the global system and in its underlying paradigm. The breach between the US and the USSR may be healed, as were the conflicts with our earlier "enemies" — Germany, Japan, and China. But a far more fundamental and long-lasting breeding ground for conflict is present in the gap between the rich North and the impoverished South. The basic concepts of national and global security in a nuclear age have to be reexamined, as does the present economic and political world order.

2. The need for widespread change of mind to bring it about.
Fundamental societal change occurs when vast numbers of people change their minds. Fundamental social system change has historically come about only "from the bottom." The initiative has not come from society's "powerful" leaders. A growing group of planetary citizens are changing their minds about the acceptability of the nuclear "balance of terror," with or without the embellishment of "Star Wars."

3. A general desire for peace. People, by and large, want to affirm a goal of peace and common security — peace that works. They are, however, wary of a goal of peace that implies weakness or invites future betrayal or seems dreamily unrealistic.

4. Doubts that the goal is realistic. People, by and large, do not believe that sustainable peace is an achievable goal, at least in the near future. They are convinced that the issue is incredibly complex, that the forces toward war are strong, that the necessary leadership is not forthcoming, that we do not know how to bring about peace and hence its achievement requires far more research. Hopefully this book will help change that.

5. Underappreciated power of imagery. People, by and large, are unaware of the power of collective imagery and affirmation. They are relatively unaware of the power of individual inner imagery and affirmation (self-fulfilling belief) to actualize chosen goals, although this is becoming more widely recognized — largely through reported successes in healing, athletic training, business entrepreneurship and management; also through such contemporary spiritual movements as Religious Science, Unity, etc. However, people tend not to extrapolate to the potentiality of collective imagery and affirmation, although the specific examples with athletic teams and nation-states are well known.

6. Negative use of this power. Hence they tend to be unaware that this power is presently being used negatively in the form of collectively affirmed beliefs about the infeasibility of sustained peace on the planet. (Fear of a nuclear holocaust is such a belief; so is the feeling of powerlessness in the face of the nuclear war possibility; so is a confidence, secret or expressed, that though we can't get rid of the weapons, they will never go off.)

7. Power greater than assumed. The power of imagery and affirmation is potentially far greater than is ordinarily assumed. Through changing the unconscious "programming" of the individual it changes perceptions, and hence, behavior. If persons affirm a world at peace, they tend to see a world at peace, and hence to act in ways that tend to bring that about. Their political effectiveness can be enhanced by the realization that the legitimacy of all institutions comes from the perceptions of people: If people change their beliefs about the legitimacy of institutions or the behaviors of those institutions, the institutions in turn change. But beyond these links there appear to be still more subtle ways, little understood scientifically, in which our reality changes when we change our unconscious beliefs about reality. It must be said, we do not know the ultimate limits of the power of the beliefs we affirm and the images we contemplate; evidence points to its being greater than generally assumed.

8. The need for a shift from negative to positive use. Thus among the most important tasks in the world today is that of spreading the understanding of this neglected tool, and shifting the prevailing affirmation of the possibility of peace from negative to positive.

9. The need to affirm a realistic scenario. This will be facilitated by having a realistic scenario to affirm. The effectiveness of an affirmation regime is enhanced if what is being affirmed can be assented to by the rational mind. A scenario can be believed if it seems to anticipate and deal with the person's prior reasons for judging peace to be an infeasible goal, and if it has reassuring endorsements from persons whose judgment one has reason to trust.

10. The coming global wave of awakening. Such an affirmation, with the knowledge of the potential power of a positive image collectively held, could contribute to a global wave of awakening to the choice that we have. It is we the people of the planet who, throughout history, have given legitimacy to war and preparation for war as an instrument of national policy. We can take it away. Mass challenge to legitimacy is the most potent instrument of social change to be found in history.

It may at first thought seem unsatisfying to argue the existence of a workable strategy for achieving peace within a generation, and then stop short of defining that strategy. But if the above premises are accurate, the eventual strategy will have to be emergent — that is, it will emerge out of the composite of the intuitively-led actions of vast numbers of people who sense that something like these premises are true in their experience. In other words, being led to a strategy by the shared conviction that one is possible is more trustworthy than being led by a specific strategy put forth by some persuasive ideologue.

What Can I Do?

If the entire strategy is not yet visible, how can I find my part? The strategy we seek is in fact the composite of the actions of great numbers of people, each carrying out some kind of (1) inner work, (2) outer work, and (3) systematic positive imaging.

1. Inner work. The primary objective in the inner work is to discover that it is possible to *shift to a more positive perception* of the world, no less realistic than the previous perception, but far more likely to lead to a constructive response.

The state of publicly accessible knowledge regarding this inner work has improved dramatically in recent decades. Half a century ago, a reductionistic and positivistic science seemd to be making a very effective argument that only the sense-perceived and measurable world is real, and that the capabilities of mind are limited by the physical dimensions of the brain. It seemed that the more science one learned, the less plausible was any kind of religious or spiritual story; and the more education one had, the more skeptical one became regarding the further reaches of the mind and intuitive powers. The turnaround in this regard has been remarkable. It now seems that with further scientific advance some sort of spiritual accounting of humankind becomes increasingly plausible, and less in conflict with scientific findings. Age-old meditative exercises and spiritual practices are being reassessed. From a variety of scientific and scholarly disciplines — experimental psychology, psychotherapy, cultural anthropology, parapsychology, comparative religion — come evidences that the main if not the only limits to the human consciousness are in the inner beliefs. There is a gradually unfolding realization of the powers and the profound wisdom of the hidden mind.

For the *discovery and appropriation of the hidden inner resources*, a variety of meditative approaches are easily accessible. Through these, one learns to be conscious of oneself in new and transcending ways, and to discover potentialities for inner peace that seem ultimately authentic and universal.

In addition to the meditative approaches, some other techniques are useful in dealing with the kinds of *unconscious beliefs that generate conditions of individual non-peace* — of fear, distrust, and hostility. These unconscious beliefs we pick up, mainly, from childhood socialization and through the "hypnotic" suggestions of the surrounding culture. They sometimes change spontaneously or through traumatic life experiences — coming close to death, or a great grief, for example. Many people are led to one or another kind of psychotherapy because these "inner maps of reality" are disadvantageous in terms of causing pain and feelings of separation. Approaches involving guided imagery and positive affirmation (autosuggestion) can be very powerful.

As described earlier, each of us inevitably has complicity in world conditions because of "buying into" the collective beliefs that create those conditions. To discover this in oneself is absolutely essential for clear sight and effective work. Yet each of us has a strong resistance to this discovery, besides which the old beliefs are continually being reinforced by the surrounding culture. One of the more helpful techniques here is deliberately exposing oneself to different points of view (e.g. Third World, Soviet, feminist, Native American Indian) with the attitude that they are not wrong, just different perceptions.

This inner work is unsettling at first — both the work with self-image and the uncovering of pathogenic collective beliefs. Yet as it progresses it becomes exhilarating. As the negative, separating beliefs are brought to light, the positive vision will strengthen of a world that could be — and the actions to help bring it about will become more sure-footed.

2. Outer work. To understand how a variety of kinds of outer work may all contribute to achievement of peace, it is critical that there be an adequately comprehensive picture of the interconnected aspects of global non-peace, for they must be understood together. Global non-peace includes at least the following:

•The ever-present threat of triggering a nuclear exchange, with massive loss of life and mass creation of human desolation;

•Persistent "local" wars with "conventional" weapons leaving a steady wake of human misery;

•A global arms race involving expenditures of over a billion dollars a day, with some of the poorer countries spending more on military preparation than on health care, education, and human welfare all together;

•Widespread poverty, with accompanying disease, malnutrition, and starvation, and with strains on the natural environment that include overgrazing, deforestation, soil erosion, and surface water pollution.

•Environmental degradation and resource exploitation stemming from the economic activities of the industrialized societies;

•Increasing tensions between the industrialized, mass-consuming North and the poverty-stricken South.

It is important to keep in mind these broader dimensions of non-peace because many of them are much longer-lived than the US-Soviet enmity. But even more importantly, it is through seeing these dimensions of the problem of non-peace and their underlying origins in our collective belief systems that the whole-system-change nature of the solution is seen. (This may appear to make an already complex problem seem even moreso. It is helpful to think of an analogy in human illness. A person may have a bewildering array of symptoms that come and go, which all make more sense when they are traced to their common origin, stress — which in turn is a product of the internalized belief system. Similarly, the problems of the planet can appear simpler when viewed as a whole than when seen in isolation.)

Our enemy is not another nation, or another religion, or another ideology . . . but a mind-set. Behind all the components of global non-peace are the tacitly held premises, conscious and unconscious, that shape the institutions and the policies and the "laws" of

Changing Our View of Reality

Each of us has a unique mental picture or map or model of reality based on the things we've seen, heard, experienced and learned during our life. No one has ever had a complete, flawless model because reality is large and complex beyond human comprehension. So we each accept our own limited version as reality . . . often blanking out those things around us that do not fit neatly into our model.

Major changes to our model do not occur often and they do not come easily . . . but they do happen to most of us at some time in our lives. They can occur in the face of crisis, when a flawed vision of reality leads us to one of life's dead ends — drug addiction, alcoholism, emotional breakdown, heart disease . . .

Transformations can also come about in a less destructive fashion when two or more people with very different backgrounds are involved in a joint project requiring a pooling of their diverse knowledge.

economics, and yes, even the sciences and technologies. As that awareness becomes ever clearer, it will illuminate and guide the outer work, making it more effective at achieving the real goal.

If indeed the solution to the nuclear weapons dilemma, and the achievement of peace, are to be found in whole-system change, then this involves a vast number of specific tasks. Each of us has our own unique role to be discovered and played. It may be a significant public role, or it may be a small, quiet inconspicuous one. Whatever it is, it is important, not just because of the work itself but because the activity is sensitizing. It preserves one from indifference. It also keeps the inner work from becoming too introspective.

3. Systematic use of imagery and affirmation. As one becomes more convinced of the power of self-suggestion and inner imagery in achieving individual goals, it becomes easier to believe this might extend to collective beliefs and collective goals. (A good football coach knows how to make this work with team beliefs; charismatic leaders have influenced entire societies.)

Think of this now in application to the nuclear weapons dilemma:

Imagine, for example, that a group of attorneys and a group of computer engineers faced the awesome task of designing a computerized legal system that would be fairer, faster, and less prone to human error than traditional systems. Because of their education, the attorneys and engineers live in two completely different realities. As time passes, however, the two realities gradually overlap as the attorneys learn more and more about computers, and as the engineers learn more and more about law. In essence, they are transforming their values and realities for the sake of collaboration.

Today we live in a world of rich cultural, religious, economic, political, and social diversities. We have been assigned by destiny the joint project of bringing peace and order to a world in crisis. For us to be successful, transformations must occur to our world, our nations and religions, our social groups and ourselves . . . as we all broaden our pictures of reality, learning more and more about the diversified world around us.

We all must transform our values and realities for the sake of collaboration.

— *Adapted from existing Earthview Press Publications.*

We can't afford to live with them, and we feel we don't dare live without them. Some respond to this dilemma with anxiety; some with avoidance or denial; some by convincing themselves the weapons will never go off; some with faith in a "Star Wars" preventive. *All of these responses are in fact denials that the goal of sustained peace is feasible — negative affirmations.* When we fear the bomb, when we feel despair, when we feel impotent and frustrated before the enormity of the problem, when we deny the reality of the problem, when we seek a "technological fix" — we are contributing to the negative collective image that will bring about the very thing we fear.

On the other hand, if we positively affirm and image a world in which peace has already been achieved, devoting time each day vividly imagining that to be a fact, then we make a powerful contribution to bringing about that state, even if we do nothing else. (Persistent repetition and discipline are important. It helps to bear in mind that those who are affirming the negative images of fear, despair, perplexity, confusion, cynicism, and hate are doing that diligently and persistently, however unintentionally they may be adding their weight to the destructive side of the scales.)

An example positive affirmation is the following:

"I see a world in which there is a global commonwealth, with war having no legitimacy anywhere. There is universal support of appropriate peace-keeping institutions. Each of Earth's citizens has a reasonable chance to create, through his or her own efforts, a decent life for self and family. Men and women live in harmony with the Earth and its creatures, cooperating to create and maintain a wholesome environment for all. There is, around the globe, an ecology of different cultures, the diversity of which is appreciated and supported. Throughout, there is a deep and shared sense of meaning in life itself. This world exists. It exists because it exists in my mind."

It may seem difficult at first to convince oneself that by such an affirmation one is actually doing anything. People sincerely busy with some sort of peace activity often fail to recognize the subtleties of the principles involved here. Holding a negative image — dwelling on and even trying to generate the fear that a nuclear exchange might come about, or holding anger toward our leaders who continue to escalate the numbers of missiles — contributes very directly to bringing about what is feared or hated. *Being against war is not at all the same thing as affirming peace.* Holding a positive image, vividly imagining a state of peace to exist, contributes to that state coming about in ways that may seem quite mysterious if we have too limited a belief about the capabilities of the human mind. Because of the interconnectedness of all minds, affirming a positive vision may be about the most sophisticated action any one of us can take.

It is true that it may be simplistic to believe that if we just all love on another and speak peace, peace will come into the world. It may be simplistic because powerful unconscious forces make our love ambivalent, and our peace tinged with hidden conflict. *Collectively held unconscious beliefs shape the world's institutions, and are at the root of institutionalized oppression and inequity. "Peace" will always be no more than a temporary truce if there exist widespread perceptions of basic injustice, needs unmet, and wrongs unrighted.*

Thus to give power to our affirmations we need to be as specific as possible, and as willing as possible to look honestly at the kinds of institutional and attitudinal changes that will have to precede or accompany sustainable peace. It helps to have thought through a "plausible scenario" of achieving "operational" peace and the delegitimation of war within a couple of decades, identifying specific steps and phases necessary to make the scenario "feel" *possible*. (It need not be probable.)

Some day soon we will all look back on these years during the late 1980s as the time when the tremendous momentum of the global arms race and the related planetary dilemmas finally began to show signs of turning around. By then it will have become much more apparent that the critical battleground was not in the Middle East or Central America, but in our minds.

Chapter 11
Peace,
beliefs
and
legitimacy

141

Chapter 12

Peace Values for a Better World

by Hanna Newcombe
Co-Director, Canadian Peace Research Institute — Dundas
Ontario, Canada

Background. Numerous honors and leadership positions in peace organizations for her peace efforts. The high pitch of her efforts started in the 1960s, when she joined the United Nations Association, the Society of Friends (Quakers), and the Voice of Women. In the same period, she along with her husband Alan helped found the Canadian Peace Research Institute and started the Canadian Peace Research and Education Association. Her research work has centered around UN restructuring.

Her article. For thousands of years philosophers have puzzled over what types of values keep people happy and society peaceful and stable. Today, psychologists and social scientists have gathered a valuable storehouse of information on values. This chapter traces through a cross-section of values for a better world advocated by leading social thinkers of recent times, before the author's own wise, sensitive worldviews come to light at the end of the article.

To provide a peaceful world we must control not only our aggression, but also our conformity and obedience to authority.

Peace Values for a Better World

by Hanna Newcombe

*T*his is a survey of needed values as gathered from literature by the authors mentioned throughout the article. It is presented in three groups — social cement values, human dignity values, and global values — and then it is pulled together.

Social Cement Values — For the Good of the Group
Johann Galtung, in connection with the Global Indicators program, compiles values into 10 categories:

•Personal (survival, basic needs — physiological, ecological, and social; and almost-basic needs — creativity and freedom.).

•Diversity and pluralism (cultural and structural).

•Socio-economic growth or production, to overcome poverty and scarcity.

•Equality, to overcome disparity.

•Social justice, to overcome any disparity in benefits for different groups or classes.

•Equity, to counteract exploitation or asymmetry in the accumulation of value.

•Autonomy, to counteract penetration, foster self-reliance and self-respect.

•Solidarity, to overcome fragmentation, foster multilateral links, especially among the oppressed.

•Participation, to overcome marginalization.

•Ecological balance, to overcome resource depletion and pollution.

Ervin Laszlo and his associates compiled a "World Atlas" of international and transnational goals; not only of the main nations and regions, but also of the United Nations, the transnational corporations, the World Council of Churches, other great world religions, and so on. Within each main nation, the goals of various sub-groups are represented in diagrams by different-size circles.

•Nations: Conservation policies, economic policy, energy policy, agricultural policy, foreign aid, life-styles, demographic balance, and arms and defense.

•United Nations: World security, disarmament, peace-keeping, settlement of disputes, human rights, development assistance, energy and resources, food, health, education, population, environment, world law, social justice, and employment.

•Transnational Corporations: Growth, profitability, efficiency, and global rationalization.

The goals and relative priorities were compiled by examining documents and statements issued by each nation, agency or organization.

Donald Evans refers to 10 principles of ethics in international affairs:

•The basic principle — any moral decision takes into account the interests of all those concerned.

•The nationalist principle — the national interest has a pragmatic priority in decisions concerning foreign policy (just as it is useful for a person to look after his/her family first, because then all families have someone to look after them).

•The underdog principle — the interests of the powerless have priority over the interests of the powerful.

•The principle of non-violence — killing people is always evil (though it may sometimes be a lesser evil).

•The materialistic principle — everyone has the right to the basic necessities of life.

•The humanist principle — a variety of human values should be not only tolerated, but promoted, as long as they are not destructive or inhumane.

•The principle of reconciliation — reconciliation, not hostility, should be promoted between nations.

•The international law principle — respect international law and order; submit disputes to arbitration.

•The utilitarian principle — do whatever will bring about the most useful consequences in each particular situation.

•The democratic principle — the general public has a right to participation and protest in matters of foreign policy.

Human Dignity Values — For the Good of the Individual

John Burton, in "Dear Survivors," presents a list of human needs which, he says, people will always strive to satisfy with such single-minded determination that they will not shrink from any extremes of violence in the struggle for them. His list contains:

•ethnicity,

•identity,

•recognition,

•stimulation,

•security,

•control,

•participation.

Abraham Maslow. Human needs are closely related to the values by which we must live, for we must be careful not to deprive each other of them if we are to prevent explosions fed by frustration. A related scheme is Maslow's hierarchy of needs:

The basic needs for food, water, air, shelter, and warmth form the bottom of the pyramid. "Man does not live by bread alone," true, but without bread he does not live at all.

The intermediate and top layers of the pyramid (or the higher rungs of the ladder) are concerned with the higher needs, those which the Biblical phrase above suggests.

The next higher need is really just as fundamental as the physiological needs: the need for safety, or personal security. We must be assured that fellow-beings are not out to kill us. If they are, we must devise means of self-protection (which may quite effectively be flight rather than fight). If they are not, we must learn to trust, or our human relations will be forever poisoned by fear. To know our fellow-beings' intentions is our first and quite difficult intellectual task. The first stage in a baby's mental and emotional development is to learn "basic trust." This learning is emotional, not fully conscious, but nevertheless forms the basis of all future behaviour. A baby must be assured that it will be nurtured and not abandoned by its parents or killed soon after birth. (After all, some infants are still killed in some parts of the world.) The basic trust is built and then confirmed and re-confirmed by touching and fondling, which is so important in the first moments and years of life (and even later). "Love casts out fear."

Naturally enough, love, affection, belonging, affiliation — call it what you will — is the next rung on the Maslow ladder. It is not quite a physiological need, it is an emotional need; although evidence is accumulating that the loving tender touch is actually even a physiological necessity for the small infant, without which it does not grow and prosper; the development of the cerebellum, in particular, is stunted. Babies who receive only impersonal care without fondling sometimes even die — as if life without love is not worth living. They simply seem to give up.

On the next rung is respect, recognition, self-esteem, achievement.

The final Maslow stage is self-actualization, the full development of one's potential.

Marilyn Ferguson. Many have talked of advancing beyond the ego (for example Jung in his concept of "individuation"). Consider for a moment the views of a recent exponent of spiritual enlightenment, Marilyn Ferguson. According to her, those who discover the awakening discover some of the following features:

•a larger self (that presumably does not need the constant reassurance of social recognition),

•the importance of process rather than goal,

•the body-mind connection,

•freedom (beyond grief and danger),

•freedom from monochronic time,

•freedom from attachment (as in Buddhism),

•tolerance of uncertainty,

•sense of mystery,

•need to liberate others,

•a sense of vocation rather than career,

•synchronicity (the simultaneous occurrence of two meaningful, but not causally related events),

•a sense of mission,

•responsibility (but not either guilt or duty),

•and the transformation of fear (e.g. the discovery that personal failure no longer matters).

Global Values — For the Good of All
William Eckhardt's "axiological standards" are stated as follows:

•Universality: values which are good for others as well as oneself are more valuable than those which are good only for oneself.

•Eternity: values which are good in the future as well as the present are more valuable than those which are good only for the present.

•Unity: values which are in harmony with other values are more valuable than those which are in contradiction with other values.

•Honesty: values which find expression in actions as well as in words are more valuable than those which are expressed in words only.

•Freedom: values which are freely chosen are more valuable than those which are chosen under coercion.

•Nonviolence: values which are actualized without violence are more valuable than those which require violence for their actualization.

David Orr. Ecological ethics is the best example there is of the expansion and generalization of values which we are now discussing. Orr has compared the nuclear-war crisis and the ecological crisis, and has come up with the following similarities: both are global; unprecedented; survival-related; permanent (i.e. will have to be managed forever); problems of macro-structure; dilemmas rather than problems (have to be avoided rather than solved); and have causes in history and culture, not primarily technology, although at first glance they seem to be technological.

Some of the historical and cultural causes are:

•The West lacks balance between male and female, the rational and creative.

•Secularization took away our steering mechanism; and we have simply increased our speed.

•There has been a decline in participation, and an increase in passivity and dependence, for example with regard to food, energy, information.

•We have been bought off with material goods.

•We are victims of abstraction and alienation in language, for example "mega-death."

Some of Orr's prescriptions are:

•Shorten the path, the volume, and the speed of physical flows (of food, water, energy, waste, soil erosion).

•Become different persons: proud, self-reliant, in control, wise, cooperative, with commitment to life, to health, to balance, to diversity, to wholeness; loving and nurturing; promoting connected (trans-disciplinary) learning; include a sense of the sacred, the tragic, the heroic (e.g. there is no guarantee of survival — we have existential responsibility like the hero of a Greek drama); cultivating a "sense of place," in contrast with our present up-rootedness and displacement.

Jack Vallentyne describes three levels of depth of our ecological concerns: The first, most superficial level is concern for the human environment; here we are still focused primarily on human society, with the "environment" being something out there, which unfortunately needs some care, for our own protection.

The next stage is "ecological awareness," when we begin to grasp some of the links and connections, and realize that we cannot really fix or control one thing at a time, because of the interconnectedness of parts.

The final stage is awareness of the biosphere, as a web of life of which we are but a small part, and whose continuation is itself a value, quite apart from the human species. We may even conceive of Gaia (the Earth) as a supra-personal being, with homeostatic cycles of her own, and of ourselves as cells or tissues or organs in her body.

A CROSS-SECTION OF VALUES AND OUR RESPONSIBILITIES

Human Rights. In the 18th century, human rights were thought of in terms of "natural rights" that were somehow God-given and "inalienable." This concept is probably untenable. There is nothing "absolute" about human rights; they evolve along with our awareness; they are socially conditioned; they respond to human needs. In other words, they are, in each historical epoch, an expression of the stage of development of collective human ethics. What is essential and urgent is the implementation of the human rights already formulated. The gap between proclamation and implementation is tremendous, and in many parts of the world may be widening. We need to recover the ground lost, as well as attempt to advance into new territories.

The Universal Declaration of Human Rights of the United Nations (approved unanimously by all nations in 1948, and since made into a series of binding Covenants which have the status of international treaties) is divided into two main sections: civil and political rights, and economic and social rights. A third concept which is implicit in the others is equal applicability to all regardless of differences in nationality, race, sex, religion, ideology, or any other ascribed or achieved trait.

Civil and political rights include such traditional Western concepts as right to life, absence of slavery, no torture, equality before the law, freedom of thought, freedom of conscience, freedom of religion, peaceful assembly and association, the right to vote, freedom from arbitrary arrest, right to a fair trial.

Social and economic rights, insisted upon prior to 1948 by the Soviet countries, include such rights as the following: right to employment, right to social security, right to form and join trade unions, right to rest and leisure, right to holidays with pay, right to an adequate standard of living, right to medical care, right to education, special care of children and mothers.

Some people regard the social and economic rights as goals, which many countries cannot yet fulfill because of general poverty; however, the civil and political rights are usually not implemented in the very poor countries either; maybe they, too, are luxuries when survival is not even assured.

It could be argued that, in a situation of extreme poverty, economic concerns should be uppermost, before political ones; however, fulfilling the economic obligations to citizens is costly in resources. Proper (more equal) distribution of the scarce goods is probably the key to at least partial fulfillment.

Freedom and Equality. Research has found that autocratic socialists (communists) tend to put equality high and freedom low, democratic capitalists tend to put freedom high and equality low, autocratic capitalists (fascists) tend to put both freedom and equality low, and democratic socialists tend to put both freedom and equality high.

Wisdom and Self-Actualization. With reference to the Maslow stages, self-actualization may not be reached by everyone, but the need for self-esteem level is universally reached. People feel the need to defend the ego just as strongly as the need to defend the body and its physical existence, and integrity is felt at the lower level of the Maslow hierarchy. The defense of the ego and its values can become strong enough to acquire the capacity for extreme destructiveness, when thwarted, which Burton ascribes to it.

Would this situation change if more people were able to reach the stage of wisdom? It is an intriguing thought. If we reached the insight that the ego is not the end-all and be-all, that we are part of a higher reality, then we could drop our petty defenses and relax our frantic striving. This may be the most secure basis of peace we could have.

Until that "most great peace" is reached, we had better apply ourselves to build the "lesser peace" by accepting the foibles of humanity's childhood, and pay attention to the tender ego needs of one another.

There are several stages of wisdom, each reached after a "crisis" (like the mid-life crisis at 40, and several later ones) and subsequent re-integration. Developmental psychologists are too much oriented to youth, and tend to see old age as a time of decline rather than development . . . which may not be so at the spiritual level. However, as we said earlier, not all persons reach the last stage of self-actualization (that is, wisdom), so perhaps distinguishing its sub-stages would be extravagant. What would be interesting to find out, by some empirical method, is what proportion of the population gets stuck at which stage, and what the inhibitors and promoters of further development might be.

Universality and Eternity. Let's focus for a moment on Eckhardt's first two values — universality and eternity. Most people think only of their own families and of people in their immediate vicinity, not of people faraway. Also, most people think only of the present and the immediate future, not of the distant future. All this is natural, but highly unsatisfactory in our interdependent world, and a world in which our present actions (for example regarding the environment) may foreclose the future. We begin life, as infants, with an exclusive concentration on the self and the present moment; one has to begin that way.

We expand our horizons, as we mature, by including the neighborhood, the school, playmates, the community, eventually the nation — but most people stop there, though a few expand to a feeling of belonging to humanity. We also expand our horizons in time; we become capable of planning for tomorrow, then for next week, for next year, maybe for a life-time; many of us plan for our children, even fewer for our grandchildren . . . but soon our concern peters out; we heavily discount the future in favor of the present, even within our own lifetime.

When it comes to a concern for centuries, for millennia, for the millions of years for which human life on Earth could continue if given a chance, we give up. It is too difficult to imagine. And when it comes to concern for non-human species, we might love our pets, but have little concern for wildlife; we may love birds, but hate rodents or snakes; and most insects (except bees and butterflies) are our sworn enemies; worms are too lowly to worry about; and plants are hardly perceived as alive. A few sages (such as Schweitzer) attain respect for all life; but many of us would actually condemn not killing flies. How far do we carry universality? How would we react to extra-terrestrial life if we should meet it and recognize it? Would we be killers or friends?

Obviously, the expanding circles do not expand forever for most of us, and maybe they should not, but at least we should think about it, give it a chance, try to figure out the limits. Most forms of earthly life use each other to survive, as prey, or compete for necessities . . . and we are part of the natural order. Universal love for all life forms may not be attainable in practice. But at least, if we have to kill or exploit, some thought should be given to alternatives that might avoid it. The prohibition of killing may not be absolute (probably nothing is), but killing or exploitation should never be thoughtless; life is too precious for that.

The metaphor of expanding circles has been called "the onion view of the world" by Chadwick Alger (1974), who advocates instead the alternative of a "cobweb" image. In the cobweb, we can reach out directly, across levels, to those distant from us in space, as in transnational cultural exchanges, without necessarily going through the governments of our own cities or nations, which in the onion model would be closer to us. We all do this at times in transnational networking (a "network" is just a more elegant term for a "cobweb"), and it is a valuable alternative. Yet it is just a different form of the "universality" we seek, in reaching beyond our own narrow circle (beyond being "parochial"). It is said that "peace begins at home," but it cannot end there, for the links of interdependence are too strong and too dense — though not always of a sufficiently caring and sharing quality.

In this sense, then, "solidarity," which has been cited as a value by many, must expand to "universal human solidarity," at least. We are beginning to consider group rights in addition to individual rights, but not many have considered the rights of humanity as a whole, its right to survival and a satisfactory quality of life reasonably distributed to all its members.

With respect to thinking in the time dimension, again we need a tremendous change in values. People centuries from now are real — and we need to feel this.

Time-expanded thinking is especially important when we consider ecological values, but spatial universality is too. From Orr we can extract the following ecological values: balance between rationality and creativity, a sense of direction, participation, opposition to mindless consumption, clear use of language, self-reliance, control, cooperation, commitment to life, diversity, love, connectedness, beauty, rootedness. Among these values, we recognize some of our old friends: rationality, participation, control, diversity, love. But there are also some new ones.

Rights and Responsibilities. We need to pay some attention now to our obligations and responsibilities (for "rights" always imply "duties") and to the resources that make it possible for us to carry out these obligations.

Existential inner-directed responsibility is very different from duty imposed from the outside. We carry out duties for a master only as long as he stands over us with a whip, or otherwise exerts at least implicit coercive power. We may also conform to duties in order to gain the approval of our superiors or our peers, or out of habit or reluctance to change. Existential responsibility, on the other hand, comes from the spirit. It is only partly intellectual; it has also a large emotional component, but there is something else, which is of a volitional nature: the commitment to act on our beliefs.

Eckhardt touches on it in his fourth axiological standard, "honesty": to be truly valuable, a value must be actualized in action, otherwise it cannot affect the world. And who is to act? The experts? Our elected representatives? Our intellectual or spiritual mentors? No, in the end, the actualization of values rests upon our own shoulders. We can only do so much, of course; but that which we can do, we must do. Kant's categorical imperative tells us so to act that we would be willing for our actions to become the general norm.

Well, if we fail to act, we must be willing that no one else should act either, in which case the task will not be done. We cannot, if we listen to our conscience, be "free riders" in the global striving for a just sustainable future. It is true that, if a certain percentage of us act to actualize our values, it may happen, for it only takes an (as yet unknown) critical mass to move society; but if we do not participate, the critical mass may not be reached, or if it is, how can we then live with our conscience, being the beneficiary of this larger good which we did not help create? Our consciences may not be sufficiently developed to even feel this, but once we do, no obstacles can stop us from at least trying.

To act, we must be empowered to act. If we have been conditioned to a feeling of our own powerlessness, we may never be able to summon up the courage. If we do have the courage, then part of our responsibility is to empower others. This cannot be done too well by direct admonition or preaching, but is better done by example. We thus have a double reason to act on our beliefs: to help change the world, and to act as a role model for the hitherto powerless.

What, specifically, do we have to do? There are certain tendencies to control, and there are some others to foster. To provide a peaceful world, it has been shown that we must control not only our aggression, but also (and perhaps especially) our conformity and our obedience to authority. Our aggressive tendencies (it is somewhat useless to argue whether they are innate or learned; they exist) stem either from frustration (so-called irritability aggression, which may be impulsive rather than instrumental) or from the competitive drive for power (when it is purely instrumental, as in premeditated murder), or from fear (defensive aggression, as by a cornered animal).

Actions suggested by this are:

1) Avoid frustrating others.

2) Be aware of the frustration-aggression link, in yourself and others, in order to act as "chain-breaker." Mutual escalation (tit for tat) can sometimes perpetuate itself in a hostile pair; or worse, can be passed on to an innocent bystander in so-called "displacement aggression." But, as in other cases, "truth can set us free," and self-knowledge can break out of these vicious cycles by the "self-falsifying prophecy" mechanism. If all else fails, we must be prepared to absorb the suffering to stop the chain of fear and hate, like Jesus on the cross. Even that may be demanded of us, as part of our existential responsibility. We are not alone; many martyrs have preceded us.

3) Redefine "power" as "competence" rather than "domination over others."

4) Avoid "cornering" anyone, even an opponent. In negotiations, provide a "yesable" proposition, or at least an honorable way out without loss of face. When cornered yourself, make creative use of Gandhian methods — there may be a way out.

Continuity and Change. Finally, let's address questions about continuity and change. There needs to be a balance between them, for each has advantages and disadvantages. The good points about continuity are:

1) There is less risk-taking; "adventurism" can be counter-productive.

2) Cultural inheritance, somewhat like genetic inheritance, has been tested by time and experience; while it might be improved-upon, it should not be discarded lightly.

3) Continuity is related to "conservationism," as opposed to waste and profligacy.

4) Too much change in one area of our life, namely technology, is one of our main problems. Not enough testing of new chemicals, for example, can be done at the rate at which new ones are pouring into production.

5) Continuity is more "natural."

Most processes in nature are continuous or cyclic, only occasionally punctuated by discontinuities (most of which turn out to be disastrous, like mutations, although the few beneficial ones are needed to drive evolution). Individual development, like historical development, proceeds in a series of steps, far more time being spent on "plateaus" than on rises.

The good points about change are:

1) Without it there would never be any breakthrough to new forms. Even life itself would not have begun.

2) The potential for change provides insurance of adaptability in case of breakdown of the old forms.

3) Change provides insurance against stagnation and overspecialization, or bureaucratic ossification in society.

4) If the environment changes, we must change with it or perish.

5) Changes in society may lag behind changes in technology or in the environment; this lag must be overcome to stay in phase.

Notes

Alger, Chadwick, *Your Community in the World, the World in Your Community*, Mershon Center, Ohio State University, November 1974, 155 pp.

Burton, John, *Dear Survivors*, Pinter (London) and Westview Press, Boulder, CO, 1982, 137 pp.

Eckhardt, William, *Compassion: Toward a Science of Value*, Canadian Peace Research Institute, Oakville, Ont., 1972, 311 pp.

Evans, Donald, "Ten Principles of International Ethics," Chapter in *Peace, Power and Protest*, edited by Donald Evans, Ryerson Press, Toronto, 1967, pp. 14-40.

Ferguson, Marilyn, *The Aquarian Conspiracy*, J.P. Taracher, Los Angeles, 1980, 448 pp.

Galtung, Johan, "Measuring World Development," *Bulletin of Peace Proposals*,

1975, No. 2, pp. 156-159.

Laszlo, Ervin, et al., *Goals for Mankind,* Signet, New American Library, 1977, 374 pp.

Maslow, Abraham, *Motivation and Personality,* 2nd edition, Harper & Row, New York, 1970, 369 pp.

Orr, David, (Meadowcrest Project), "Sustainability and Nuclear War Prevention," Paper, COPRED, Little Rock, Ark., October 28-31, 1982. Also his paper to COPRED, LeMoyne College, Syracuse, N.Y., October 29, 1983.

Vallentyne, Jack R., "The Role of the Biosphere in International Affairs," address to World Federalists, Hamilton, Ontario, February 7, 1982.

Four works by the author, Hanna Newcombe, were also used as reference material:

1. "Cooperation in the Light of Peace Research Theories," pp. 310-331, in *Key Issues in Peace Research,* edited by Ruth Klaassen and Yoshi Sakamoto, publ. by Peace Research Institute — Dundas and Conrad Grebel College, University of Waterloo, 1983, xvi + 331 pp.

2. *Design for a Better World,* University Press of America, Lanham, MD, 1983, 362 pp.

3. "Escape from the Dilemma," *Peace Research*, Vol. 9, No. 1, January 1977, pp. 51-59.

4. "Venn Diagrams of Values: Peace, Justice, Freedom, Love,"

Chapter 13
Redefining Sovereignty
in an Interdependent World

by Gerald Mische
President, Global Education Associates (GEA)
New York, USA

Background. Writer, lecturer and coordinator in the move toward global interdependence and world order. A graduate of Columbia University's Graduate School for International Affairs. Currently organizing a new Center for World Order Alternatives in New York City to facilitate and coordinate worldwide dialogue and research through a growing network of GEA associates in over 60 countries. Has conducted world order workshops on five continents.

His article. Our species has entered an era of increasing economic, monetary, and environmental interdependence, but government leaders and their arms negotiators dangerously assume that nations are still territorially sovereign. A transcultural project is needed to develop international institutions to deal with global problems that have grown beyond the grasp of nations.

(Developing a new world order) must not be left solely in the hands of the acclaimed experts; significant new ground must be broken.

Redefining Sovereignty
in an Interdependent World

by Gerald Mische

*I*f the leaders of the USA and USSR could be made to understand the insanity of the arms race and transcend simplistic ideological worldviews, then their negotiators could sit down around the table to agree on the practical transitional steps for turning swords into ploughshares . . . right? Probably not.

There are inexorable linkages between economic and military security problems. Neither can be solved separately. Yet that is what we are trying to do. Arms negotiators assume that nations are still territorially sovereign, that territories can still be impenetrable, and that national legislation and institutions are adequate for providing security for their people.

These assumptions are not shared by most persons sitting around the table of monetary and trade negotiations. The latter recognize that a radically new world has come into being. It is a world that is economically, monetarily and environmentally interdependent.

In this new world, nations are no longer fully sovereign, their territories *are* penetrable (at every level), and national legislation and institutions are not adequate (by themselves) for providing security and guiding the destinies of their peoples.

We are seeing a trend toward greater interaction, a natural progression toward a unified human species.

At the same time we are seeing a conservative reluctance to change — a desire among nations to preserve their fiction of self-sufficiency and territorial impenetrability.

Economic interdependence is not a recent phenomenon. Its impact did not begin with the OPEC oil-price crisis. Its seeds were planted more than a century earlier.

Nineteenth century colonialism was an effort to regain the sovereignty and reestablish the self-sufficiency and territorial impenetrability that was breaking down as a consequence of the Industrial Revolution's new dependency on foreign resources and markets. What has energized the unprecedented growth of interdependence in recent decades are the new transportation and communications technologies that, in a short time, have linked the world's peoples and economies into a global village. This explosive growth in global economic interdependence has, of course, made the dependency on external sources for scarce resources, and on foreign markets for goods and foreign exchange, more acute — and ever more a central national security concern.

In today's lawless world economy, no nation can be expected to substantially reduce its armaments as long as it is dependent upon external sources for raw materials and markets. This dependency is at the heart of the linkage between disarmament negotiations and economic-monetary-trade negotiations.

Two Options

What then is the way out of our dilemma? How can national leaders — confronted by their nation's dependency on foreign raw materials and markets in today's lawless world — substantially reduce their armament stockpiles? There are two options:

• Retreat to a bygone era of economic self-sufficiency.

• Strengthen global public structures that can provide a framework within which nations can cooperatively achieve basic economic, monetary and resource security.

The first option is not a realistic possibility. Too many national economies are now substantially structured for export. Following the "successes" of the export model embraced by Japan, Taiwan, Hong Kong, Singapore and Korea — and often pressured by International Monetary Fund policies for dealing with foreign debt obligations — the great majority of African, Asian and Latin American countries are rapidly structuring their economies for export markets.

This mass movement toward the export economy is a contributing factor in numerous growing problems:

• Food and land have become prime national security tools.

Chapter 13
Redefining
sovereignty
in an
inter-
dependent
world

• Agribusiness has become a central national security partner.

- Family farms give way to corporate economy-of-scale economic units.

- Land reform is "postponed."

- Capital-intensive technology and economic models are embraced.

- Farm land is destroyed and poisoned by export-oriented agriculture.

- Urban migration escalates.

- Food imports increase.

- Prices of food and other basic commodities rise.

- Purchasing power declines.

- Malnutrition, hunger and starvation increase.

Burdened by the suffering and the economic and political instability resulting from the above, some debtor nations have considered defaulting on their loans — which, in effect, would be to follow the first option. To date, however, the domestic costs of such actions have been judged too high. Should political pressures eventually prompt them to default, the result could be a global economic collapse. The turmoil, fear, paranoia and political instability that would follow could, in turn, trigger World War III.

Which leaves us only with the second option: that of strengthening international organizations as a framework through which nations can cooperatively achieve basic economic, monetary, resource as well as military security.

Redefining Sovereignty and Security

The challenge we face is not to "give up" sovereignty, but rather to redefine it. In so doing, we will also find ourselves redefining security. In today's global village, it is only possible to regain a viable sovereignty by pooling certain functional dimensions of sovereignty. As Emery Reves has put it:

"The question is not one of "surrendering" national sovereignty. The problem is not negative and does not involve giving up something we already have. The problem is positive — creating something we lack, but that we imperatively need."

The task, then, is not to turn back to the past. Nor is it to dismantle or bypass the nation-state, or to centralize power at a global level. Rather, the task is to recognize that, in today's interdependent world, both private and public sector institutions are needed at every level. The functional institutions that are required at the international level should be structured according to the principle of subsidiarity — that is, decisions should be made at the lowest reasonable level.

This principle recognizes that many problems can and should be resolved at the local, municipal level. Others, because of social, economic or environmental interdependence at larger geographical areas, can be adequately resolved only by public sector institutions operating at the county, provincial or national levels. What makes our era different is that the circles of interdependence have today expanded beyond national boundaries. As a result, certain problems can only be solved with public sector institutions that are global in scope. Included in this category are the arms race, the international debt crisis, terrorism, international drug trafficking, and some environmental problems such as acid rain, pollution of the oceans, the destruction of the ozone layer, radiation fall-out from nuclear testing and disasters like Chernobyl.

Providing a facilitating framework for such functional public sector structures at the global level should be a broad, flexible set of global standards and values — based on justice, acceptance of diversity and respect for all life — to provide a general sense of compatibility throughout the human species. Although a significant body of such values does exist, as articulated in the United Nations Declaration of Human Rights, much more remains to be done in this area.

A world order designed according to the subsidiarity principle is not a quantum jump into the unknown. It is, rather, the next logical step in social development. For the historical process of political development did not culminate with the emergence of the sovereign national state. The concept of unlimited national sovereignty does not represent a final vision. It reflects, rather, an interim stage of human history.

Chapter 13
defining
sovereignty
in an
inter-
pendent
world

With this awareness comes a recognition that, rather than living in "End Times," we are living in "Between Times," a period of transition from national to global-scale interdependencies.

The need now is to develop international institutions that — while preserving basic sovereignty and cultural diversity — would have the functional authority needed to cope with those global problems which nations cannot handle, thereby providing a structural framework for nations to achieve security.

The formulation and development of these world order institutions must be a transcultural undertaking. Concerned persons around the world need to join hands across national, cultural, religious and ideological borders to participate in this creative task. They need to dialogue, collaborate in research, publish materials and engage in consciousness-raising efforts on what the form of the new world order structures and global security policies should be.

This task must not be left solely in the hands of the acclaimed "experts." Most have too many educational, professional, financial and political constraints to be free enough to break significant new ground. Scholars, educators and leaders of religious, business, labor and grass-roots issue constituencies must also become active and bold participants.

Traditional wisdoms and expertise are no longer adequate. Hallowed assumptions must be rethought. And our focus cannot be only on finding solutions to the problems and questions emerging from today's interdependencies: for we have not yet asked enough of the right questions.

Linking Two "New Frontiers"

Humankind now stands at the threshold of a historic thrust toward a viable world community.

Will we venture into space with "Star Wars" weaponry, or will the human community join hands in cooperative space programs to benefit all humankind?

Will we venture into today's interdependent economy with economic and monetary weaponry, or will the human community join hands in cooperative efforts to redefine sovereignty and develop viable global institutions for achieving an equitable and secure international economic order?

If you are reading this book, you surely accept the latter option in both cases.

(This article was first published in a longer version in "Breakthrough," Vol 7 nos 1-2, Fall 1985 / Winter 1986, Global Education Associates. Adapted, updated, and printed with permission.)

Chapter 14
Europe, the Link Between East and West, North and South — A New Age of World Socialism

by Jozsef Bognar
Director, Institute for World Economics, Hungarian Academy of Sciences
Budapest, Hungary

Background. Currently a university professor (economics), president of the Hungarian Scientific Council for World Economy, Parliament member, chairman of the Committee for Planning and Budget, editor of *Studies on Developing Countries* and *Trends in World Economy*. Member of a dozen national and international associations for economics, development, politics, and peace. Has monitored economic trends in East and West, writing numerous articles on the subject. Awarded Hungarian State Prize (1970) and several other national and international honors.

His article. No history-conscious person would deny the success of socialism in transforming struggling, disjointed peasant economies of Eastern Europe and Asia this century into unified, modern social systems. The rapid transformation came about through tight regulation by strong central governments. One by-product has been a backwardness in technology and sophistication. Now the socialist world, led by China, Hungary and Yugoslavia, is entering Stage Two — loosening controls and allowing regulation to disperse out into the social structure.

Europe will enjoy mutual economic interests and close cooperation only after the nations of East and West have learned to deal with the bipolar world system and its resulting Cold War and mutual mistrust.

Europe, the Link Between East and West, North and South — A New Age of World Socialism

by Jozsef Bognar

*T*he emergence of modern Europe may be summed up in the following general terms.

• Western Europe's situation in the world has been changed externally for the most part — by events and developments in the outside world — while

• The East European situation has been shaped internally — by the Soviet revolution of 1917 and the subsequent revolutions of the East European people.

In the past, Europe was the main arena of world development and change in the economic, technical, monetary and political spheres. This holds for Western Europe moreso than Eastern Europe, whose evolution had been greatly distorted by a life-or-death struggle with the Ottoman Empire. Nevertheless, both world wars were ignited by conflicts among the European nations, both Western and Eastern.

Current Trends in the World Economy

The USA played a key role in deciding the outcome of both world wars, but its role in post-war world affairs was quite different in each case. After World War I the USA retreated to decades of isolationism, but after World War II a number of historic changes unfolded:

• The USA gained ascendency over Western Europe in a number of spheres including the military, economic and political,

• The USSR became the dominant power of the East Central and East European space,

• In a process taking almost three decades, the colonial empires of the European powers fell apart,

•As the outcome of World War II, a bipolar system came to exist in the developed world,

•Japan and the Southeast Asian space developed into one of the focal regions of the world economy. This and the westward shift of the economic power centers within the USA are now leading up to a Pacific epoch in economic history, replacing an earlier Atlantic-centered world economy,

•Amid the storms of their population explosion and struggle for development, the least developed countries voice with increasing stridency such problems as stagnation and inadequate performance,

•A number of global issues and problems have emerged. Nations have become mutually interested in each other's economic situation.

A Closer Look at Eastern Europe

The Soviet Union and the European socialist countries are undergoing a modern revolution ... entering a new period of development. The previous period began in the 1920s and ended in the 1970s. The goals, norms and values of the new period are now solidifying. They include:

•new development-policy priorities,

•economic reforms, and

•a new foreign trade concept.

New priorities mean that each and every European socialist country regards economic and technological progress as the most important issue. Intellectual and material potentials will have to be reallocated accordingly. This will require that national security in Europe be realized at the lowest level of armament that serves the purpose.

Economic reforms will rationalize, and/or replace by a more suitable one, the centralized model of control of the first, catching-up-type phase of socialist evolution. The early phase was geared for social transformation and industrialization, and relied on a far-reaching centralization of funds in the hands of the state. The system of control of this first period gave rise to structures which are fairly up-to-date in their end products but rather backward in mechanization, in technology and in the sophistication of certain materials, parts, units and other industrial building blocks.

This setup encourages imports while discouraging exports. It therefore maintains a sort of built-in trade disequilibrium. At the same time, the present regulating mechanisms and techniques hamper the satisfaction of needs and confine the creativity and the spontaneous initiatives of the people.

In some of the countries, the existing model is being rationalized these days.

•Centralization is reduced as is the number of prescribed plan targets.

•Personal initiative and the individual productive pursuits are coming to be handled more in keeping with their nature (for example, by letting the cooperatives find their own best place in agriculture).

•The full centralization of enterprise income is dismantled.

•Enterprise autonomy is increased.

•Exports are encouraged in a variety of ways.

•Some forms of association with foreign capital are made possible.

A few countries have taken more dramatic steps. New models have replaced the old ones in Yugoslavia, Hungary and China. These countries are preoccupied now by things like creating a capital market, placing the banking system on a business-like basis, letting the private sector expand in certain service-type jobs, implementing price and wage reforms, and devising new systems of economic motivation. The political and social reforms that are being introduced are geared to these economic changes. They include reshaping the division of tasks between state and society, a reinforcing of the legislative branch and of the judiciary, and placing the rights of the individual on a new basis.

It is still too early to identify the exact nature of the Soviet model now being introduced; it is most likely to be a combination of the two approaches, backed up by some important social and political changes.

The new foreign trade concept is being deployed on an increasingly broad front in practice. However, it has so far been formulated theoretically in Hungary only. Its great importance in my view is that it may create new lines of communication, new bridges between the socialist economies and the world economy overall.

In the previous period, from the 1920s to the early 1970s, the economic policy-makers of the socialist countries were defensive about foreign trade. They could hardly have been otherwise in a phase of history marked by an alternation of blockades, embargoes, cold and very hot wars. Making a defensive policy work was comparatively simple in the Soviet Union whose great riches of fuels and raw materials permitted it to purchase the technology indispensable for its industrialization. It was more of a problem in the smaller socialist countries, which did not have the surpluses of fuels, raw materials or foodstuffs with which to pay for technology.

Clearly, however, the situation improves radically as soon as intensive development sets in. Foreign relations begin to play a growth-sustaining role on both the export and the import side. More manufactured goods are exported. As a result, the countries become more competitive in the world market and they adapt to modern technological standards of the trade partners, leading to increased production, investment, marketing and cooperation.

This is all part of a "change of epoch" which has made nations interdependent. It has shaped a homogeneous world economic environment which makes many-sided integration into the world economy a necessity; it has also tied up living standards with how well a country is doing in the world economy. This is why the socialist economies also need a dynamic, flexible and innovative external-economic system.

Europe will enjoy mutual economic interests and closer cooperation only after the nations of East and West have learned to deal with the bipolar world system and its resulting Cold War, mutual mistrust and the "military-strategic considerations" born of the policies of full-out armament which have hampered the development of economic relations.

Favorable changes in this respect appear rather likely. The superpowers not only want to avoid war but are also interested in maintaining the military balance on which peace is based at a lower level of military spending, because the balance of terror in the broadest sense of the term is so costly as to hamper the economic development and the international competitiveness of both superpowers. The Soviet administration in its new program intends to assign priority to economic development. It can do so only if and when it can manage a reduction of armament spending.

On the other side of the world, the massive US deficit and other signs of disequilibrium are a sure sign that the US economy too has bitten off more than it can chew, that it is called upon to handle more tasks than it can cope with. (Economic equilibrium is not the supreme good, but it is an indicator of harmony between the aims of government and the means available to achieve them.)

On pondering the long-term prospects of budget deficit in the USA, the balance-of-payments deficit, the comparative backwardness of US export patterns, and the negative balance of the flow of profits, one becomes convinced that even the USA cannot simultaneously produce both guns and butter or, in more modern language, missiles and economic vitality. This has already been demonstrated by the Vietnam war and the erosion of the dollar under President Lyndon Johnson.

Incontrovertibly, the first and decisive step in the reduction of armaments is mutual confidence. Confidence in politics is not an issue of psychology or state of mind, but a construction built out of common interests ... guarantees satisfying both parties and an active and efficient management, on a basis of joint agreements of the tensions that have arisen. In such a context, wide-ranging economic cooperation promoting the growth of both sides may well be best at generating a stock of mutual interests, a stock that will keep expanding daily. Awareness of mutual economic interests is apt to moderate decisions on international political issues, whereas a lack of such interests will inject political stress into the economy.

Another much-needed thing is the defusing of the potential danger zones and the reduction of their number. This is why a European cooperation standing on its own feet can play a very important stabilizing role in an otherwise fairly unstable world. One aspect of world instability is that the likelihood of minor and even major conflicts in a world of 180 nation-states can never be negligible. This instability, however, demands by its very nature the cool and efficient management of conflicts, which must in its turn be based on a cool and circumspect assessment of international relations.

In my analysis of a new role and new opportunities for Europe, I feel it appropriate to quote Hans-Dietrich Genscher, Minister of Foreign Affairs of the Federal Republic of Germany, who in his address to the Stockholm Conference on European confidence- and security-building measures (January 23, 1986), said:

"The European Conference on Security and Cooperation has reintroduced Europe into the arena of world political action. The Helsinki Conference, called into existence by Europe, is the tool used to lay down the foundations of lasting peace for our continent. The participating countries have the responsibility of using this tool to best advantage. The follow-up conference of the Helsinki Conference Vienna at end-1986 will provide an opportunity for assessing the evolution of the process of Helsinki."

We hope that, in the course of this very necessary assessment, the competent statesmen will realize that no such conference has as yet been convened in the matter of the second (economic) basket of Helsinki, although the analogous conferences have in fact been convened for security (in Stockholm) and for culture (in Budapest).

Europe, the Political and Economic Bridge

It is of course very important to make perfectly clear the relation of European economic cooperation to the superpowers. The superpowers are not just members but the strongest members of their respective economic groupings, the OECD on the one side and the CMEA (Comecon) on the other. Without their contributions, and without the organizational influence of their markets, it would be virtually impossible to envisage a European cooperation in anything like the full sense of the term. Even today, these two giants represent 500 million consumers and all the economic pursuits needed for their satisfaction.

At the same time, European economic cooperation would permit a better, more dynamic utilization of the facilities, abilities and resources available in the European space, a development which would benefit not only the European countries involved but also the world economy as a whole, including the Third World.

One of the political implications is that the countries would have to give up the Cold War notion of "the last (or strongest) rampart," in favor of seeing themselves, and actually acting, as bridges and channels of communication between the two halves of Europe. In a different approach, this also means that economic cooperation of the Austro-Hungarian kind or of the kind between the two Germanys should be regarded as the rule, not the exception . . . as stimuli for emulation rather than as the freak actions of mavericks.

The sort of European economic cooperation which I am envisaging demands not only a pattern of economic interests that includes mutualities or components that can be rendered mutual, nor only support by the two power centers of a bipolar world system, but also an exemplary organization, including the creation of joint

institutions. Such a system of joint institutions should be set up with active support from governments but also with vigorous contributions from the business and financial spheres.

These institutions would be called upon:

•to promote the flow of capital, technology, research and management capabilities between the countries, giving rise to joint enterprises in such areas as banking, business and research, and

•to provide the interested parties with a certain protection from abrupt changes of political climate — a buffer of sorts against any tensions or conflicts arising outside the European space that would affect the balance of the bipolar international political system.

Reinforcing economic cooperation in Europe would presuppose an injection of more invention and dynamism into those UN bodies (the UN Economic Commission for Europe, above all) which, in an unfavorable political climate marked by a lack of mutual confidence, so far has been unable to fulfill the roles envisaged by their founders. That subject is explored by other authors in this book.

Chapter 15
A Global Spirituality

by Patricia Mische
Co-Founder, Global Education Associates
New York, USA

Background. Author, lecturer and mother of three college-age daughters. Has written many articles and several books, including *Star Wars and the State of Our Souls*. Has conducted over 1,000 presentations and workshops around the world on peace, justice and other global concerns. A member of the Experimental Project on the Conditions for Peace, a think tank exploring alternatives to the arms race.

Her article. Readers are taken on a spiritual journey to a new world order. We travel inward to see personal transformation, then outward to relocate our ancestral devotion to the earth and all its living parts. Finally we look forward, beyond the dark, dangerous and polarized world of today toward an illuminated human genesis of nations developing compatibly toward a healthy future.

Our astronauts and cosmonauts go into space as technicians. Some come back as mystics . . . . We are not over the earth but are part of this single cell.

A Global Spirituality

by Patricia Mische

This is an age of tremendous problems and tremendous promise. We are at a critical point when future human survival is not guaranteed, but must be consciously sought. Old orders and systems are dying; they are inadequate to cope with the new dangers and problems of this period. A new world order has not yet been born. We are the midwives who must help give birth to this new global order.

A new world order needs to be born within us first, in a transformed consciousness; in a right ordering of our spirit, mind, heart and will. Real changes, the real transformations in history, have begun with inner spiritual changes. The great transforming agents, the formers of new culture, have been spiritual leaders: Buddha, Lao-tse, Abraham, Moses, Mohammed, Jesus, Paul . . .

This new order must also be born in the outer order of the world community in the form of new systems of greater justice and peace; in a right ordering of our international relationships and structures. A new ordering of the soul requires and seeks a new outer order in the world at large, an order rooted in wisdom and compassion.

THE GLOBAL SPIRITUAL JOURNEY

The new web of global interdependencies that binds us together, and the tremendous stresses and complex moral choices before us, require a far deeper and more far reaching spirituality than at any time in previous history. We do not need a return to the external facades of religiosity. But we do need to resume the spiritual journey with a more penetrating vision, purpose and sense of direction and within new, global parameters.

There is much that could be said about global sprirtuality and still much for all of us to discover. But in the short remaining space here, I will limit myself to three important dimensions of the global spiritual journey: the journey inward, the journey outward and the journey forward.

I. Inward Journey: Discovering the Sacred Source

The inward journey is a journey to the sacred source at the center of every being and all being. It is to enter into the deepest truth of our existence; to separate ourselves from immediate sensory experience and surrounding circumstances and enter the inner source of our life and integrity.

The inward journey is a journey through our deep past — all that has formed us. It cuts through the many layers of tradition, belief, culture, history, symbols that are part of our personal and collective experience. We travel inward through all the individual and collective sufferings, joys, struggles, discoveries, changes that have brought us to this present time; through all the history and all the choices that have separated us and divided us and broken us, and all the choices that have bound us together, healed us, made us one. We journey back and inward to a common source, into direct contact with the universal life force, or higher intelligence, or God.

II. Outward Journey: Discovering the Sacred in the World; The Great Compassion

Paradoxically, the more deeply inward we go and the more we live in deep awareness of our own sacred center and source, the more universal we become; the more we grow in awareness of our deep unity with all peoples. The joys and sufferings of the world's peoples are our joys and sufferings. We are part of one humanity. The struggles and hopes of the world's people are our struggles and hopes. Their loss is our loss. Their discovery and growth is our discovery and growth.

Forgiveness. The first step in the outward spiritual journey, in the healing of the planetary community and creation of a new world order, may be learning to forgive and to seek forgiveness. Universal love, compassion, justice and peace are not possible without a recognition of our mutual responsibility for the brokenness of the world community and our capacity to heal that brokenness. We each have hurt and have been hurt by others; we have broken trust with one another. We can each help heal the past.

This is true of nations as well as individuals. Perhaps the arms race is escalating to dangerous heights because as nations we are too proud to say we are sorry. It may be that as a first step to world peace, the people of the USA should ask forgiveness of the Japanese for dropping atomic bombs on Hiroshima and Nagasaki; and to learn to forgive the Japanese for the bombing of Pearl Harbor. It may be that the people of Japan need to ask forgiveness from the Koreans and Chinese for their past invasions and brutal occupation; that the Germans need to ask forgiveness for the genocide of six million Jews and their invasions in Europe; that the Soviets need to seek forgiveness for their transgressions in Afghanistan and Eastern Europe. Each nation has spiritual scars which need to be healed before we can build a healthy world community together. Learning to seek and grant forgiveness between national societies is an important part of the outward spiritual journey; a part of national ego transcendence needed for a more human world order.

A Spirituality of the Earth. Any spirituality deep and large enough for this new global age also needs to include a profound sense of our common dependency on the earth. We are not over the earth. We are of the earth. We will live and die as the earth lives and dies.[1] And any authentic global spirituality will also have a profound sense of the divine consciousness that informs every species and every atom of the earth and universe.

A world order is more than just a human order. It is order in which humans learn to bring their lives into communion with the earth processes — material, plant, animal of which we are an interdependent part. A global spirituality rejects the dualism between spirit and matter, between spirit and body, between human and non-human. An authentic global spirituality recognizes what the Native Americans recognized when they spoke of a united planet of nations which the human nation needs to live in right relationship with the tree nation, the water nation, the bird nation, the buffalo nation, etc.[2]

Our Shinto and Buddhist and Hindu and Taoist and tribal African and Native American ancestors intuitively understood the divine presence in the earth processes and our spiritual kinship with all life forms. Thus when Chief Seattle, leader of the Native American Squamish tribe was asked to sell tribal lands to the US government in 1854, he responded:

"How can you buy or sell the sky, the warmth of the land? The idea is strange to us.

"We are part of the earth and it is part of us. The perfumed flowers are our sisters; the deer, the horse, the great eagle, these are our brothers. The rocky crests, the juices in the meadows, the body heat of the pony, and man — all belong to the same family.

"If we sell you our land . . . teach your children what we have taught our children, that the earth is our mother. Whatever befalls the earth, befalls the sons of the earth. If men spit upon the ground they spit upon themselves.

"This we know. The earth does not belong to man; man belongs to the earth. This we know. All things are connected like the blood which unites one family. All things are connected.

"Whatever befalls the earth befalls the sons of the earth. Man did not weave the web of life; he is merely a strand in it. Whatever he does to the web, he does to himself.[3]"

Thus, too, these lessons from Zen Buddhism:

"Once when Joshu was still with Nansen, Nansen took an ox into the Monk's Hall, and led him around. The head monk whacked the ox on the back three times, and Nansen took a sheaf of grass and put it in front of the head monk, who said nothing.
Has an ox the Buddha Nature?
Had the head monk the ox nature?[4]
Rain, hail, snow and ice
are divided from one another;
But after they fall,
They are the same water
of the stream in the valley.[5]"

Thus also in Taoism:

"The universe came into being
with us together; with us, all
things are one.[6]"

We need to relocate the deep awareness our tribal ancestors had of the sacredness of the earth and all its living parts; their sense of oneness and interdependence with the earth and each other.

This does not mean going back to the past. We cannot go back. The world of today is far too complex for that. But we must bring the best insights of the world's spiritual traditions forward into our new global context and add to these a new spiritual inquiry appropriate to our times. Even in this more complex, modern world we must come to see how we are bound together; and what we do to the earth and to each other we do to ourselves. We live and die as the earth lives and dies. We live and die as our brothers and sisters live and die.

Unity of Life. The world has long been divided by the external differences between religious belief systems. Bitter and bloody wars have been fought over these differences. But in the inner or mystical vision of all the authentic religions has been the universal discovery that all are bound together in one life force. In fact the English word religion is derived from the Latin religare, meaning "to bind together; to make whole; harmony." In Sanskrit one of the original meanings of dharma (external religion) is the same: "to bind together as one the whole universe."

The discovery and affirmation of the unity of all in one Spirit, one sacred source and divine consciousness, is a recurrent theme not only in tribal spirituality and the Eastern religions, but also in the mystical streams of Judaism, Christianity and Islam. It is central in Sufi and Baha'i spirituality which grew out of Islam. It is the essence of Christ's teachings:

• "That all may be one as I and the Father are One"

• "Love one another as I have loved you"

• "I am the vine, and you are the branches"

Our astronauts go into space as technicians. Some come back as mystics. From the darkness of space they have seen the earth in a new way. This new vision of the earth as a sub-system of one minor solar system in a remote galaxy of a vast cosmos brings with it a new humility. We are not so powerful after all. We did not create the Earth. We are not the masters. We are not *over* the earth but are part of this single cell we call Earth. "We will live or die as this cell lives or dies." [7]

III. A New Genesis: The Forward Journey

The forward journey begins with the recognition that the present order, however dark, dangerous and polarized, is not the last word. Human genesis, like the cosmogenesis of which it is a part, is still in process. We have not finished our journey. We are unfinished humans and unfinished communities. There are no developed nations. We are all developing nations, part of a developing world community. We are called to grow, to become more.

A new human order will be created in the meeting ground between contemplation and struggle, reflection and action. The personal spiritual journey takes on meaning and purpose when we struggle to find an adequate response to the real life and death questions which life puts before us. As Victor Frankl noted in *Man's Search for Meaning*, we find meaning or fulfillment not when we seek our own spiritual realization, but when we transcend ourselves in response to the larger questions which history constantly puts before us.

He made the following observations about the brutal experience he and others suffered in a Nazi concentration camp, when many were tempted to surrender their will to life:

"What was really needed was a fundamental change in our attitude toward life. We had to learn that ourselves and furthermore, we had to teach despairing people that it did not really matter what we expected from life, but rather what life expected from us. We needed to stop asking about the meaning of life, and instead to think of ourselves as those who were being questioned by life — daily and hourly. Our answer must consist, not in talk and meditation, but in right action and in right conduct. Life ultimately means taking the responsibility to find the right answers to its problems and to fulfill the tasks which it constantly sets for each individual ... "[8]

He also wrote:

" ... Self-actualization cannot be attained if it is made an end in itself, but only as a side effect of self-transcendence."

What a desperate collection of people recognized and asked of themselves in the shadows of the gas chambers and mass extermination, we who live today in the shadow of nuclear genocide need to ask ourselves: "What is life asking of us?"

Today life is putting before us some very critical questions. They are life and death questions. They are not being adequately addressed in any national or international political forum. But they remain to haunt us all the same, crying out for some form of adequate response.

"Who are we? Are we capable of the psychological, spiritual, mythic growth required for the next stage of our journey? Are we capable of becoming and living as world community?"

While some scientists have been exploring outer space, others have been exploring the inner space of the human psyche and soul, the inner reaches of human nature. They have also been doing brain and mind research, understanding the different functions of right and left brain hemispheres and the human capacity for both intuitive and rational modes of knowing. They have been discovering that we have vast untapped potential; that we haven't begun to reach the limits of our mental, psychic, spiritual capacities; that we may still be in an early stage of our evolution. We are still in a process of becoming human. And we are still in the process of becoming a human community.

The work of psychologist Abraham Maslow[9] is especially relevant to the image of The Becoming Human. It is an image which, in Maslow's vision, is inseparable from an image of The Becoming World Community.

Maslow describes human potentialities in terms of inherent human needs and capacities that include not only Basic needs (food, shelter, security, belonging, affection, esteem) but also meta or Being needs. The Being needs/values include a long list of about 40 attributes such as Justice, Peace, Love, Unity, Beauty, Truth, Goodness, Simplicity, Joy, Playfulness. These are part of the inherent ground of our being withou which we feel incomplete, deprived, not fully human.

These Being needs are also the words which, through centuries of spiritual search, people in different cultures have come to use to describe God, the Buddha nature, the Christ nature, Atman, the divine. Ultimately, these Being needs must be taken into account as we design the social systems of the future.

Maslow felt that the "actualization of the highest human potentials is possible — on a mass basis — only under "good' conditions; that we need a good society in which to grow." By "good society" he said he meant "one species, one world."

Like Frankl, Maslow concluded that self-realization is not attainable as an end in itself. Only through self-transcendence, through responding to issues larger than self do we become fully human. In a sense we can look at the issues history is putting before us and say with Christopher Fry, "Thank God we live in times when problems are soul sized," when so much is demanded of us, when we are challenged to stretch ourselves and become more.

Maslow saw the long range goal as world peace through one world, one law. [10] For him the development of the fully human person and the development of world order were inseparable from each other. He put it this way:

"There is a kind of feedback between the Good Society and the Good Person. They need each other, they are *sine qua non* to each other. I wave aside the problem of which comes first. It is quite clear that they develop simultaneously and in tandem. It would in any case be impossible to achieve either one without the other. By Good Society I mean ultimately one species, one world." [11]

A more just and peaceful world order can be viewed as a necessary pre-condition for the full flowering of the human person and the full flowering of an authentic, lived spirituality. It can also be viewed as the natural outcome of the human search for completion and fulfillment, of an authentic spirituality.

For Maslow the far goal was world peace through world law. For Sri Aurobindo, the Indian mystic and philosopher who was a spiritual force in India's struggle for independence, a world political order or world government was a necessary step in the larger spiritual journey of the human community. The far goal he saw was spiritual union; a spiritual order. But he saw political unification as an essential middle step that could not be separated from or skipped over in the longer spiritual journey. [12]

What Kind of World Order?

The question is not whether there will be a new human order. It is rather, what kind of order? What values and world-views will it be built on? Will it be a world order based on power and domination over the earth and each other? Will it serve a few at the expense of the many? Will its successive stages lead to increasing hunger, war, deprivation and dehumanization? Will it be an order where increasing wealth flows into the hands of a few?

Or will we decide to journey on a path toward a world order that serves all humanity as a whole? Will it be a liberating and humanizing world order? Will it help us become more fully human and more fully human community?

The answer to these questions will depend upon the quality and values of people on the journey and on the quality of their spirituality. Who will be involved in the formulation and decision-making process for a new world order? Will they include men and women rooted in a global and creational spirituality? In a spirituality that is conscious, courageous, humble and bold enough to guide and support us in becoming co-creational with the Spirit of History in the work of building the earth?

Deeply spiritual persons experience the suffering in the world as their own suffering. The world is not something apart from them. Their skin is not a dividing membrane that separates them from the world but a connecting membrane, a permeable membrane, through which events of the world and events of their inner life flow into one another.

They suffer with the world. But they do not become obsessed by their suffering and the world's suffering. They do not let it overtake them and destroy their spirit, their ability to choose life. To live deeply in the Spirit is to be able to see beyond the immediate evidence of brokenness and suffering. It is to be able to imagine alternatives. It is to seek the not yet, but possible future. To live deeply in the Spirit is to find the courage to create in the midst of darkness; the faith to plant seeds in the dark ground of our times so that new life can flourish in the future.

Rubem Alves, the Brazilian author of *Tomorrow's Child*, has this to say about hope and suffering and the creative act:

"What is hope? It is the presentiment that imagination is more real and reality less real than it looks. It is the hunch that the overwhelming brutality of facts that oppress and repress is not the last word. It is the suspicion that Reality is more complex than realism wants us to believe; that the frontiers of the possible are not determined by the limits of the actual, and that in a miraculous and unexpected way, life is preparing the creative events which will open the way to freedom and resurrection . . .

"The two, suffering and hope, live from each other. Suffering without hope, produces resentment and despair. Hope without suffering creates illusions, naivete and drunkenness . . .

"Let us plant dates, even though those who plant them will never eat them . . . We must live by the love of what we will never see. This is the secret discipline. It is a refusal to let the creative act be dissolved away in immediate sense experience, and a stubborn commitment to the future of our grandchildren. Such disciplined love is what has given prophets, revolutionaries and saints the courage to die for the future they envisaged. They make their own bodies the seed of their highest hope."[13]

We must be far-sighted enough to plant seeds now toward a new Genesis so that our descendents will look back on us as ancestors who brought honor and life to them and the planetary community. We must be willing to bring whatever talents, skills, insights we have toward a new genesis in the human community. We must see and act on the knowledge that we are co-creational beings, and that, while the whole responsibility for the whole future of the world does not rest on any one person's shoulders, we each have a unique task to do in forwarding a more human world order that no one else can do for us. It is in discovering that task and taking it on in community with others that our life finds its meaning and that the world finds its direction and a basis for hope.

Everything we need to make a successful journey into the future is already available to us. We only need to have the courage to plumb our own depths and discover there the in-dwelling God who abides in us and in the world, calling us to Become.

Notes

1. Thomas Berry, "The Ecological Age," *The Whole Earth Papers*, No. 12 (1979), Global Education Associates.

2. Thomas Berry, in a presentation made at Seton Hall University, October, 1981.

3. The full text of Chief Seattle's speech is printed in a number of sources, one of which is *Power to the People: Active Nonviolence in the US* (Culver City, CA: Peace Press, 1977).

4. From *Zen and Zen Classics: Selections from R.H. Blyth*, compiled and with drawings by Frederick Franck, (New York: Vintage Press, 1978), p. 63.

5. ibid, p. 141.

6. As quoted in Alan Watts, *Tao: The Watercourse Way*, (New York: Pantheon Books, 1975).

7. Thomas Berry, "Ecological Age," op. cit.

8. Victor Frankl. *Man's Search for Meaning*.

9. Abraham Maslow. *The Farther Reaches of Human Nature*, (Harper and Brothers, 1954, revised ed., 1970), and Maslow, *Toward a Psychology of Being*, (Van Norstrand, 1962).

10. Abraham Maslow, "Politics 3," *Journal of Humanistic Psychology.*

11. Abraham Maslow, *The Farther Reaches of Human Nature*, op. cit., p. 19.

12. Sri Aurobindo, *The Future Evolution of Man*, (Wheaton, IL:

Theosophical Publishing House, 1974), and *Human Cycle, Ideal of Human Unity*, (New York: International Publishers Service, 1971). See also, A.B. Patel, *Toward a New World Order*, (Pondicherry, India: World Union International, 1974). Mr. Patel builds on the thought of Sri Aurobindo and looks at both the spiritual and global political implications for world order of Aurobindo's thought.

13. Rubem Alves, *Tomorrow's Child*, (New York: Harper and Row, 1972).

(Adapted from "Toward a Global Spirituality," originally published in "The Whole Earth Papers," No 16, 1982, Global Education Associates. Printed with permission.)

PART FOUR:
INEQUITIES —
NO EASY SOLUTION

*I*nequities seem to be a leading cause of tension at all levels of society, from families and neighborhoods to nations and the world community at large.

• Children bicker over who gets the bigger helping of ice cream.

• The "have" and "have-not" classes of society struggle over the question of who should own property (individuals, or the collective group?).

• Nations argue about the distribution and use of world resources.

Many of the world's brightest and most concerned individuals have studied the causes and symptoms of inequity down through the ages, and today one thing seems certain: There are no easy solutions.

We individuals seem to need incentive to produce, and so do our groups. To be innovative, we individuals need easy access to information and an unrestrained intellectual environment . . . and, again, so do our groups. If we have found a way to be more clever, or more productive, or more inventive than average, we may feel empty if our efforts go unrewarded and unrecognized. That seems to be our nature as humans — we like to do well, and we like to be recognized for it.

Part 4

But there is another side to our nature which sometimes gets us into trouble. In an unrestrained environment we may indulge excessively. We can easily become accustomed to excesses, protecting them defiantly while ignoring the plight of the less fortunate. When we see someone with a better lot than our own, we may feel a twinge of envy. We may be driven by an urge to keep up with or exceed the material pursuits of our neighbors. To want more, to guard our surpluses zealously, to envy others, to outdo others . . . these too seem to be aspects of our nature.

In short, human nature is torn by contradictions which seem to make some degree of inequity unavoidable whenever two or more people get together. One of the most crucial challenges in the coming decades is to deal wisely with the inequities now causing uneasiness at all levels throughout the human species.

The authors of Part Four explore ways to meet those challenges.

An explosive, storybook drama. Before international civil servant William Clark died in 1985, he wrote a parable, reprinted here, about families living in apartments of the same house. The mutual distrust between the heavily armed families upstairs, and the desperation of the poor families in the basement add up to an explosive situation.

The world is a stage. Ahmad Abubakar observes a real-world scenario of Mr. Clark's story. Mr. Abubakar, a rural development specialist, takes a look at the economic basis for mistrust and conflict between East and West, and between North and South.

First, a change of attitude. Gandhian theorist J.S. Mathur observes that a change toward international equity and world stability must begin with a change of heart. As long as we desire more, more, more, and these desires are reflected in national policies of expanding resource acquisition and heightened production, we will be forced to deal with inequities, ravaged ecosystems, dehumanization of workers, and other sources of social and world instability.

A sense of fairness. Educational consultant Howard Richards proposes that a sense of wisdom and fairness be applied to world economics. "Normative" regulation of world wealth would insure that a stable environment is maintained and that everyone's basic needs are met before the various market segments can pursue their economic goals.

A solid foundation for growth. Physicist and Nobel laureate Abdus Salam discusses the need for greater self-sufficiency on the part of Third World countries ... but national self-sufficiency in today's complex world requires a foundation or infrastructure of sound scientific education, research and development. As founder of the Third World Academy of Sciences, Dr. Salam explains how that foundation can be built.

Chapter 16
Bad Neighbors

by William Clark (1916-85)

Background. Journalist and international civil servant. Founded and ran in the 60s the London-based Overseas Development Institute. Served for 12 years at the World Bank where, as a close associate of Robert McNamara, he was vice president for external relations and played a key role in establishing the Brandt Commission. From 1980 until his death, president of the International Institute for Environment and Development. Author of *Cataclysm, the North-South Conflict of 1987* (London: Sidgwick and Jackson), an imaginative novel about the North-South rift. William Clark died in June, 1985.

His article. A short, prophetic parable that captures the troubled mood of a tense modern world.

(As forests shrink and topsoil disappears and deserts expand,) the stark fact is that the existing world order will collapse by the end of the century because we are destroying the very basis of our existence.

Bad Neighbors

by William Clark (1916-1985)

*T*he (Biblical) story of the Good Neighbor encapsulates a whole sociological treatise in about 400 words. This, then, is the parable of the Bad Neighbors:

Two families moved into a semi-detached house with a rather thin dividing wall, which permitted them to hear, but not understand, everything that went on in the other's abode. Both families became convinced that the other was attempting to break through the wall, and murder them in their beds. So they each built up a battery of alarm signals, and more and more sophisticated booby traps and explosive devices, which would enable them utterly to destroy the neighbors if they ever attempted to break through.

The cost of this burglar proofing was so great that neither family had any cash to spare to fix up the cellar and basement. There, in damp, overcrowded squalor, a large number of poor coloured tenants lived. In mid-winter the basement became so cold that the tenants used their axes to chop off bits of the joists in their ceiling to build fires to keep warm. Messages came from upstairs forbidding them to shake the building, lest the alarm systems were activated and everyone blown up; but as a concession, upstairs did promise to turn up the electric heating so that some warmth could trickle downstairs. But heat does not trickle down. So the blacks quietly and carefully sawed away the wood. After a time the joists gave way, the floors sank, the dividing wall tottered and fell, thus exploding all its defensive devices and killing everyone on both sides of the building.

I hope the parable does not need explaining, but I would like to emphasize some of its implications for today's world. The division of the world into two nuclear-armed camps is a reality which cannot be wished away, so that the de-escalation of the nuclear balance of terror is arguably the most urgent task before the governments concerned. But it is not the only task before those governments; there are other ways to make the earth a desert than a nuclear holocaust. Poverty can be as devastating as plutonium; the South presents as great a challenge as the East, and at least as urgent.

Today this poverty explosion is most devastating in Africa. The pressure of expanding population has filled up the cities, which have more than doubled in size since independence came in the sixties. Cities have to bring food from farms outside; but in Africa the agricultural sector, which accounts for at least three-quarters of the population, can only just feed itself, and the cities are largely supplied by imported food from the northern hemisphere. This is expensive. So the supplies are subsidized, to avoid the riots which follow any attempt to raise food prices to their economic level. This means that African farmers are underpaid for any food they do sell to the cities, which gives another downward turn to the poverty spiral. Because they are so poor they tend to overcultivate and underfertilize their land; they cut down more trees and bushes for fuel, instead of using kerosene; they burn the animal dung instead of employing it as manure. As a result, with increasing speed, the top soil blows or is washed away, leaving a desert of sand as in the Sahel, or of baked mud as in East Africa.

Less in the public eye but just as terrifying is the loss of topsoil in Asia. The expanding population of Nepal is denuding the Himalayas of their forests, which provide the essential sponge to make the great range the watershed of South Asia, supporting the lives of a billion people. The soil cover which is washed away, leaving bare infertile rock, will take 400 years to replace.

But, of course, mankind cannot wait 400 years, when it is destroying the basis on which it subsists at such a rapid rate. We are faced with the stark fact that the existing world order will collapse by the end of the century, because three-quarters of the earth's population are living in destructive poverty, and we are all destroying the very basis of our existence. Mankind might survive the exhaustion of our oil reserves, not of the earth's topsoil.

But is it our responsibility in the affluent world to help in creating a new order which would provide a sustainable improvement in the lot of the poorest? For every good neighbor who would answer "yes," there are two who will pass by on the other side. It is to them our parable is addressed. They live protected from the holocaust only by a delicate balance of terror, and from the cataclysm by a delicate balance of nature which is already dangerously upset. The basement squatters in the world are the majority of mankind and are in the process of destabilising the entire global order. We shall not find security by ignoring them.

(Reprinted with permission from The Tablet , London, 11 Feb. 1984.)

Chapter 17
Strengthening the Foundation
— Steps to a Stable World Economy

by Ahmad Abubakar
Deputy Director, Centre on Integrated Rural Development for Africa
(CIRDAFRICA)
Arusha, Tanzania

Background. Educated in the East (International Institute of
Management — Romania), the West (Vanderbilt University — USA),
and the South (University of Ibadan — Nigeria). Since 1974 has held
a variety of management and consultative positions for state-level
government in Nigeria before accepting his current transnational
position in rural development. Languages: English, some Arabic and
French. Has travelled to Romania, USA, Egypt, India, Malaysia,
Japan, Brazil and throughout Africa on a variety of study and
research projects.

His article. The desire to defend economic privileges contained in
high consumption levels has divided the world into two antagonistic
situations — industrialized vs. developing countries, and capitalist vs.
socialist countries. Solutions proposed by the author would be
enacted at the national and global levels to reduce incompatibilities
and tensions between adversaries . . . whether divided by
consumption levels or by ideology.

*Overconsumption has inspired experts to
coin the term* overdevelopment *to capture
the level of excess consumption in the
industrialized West.*

Strengthening the Foundation
—Steps to a Stable World Economy

by Ahmad Abubakar

We are perpetually striving to raise our standard of living. Achieving this goal requires more products and resources. Consumption is central to world instability.

The desire to defend economic privileges contained in high consumption levels has divided the world into two types of antagonistic situations: Industrialized (capitalist and socialist) vs. developing countries, and capitalist vs. socialist. Both types of conflict threaten world peace, but the latter is the more immediate danger because the potential combatants can destroy human civilization in a very short time.

A Backward Situation: The Poor Feeding the Rich

The benefits of industry, science, and technology — such things as elimination of diseases, and living standards unheard of in human history — are concentrated in the industrialized countries of the West and Japan. They have extended only in limited degrees to other countries of the world.

This unprecedented living standard in the West feeds on vast quantities of natural resources. Science and technology use natural resources to produce both capital and consumer goods. Capital goods produce other capital goods which in turn produce consumer goods. It is clear that the ultimate aim is to improve goods and services, which are expected to enhance the chances of survival, good health and happiness.

However, as the level of consumption rises drastically, waste sets in. Overconsumption has inspired experts to coin the term *overdevelopment*, to capture the level of excess consumption in the industrialized West. As evidence of excess consumption, researchers have established that an average US citizen consumes four to five times the average consumer in the developing countries. Industrialized countries in total consume 20 times more resources per capita than poor nations.[1]

This excess consumption requires a vast amount of natural resources. While science and technology have continued to rise to higher levels, Western natural resources have diminished more quickly. Today the West cannot satisfy its own demand for such huge quantities of resources. And even if it could, why not conserve and exploit cheaper resources of other countries? Hence, a growing dependence of the industrialized countries on the Third World. Thus Alvin Tofler says,

" . . . industrial civilization has to be fed from without. It could not survive unless it integrated the rest of the world into the money system and controlled that system for its own benefit."[2]

This heavy dependence of the industrialized countries on the natural resources of the Third World to sustain excess consumption has occasioned fierce competition among those countries.

The economic struggle drew in UN (United Nations) agencies such as IMF (International Monetary Fund), IBRD (International Bank for Reconstruction and Development) (World Bank), and GATT (General Agreement on Tariffs and Trade). These are UN institutions in name only. In reality, they have been instruments of the industrialized countries, especially the USA, prior to the changes in the 1970s. From the creation of these institutions up to the 1970s, the USA had wielded 40% of the power in the World Bank, for instance.[3]

The establishment of these institutions was planned by the USA before the end of World War II. After the war, the USA emerged as the strongest Western Power and the sole creditor to the war-ravaged European nations. The belligerents would need infusion of capital to reconstruct their war-ravaged economies. Hence the US-inspired Marshall Plan.

In addition, the world would require a peaceful environment for economic activities. No protectionism, trade wars, or currency wars, which were the characteristics of the 1930s and in fact part of the causes of the War itself. Such a peaceful global trading climate would require three institutions to perform some functions:

•Liberalization of trade by removal of barriers needed the GATT.

•The creation of credit to stimulate economic development and demand for export of industrialized countries in the Third World required the World Bank.

•IMF was assigned the role of stabilizing the world's financial system by managing the exchange rates.[4]

To complete this arrangement, the dollar was established as a global currency. Yet this elaborate arrangement did not prevent global skirmishes here and there. It did not eliminate the need for secret intelligence agencies. It did not stop intervention and bullying by the industrial powers in the race for raw materials and markets. I will discuss this aspect of global instability in the next section. Meantime, suffice it to say that all the arrangements to manipulate and impose political authority in the world have as their underlying explanantion the desire to maintain the ever-rising consumption levels attained by the industrialized countries at the expense of the Third World countries.

East Vs. West

In the course of the evolution of industry in the North, two important persons came to the scene — Adam Smith and Karl Marx — whose 200-year-old ideas represent the two opposing forces threatening world peace today.

In 1776 Adam Smith published the revolutionary work, the *Wealth of Nations*, a philosophy that expounds and defends free trade, the basis of capitalism.

A half-century later Karl Marx introduced another revolutionary social philosophy — dialectical materialism — in which capitalism is merely an early stage in the evolution of society. The ultimate destination of society is communism, a stage in which there will be no class. But between capitalism and communism is socialism. This stage is attained when the workers revolt to establish a dictatorship of the people. In this form of social organization, business and industry are owned by the State. There is no free enterprise, no exploitation of workers by a few capitalists. This will be the beginning of elimination of classes. And ultimately, even the State is expected to wither away, thus arriving at a classless society.

It was the Russian Revolution and World War I which crystalized the influence of Karl Marx. For the first time, Europe found a communist state at its doorstep. This development awakened some fear in the forces of power and privilege. These forces committed themselves to the defense of the status-quo, and in this they found an ally in the

USA. As socialism started to spread globally, the conflict between the European powers and USA on one hand and the Soviet Union on the other, sharpened. This was the beginning of the sharp ideological conflict which is, more than anything else, threatening world peace and, indeed, human civilization.

North Vs. South

Powers on both sides of the East-West ideological divide are guilty of destabilization or crude intervention in their dealings with their Third World neighbors to the South. Neither superpower has had much experience in acquiring colonies outside their boundaries. But they have what one may call sphere of influence in this age of imperialism.

US adventurism. The USA has maintained a few colonies of sorts. I know the Philippines is one of them. But Latin America has been USA's backyard for a long time. The ostensive US policy in Latin America is based on the statement that security in the latter is indispensable to the former's security. The truth is that Latin America is merely a quarry of US capitalism. In exploiting Latin America, the US uses four major forms of instruments:

- multinational companies,

- the comporador elite in Latin America,

- covert and overt intervention,

- the World Bank and the debt weapon.

The multinationals do the exploitation and the milking through Latin America's labor force. The other institutions are used to subjugate the governments of Latin America.

Here, of special interest is the role of the World Bank and the debt. The World Bank, along with IMF and even GATT, have become instruments of blackmail. Third World countries cannot qualify for membership of the World Bank without being members of the IMF. And of recent, this blackmail has become very prominent in the prevailing global recession. Third World member countries are forced to implement IMF conditionalities before qualifying for an IMF loan. The World Bank is also increasingly, but subtly, basing its loans on IMF conditionalities. Western banks have categorically stated: "no IFM conditionalities, no loan." Yet evidence has shown that IMF prescription is a recipe for instability in Third World countries. There were instances where lives were lost and governments collapsed in their bid to implement IMF prescriptions. And it is also being revealed that the World Bank is increasingly playing a role in the Western strategy of increasing world supply of minerals on favorable terms to multinational companies and industrialized countries.[5] Yet these are supposed to be UN institutions.

As to the question of debt, the subservience it promotes is obvious to any layman. In recent times, indebted governments have been forced to seek more loans in the effort to continue paying the past loans, but have instead found themselves sinking into deeper debt. In addition, IMF is ever present around the corner imposing its conditionalities for qualifying for further loans.

I have been talking about the USA's peaceful intervention in Latin America. There are also many examples of crude interventions, such as Chile, El Salvador, Nicaragua, and Bolivia (the CIA murder of Che Guevera) . . . Vietnam, Grenada, Lebanon, and Libya, just to mention a few prominent ones.

In Africa, the USA is continuing to destabilize Angola and preventing the independence of Namibia. In South Africa, the USA is being supported by Britain, France, and probably West Germany to preside over apartheid and the extermination of the black race simply because their multinationals are reaping the greatest net profits in the world. Labor is cheaper in South Africa than anywhere else in the world. And in all this crude and dangerous adventurism, Britain is enthusiastically supporting the US in its (Britain's) futile attempt to salvage its decaying civilization which was for the most part built on exploitation.

Soviet adventurism. As to the colonial adventures of the USSR, there is nothing to say because they had no colonies. But as to their imperialist adventures, there is, as in the case of USA, much to be said. In a similar fashion, the Soviets have created a ring of satellites in Eastern Europe (COMECON — Council for Mutual Economic Assistance) as a countervailing force to NATO. Again the reason given for this is Soviet security. One could help justify this situation with Soviet experience in World Wars I and II. But in practice the intention has gone beyond mere security; it has also embraced economic and power relations. The Soviet Union is deriving the benefit of a monopolized market in Eastern Europe. It is likely that the USSR is obtaining raw materials from the COMECON countries.

The USSR also has its record of covert and overt intervention, but, unlike in the case of the USA, only the more overt intervention is widely known. There are two well-known examples of crude Soviet interventions — Czechoslovakia and the prevailing one in Afghanistan. In comparing the superpowers, the only credit the USSR has is that its number of known interventions has been much fewer. But in principle the crime is the same in gravity. In addition, what the USSR might have gained in engaging in fewer instances of covert and overt interventions, it is likely that it has neutralized that lead in its sad records of human rights. There seems to me to be no freedom of speech or press whatsoever in the USSR.

The Staggering Cost of Superpower Rivalry

In their bid for intervention, both superpowers have committed one or another serious crime in common. They succeeded in dividing the people of Vietnam, Korea and Yemen with the attendant destruction of lives and resources, and the inflicting of pain arising from separation of relatives. Only Vietnam has succeeded in healing this wound. I hope the other two countries will be allowed to heal their wounds by reuniting their people.

The cost of these adventures in money, products, resources, and human life is staggering. According to Fidel Castro, President of Cuba, the cost of a Trident nuclear submarine could pay the annual bill for educating 16 million children.[6]

Another source reveals that superpowers account for 50 per cent of world military expenditure since 1976.[7] These monstrous expenditures on armaments are incurred when Third World debt is approximately US $1000 billion,[8] and 40 million people, half of them children, die of hunger and malnutrition every year.[9]

If global resources are managed properly, there is no need for anybody to die of hunger and malnutrition and ill health, and also there is no need for the Third World to incur the debt they did. Surely, this debt could be written off as alternative to expenditure on armaments.

Conclusion

The competition for strategic resources and the determination to defend the status quo have generated two areas of serious tension in the world — North vs. South, and East vs. West. Both situations are almost equally liable to escalate to very dangerous proportions, but the one of immediate danger is the ideological conflict between the socialists and the capitalists. As to North-South tension, there is enough time to defuse it if the North is willing to make some concessions and the South is willing to reexamine critically its development policies.

The United Nations Organization rose out of the debris of World Wars I and II. Its role in the world is to prevent another holocaust by making the world a home for all races, genders, religions, and ideologies to coexist peacefully. The UN has done well in the area of socio-economic development. Since its founding, it has uplifted the living standards of millions of citizens of this globe.

But in regard to world security, the main purpose for which it was founded, the UN has achieved relatively little. The responsibility for global security has forcibly passed into the hands of the superpowers which use such responsibility crudely to settle scores.

Furthermore, there is growing evidence of efforts to further weaken the UN. Its resolutions are being flouted more than ever before. Some countries have withdrawn and some have threatened to withdraw from some institutions. Some are refusing to contribute to its budget or are cutting their contributions. From this, it is clear that the problem of the UN is that of enforcement and by extension such is the problem of global instability. So, some very basic, crucial questions arise:

•How do we organize global security and how do we enforce it?

•How do we share the world resources?

•How do we conserve such resources?

•How do we persuade some people, groups and nations to lower their living standards?

•How do we defuse intense competition?

It will be observed that these questions are fundamentally economic in nature, and until they are answered satisfactorily, both theoretically and practically, global security will continue to elude us until finally we destroy ourselves and our civilization.

To answer these questions let me make some proposals as to how to obtain world security. They are divided into two parts. The first is what I call the national level proposals. The second part is what I call the international or global level proposals.

National Level Proposals
•Consumption levels should be reexamined with the view to eliminating waste, thereby raising the living standard of others to a reasonable level.

•Some resources should be diverted from space and military research to solving prevailing global problems such as disease, hunger, malnutrition, ill health, and natural disasters.

•Greater efforts should be made to conserve energy and natural resources, thereby eliminating dangerous competition and avoiding environmental degradation and pollution.

•Noting the breakdown of correlation between the application of knowledge and building civilization, application of knowledge should be shifted from military to civilian purposes.

•The citizens of superpower countries should impress upon their leaders the need for reducing nationalism and cutting military expenditure.

•In the words of Emery Reves, "Those in power have no time and incentive to think. And those who think have no power whatsoever." [10]

In this regard, perhaps scientists who are fully aware of the dangers of nuclear holocaust should start participating in government as politicians, hoping that they will not get so power-drunk as to cease to have the time and incentive to think. It is hoped that such people will bring sanity to the top-level political hierarchy.

Global Level Proposals
•Going with Bertrand Russell, we should have a world government. The UN should be transformed into such government by equipping it legally and materially with enforcement capacity.

•Nationalism should take second place to the sense of globalism.

The grave situation in the world has made me come to the conclusion that the greatest challenge we face is not the conquest of vast interstellar distances, but the capacity to save ourselves from extinction.

Notes

1. Jan Tinbergen, *Report to the Club of Rome*.

2. Alvin Toffler, *The Third Wave*, 1980, p. 90.

3. D. Wadada Nabudere, *The Political Economy of Imperialism*, Zed Press and Tanzania Publishing House, 1987, p. 150.

4. *Monthly Review*, Volume 35, October, 1983, p. 8.

5. Michael Tanzer, *Monthly Review*, Volume 35, April 1984, p. 27.

6. Quoted by Michael Tanzer in *Monthly Review* Volume 35, December, 1983, p. 59.

7. Ibid (2)

8. *Monthly Review*, Volume 36, July-August, 1984, p. 35.

9. Ibid (10), p. 59.

10. Emery Reves, *The Anatomy of Power*, 1946, p. 202.

Chapter 18
New Values for Equitable Growth

by J.S. Mathur
Director, Institute of Gandhian Thought and Peace Studies
University of Allahabad
Allahabad, India

Background. Writer, editor, professor and international lecturer on social, industrial, economic and peace issues. Author of dozens of articles and 20 books, some highly acclaimed by scholars and media in India, Europe and the USA. As Institute director, hosts many visits by professional, political, scholarly and spiritual dignitaries, including Mother Teresa. Edits the quarterly *Journal of Gandhian Studies* with an international list of subscribers and contributors.

His article. Bringing equity to a modern world where starvation coexists fitfully with luxury must begin with a change of heart. The assumption that ever-increasing wants should be continually satisfied by ever-increasing production is leading to the suicide of civilization. It is time to readjust our priorities from a mad pursuit of material affluence to a more rational, more humble pursuit of peace and healthy world development.

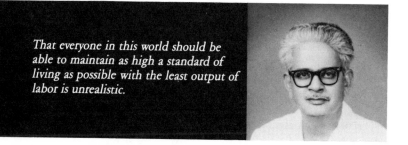

That everyone in this world should be able to maintain as high a standard of living as possible with the least output of labor is unrealistic.

New Values for Equitable Growth

by J.S. Mathur

*I*n our times when everyone thinks in terms of material comforts and welfare, it may sound paradoxical to write about non-economic aspects of growth and development. But the world is at a point where it is imperative to think about the dangers facing humanity because of the dominance of purely economic interests, motivations and welfare. It is no exaggeration to state that the existing economic structure cannot sustain itself if we lose sight of less-economic, more esoteric values.

Albert Schweitzer remarked,

"It is clear now to everyone that the suicide of civilization is in progress. What yet remains of it is no longer safe. It is still standing, indeed because it was not exposed to the destructive pressure which overwhelmed the rest, but like the rest, is built upon rubble, and the next landslide will very likely carry it away."[1]

Humanity faces these dangers because the present economic system is based upon a wrong appreciation of basic human instincts and is driven by dangerous, improper values. One of the basic assumptions of the modern economic structure is that ever-increasing wants should be continually satisfied by ever-increasing production and organization. That is, the quantity of growth rather than the quality is equated to a healthy society. As a result people are judged not by their human qualities but by their material affluence.

"The expansion of machine during the past two centuries was accompanied by the dogma of increasing want. Industry was directed not merely to the multiplication of goods and to an increase in their variety; it was directed towards the multiplication for the desire for goods. We passed from an economy of need to an economy of acquisition."[2]

The economy of acquisition has become the everyday mode.

Everyone knows what grief befell the mythical King Midas, whose mere touch turned his surrounding to gold. The same is happening to modern society in many lands. Our concept of heaven today is most likely to be a big department store providing new things every day, and us with enough of money to buy everything we please. Our technology — and leisure-oriented societies — keep on producing all sorts of wants within us . . . followed by things to satisfy these wants. Production and consumption have become ends in themselves.

But why do we want to produce more? Why do we want this, that and the other? These questions are rarely asked.

In a society where reputability depends upon the variety of goods a person possesses and consumes there shall remain a constant competition to possess something more than friends, neighbors, colleagues and others with whom one is in the habit of comparing one's self.

"In the nature of the case the desire for wealth can scarcely be satiated in any individual instance and evidently a satiation of the average or general desire for wealth is out of the question. However widely or equally or 'fairly' it may be distributed, no general increase of the community's wealth can make any approach to satiating this need, the ground of which is the desire for everyone to exceed everyone else in the accumulation of goods — since the struggle is substantially a race for reputability on the basis of an invidious comparison, no approach to a definitive attainment is possible."[3]

This mad pursuit of material affluence has given rise to a system of production dominated by machine culture . . . a factory civilization. Production is becoming more and more roundabout, mechanized and centralized. This in turn leads to misuse and exhaustion of natural resources — the nation's nutrients — the source of our products and energy.

"There can be no talk of riches produced by technology. What really happens is rather a steady, forever growing consumption. It is a ruthless destruction, the like of which the earth has never before seen. A more-and-more destruction of resources is the characteristic of our technology. Only by this destruction can it exist and spread."[4]

That is why the inevitable outcome of today's form of industrial society can only be exhaustion of natural resources and ultimate impoverishment of the human race.

"This poverty cannot be overcome by technological efforts; it is inherent in technology itself, it has marched in step with the industrial age and it will be so to the end."[5]

Exhaustion of resources has also resulted in the progressive rationalization of organization, the comprehensive administration and management of humanity by a bureaucracy of experts especially trained for the task.

"And as poverty spreads, the pressure of the organization upon us increases, for it becomes more urgent to squeeze from us the last drop. This mercilessness is characteristic of all moments of human distress. Beleaguered towns, blockaded countries, ships whose food and water are running low have shown like conditions."[6]

Industrial organizations increasingly require an enormous personnel, a personnel which is wholly unproductive, yet increasing in number all the faster. Burgeoning organization and its perfection have opened new fields of exploitation. The expert, even in socialist societies, acquires increasing regulatory power over others. This is the inevitable result of greater degree of organization that scientific technique brings about. It is apt to be irresponsible, behind-the-scenes regulation.

"This tyranny of the officials is one of the worst results of increasing organization, and one against which it is of the utmost importance to find safeguards if a scientific society is not to be intolerable to all but an insolent aristocracy of Jacks-in-office."[7]

In such a socioeconomic set-up an individual feels lost and isolated. With medias of mass persuasion, rather hypnotism, we have been able to persuade the large masses that their welfare can best be decided by those in authority. For two or three generations large numbers of individuals have been living as workers, not as human beings. The feeling of helplessness and insecurity have increased with every change in technology.

This emptiness has manifested itself as extreme self-centerism and selfishness. We are unmindful of the problems of others and do not pause even for a moment to think of the consequences our actions on other members of the community.

Describing American society, a sociologist of repute remarked,

"The typical American citizens today are concerned almost exclusively with private problems. By 'concerned' I mean enough interested in a problem to lose one's sleep sometimes, not merely just to talk about it. They lose their sleep about health, money and family problems. They do not lose their sleep about problems, of the society, because they have cut themselves off from the experience of social concern, from relatedness to others as part of their lives. They are private individuals with only private interests." [8]

Another social scientist broadens the scope to a world view:

"Society within the nation and without it is breaking down in groups that show ever increasing hostility to each other, irrational hates are taking the place of cooperation. This, historically, has been the precursor of downfall for many valiant civilizations. There is no reason to suppose that our own fate will be otherwise, if we do not at once state explicitly the problem and struggle to develop a better elite than we can at present show in public, private or academic life. Social life resembles biological life in at least one aspect, when normal process ceases, pathological growth begins. It is a short step from friendship or tolerance to distrust and hatred when the normal social relationships disintegrate." [9]

It is clear that such self-centeredness and lack of concern for the society of which one is a part and parcel cannot sustain the society. This may cause serious dislocation and therefore some external agency has to come into existence to curb these values which motivate large numbers of individuals.

Collectively we think in such terms as "welfare," "equity," and "fairness," but such movements get little or no momentum of their own because of the inherent contradiction in individual values and traits, and collective or group norms and standards. If the individual is not trained by moral values to look to the good of others, then some omnipotent external agency i.e. the government or state has to bring about collective good.

In other words, as people lose their sense of moral responsibility so do they lose their freedoms.

Gasset refers to this tendency as "the greatest danger threatening European civilization ... this is born of civilization itself. More than that, it constitutes one of its glories ... In our days the state has become a formidable machine which works in marvellous fashion, wonderful efficiency by reason of the quality and precision of its means. Once it is set up in the midst of society, it is enough to touch a button for its enormous levers to start working and exercise their overwhelming power on any portion, whatever of social framework." [10]

State intervention is one of the gravest dangers that today threaten civilization. In fact a time has arrived when it appears that society will have to live for the state, people for the governmental machine.

Gandhiji remarked,

"I look upon an increase of the power of the State with the greatest fear, because although apparently doing good by minimizing exploitation, it does the greatest harm to mankind by destroying individuality which lies at the root of all progress." [11]

For him the state represented organized and concentrated violence.

These tendencies that threaten civilization today have made serious-minded thinkers skeptical about the present society and its future.

Gandhiji advocated that we must deliberately put a stop to this desire to keep on increasing our wants ad-infinitum. He emphasized, "Our civilization, our culture, our Swaraj depends not upon multiplying our wants (self-indulgence) but upon restricting our wants, (self-denial)." [12]

Gandhiji quoted from the Christian Bible to drive home his point: "How hardly shall they that have riches enter into the kingdom of God ... It is easier for a camel to go through the eye of a needle than for a rich man to enter the kingdom of God."

Our happiness really lies in contentment. We who are discontented, however much we possess, become slaves to our desires. That everyone in this world should be able to maintain as high a standard as possible with the least output of labour is grotesquely unrealistic. Luxurious living is an impossible proposition for any society as a whole. And when there is no limit to luxury where shall we stop? When the resources run out, and intense competition leads to riots within nations and war among them, perhaps?

Therefore we must think in terms of regulating our wants. We must regulate them within before they are regulated from without.

"A certain degree of physical harmony and comfort is necessary, but above a certain level it becomes a hindrance instead of help. Therefore the ideal of creating an unlimited number of wants and satisfying them seems to be a delusion and snare. The satisfaction of one's physical needs, even the intellectual needs of one's narrow self, must meet at a certain point a dead stop, before it degenerates into

physical and intellectual voluptuousness. A man must arrange his physical and cultural circumstances so that they do not hinder him in his service of humanity on which all his energies should be concentrated." [13]

Nay, we need go a step further and identify ourselves with all forms of life, not only human life, but even with inanimate objects.

This may mean a complete change in and overall simplification of our system of production. It may mean abandoning much of technology and much that it represents. In the words of Lord Russell,

"The idolatry of the machine is abomination. The machine as an object of adoration is the modern form of satan, and its worship is the modern diabolism." [14]

Another sociologist remarked,

"The control of technology means a severe limitation of its hitherto unchecked growth, a limitation demanding an almost savage asceticism on the part of an age drunk not merely with synthetic emotions and pleasures manufactured hourly by entertainment factories, but with dreams of power and of conquest of outer space." [15]

It was for these reasons that Gandhiji wanted India to adopt a system of economic development which will shun industrialism and develop its cottages and villages. His belief was that

"Independent India can discharge her duty towards a groaning world by adopting a simple but ennobled life, by developing her thousands of cottages and living at peace with the world." [16]

His message of the spinning wheel has to be viewed in this light . . .

"the message of the spinning wheel is much wider than its circumference. Its message is one of simplicity, service of mankind, living as not to hurt others . . . The larger message is naturally for all." [17]

Similar sentiments were expressed by Lord Russell,

"The root of the matter is very simple that I am almost ashamed to mention it, for fear of the derisive smile with which wise cynics will greet my words. The thing I mean — please forgive me for mentioning it — is love, Christian love or compassion. If you feel this, you have a motive for existence, a guide in action, a reason for courage, an imperative necessity for intellectual honesty. If you feel this, you have all that anybody should need in the way of religion. Although you may not find happiness, you will never know the despair of those whose life is aimless and void of purpose, for there is always something that you can do to diminish the awful sum of human misery." [18]

Gandhiji trained leaders in his Ashram to accept these values. The vows that the members of his Ashram were to adopt were non-possession, voluntary poverty, non-violence i.e. love, compassion and reverence for all living beings ... nay, even towards nature. This is quite contrary to accepted and current values.

"As a matter of fact, the most utterly inhuman thoughts have been current among us — in all the ugly clearness of language and with the authority of logical principles. There has been created a social mentality which discourages humanity in individuals ... The stand-off-ishness and want of sympathy which are shown so clearly in every way to strangers are no longer felt as being really rudeness, but pass for the behaviour of the man of the world. Our society has also ceased to allow to all people, as such, a human value and a human dignity, many sections of the human race have become merely raw material and property in human form." [19]

May we dismiss these values as religious or ethical ideas? Gandhiji felt otherwise.

"I must confess that I do not draw a sharp or any distinction between economics and ethics. Economics that hurts the moral well-being of an individual or a nation are immoral and therefore sinful." [20]

Albert Schweitzer agrees that ethical progress is, then, that which is truly of the essence of civilization ...

"We shall not succeed in re-establishing our civilization on an enduring basis until we rid ourselves completely of the superficial concept of civilization which now holds us in thrall, and give ourselves up again to the ethical view." [21]

To quote Gandhiji once again:

"Economics, to be worth anything, must also be capable of being reduced to terms of religion and spirituality." [22]

A world community can be created in which human beings can live comfortably and in peace with each other. Today the destiny of humanity is at stake. We need new training so that we can subjugate selfishness to generosity, ignorance to wisdom and hate to love.

"Civilization can only revive when there shall come into being in a number of individuals a new tone of mind independent of the one prevalent among the crowd and in opposition to it, a tone of mind which will gradually influence over the collective one, and in the end determine its character. It is only an ethical movement which can rescue us from the slough of barbarism."[23]

We need individuals who can swim against the current. No society can be progressive without a leaven of rebels. Let us hope a large number of dedicated souls will rise and be inspired by the song of Gurudev Tagore —

'Walk Alone.
If they answer not to thy call, walk alone,
If they are afraid and cower mutely facing the wall,
O thou of evil luck,
Open thy mind and speak out alone.
If they turn away and desert you
when crossing the wilderness,
O thou of evil luck,
trample the thorns under thy tread,
and along the blood-lined track travel alone.
If they do not hold up the light
when the night is troubled with storm,
O thou of evil luck,
with the thunder-flame of pain ignite thine own heart
and let it burn alone.

Notes:

1. Albert Schweitzer: *Decay & Restoration of Civilization* p. 16

2. Lewis Mumford, quoted in Harris Brown: *The Challenge of Man's Future* p. 187

3. Veblem: *The Theory of Leisure Class* p. 32

4. Juenger, F.G.: *The Failure of Technology*, p.20

5. Ibid., p. 13

6. Ibid., p. 17

7. Bertrand Russell: *The Impact of Science on Society*, p. 72

8. Erich Fromm: *Freedom in Work Situation*, pp.6-7

9. Mayo: *Social Problems of an Industrial Civilization*, p.119

10. Ortega Y Gasset: *The Revolt of the Masses* pp. 85-87

11. Mathurs: *Economic Thought of Mahatma Gandhi*, p. 579

12. ibid., p. 527

13. ibid., p. 583

14. *The Impact of Science on Society*, p. 106

15. Juenger F.G., *Failure of Technology* (vi)

16. Mathurs, *Economic Thought of Mahatma Gandhi*, p. 517

17. ibid., p. 477

18. *Impact of Science on Society* p. 149

19. *Decay & Restoration of Civilization*, p.32

20. Mathurs: *Economic Thought of Mahatma Gandhi*, p. 528

21. *Decay & Restoration of Civilization*, p.6

22. Mathurs: *Economic Thought of Mahatma Gandhi*, p. 86.

23. *Decay & Restoration of Civilization*, p.68

Chapter 19
World Values for Economic Justice

by Howard Richards
Professor of Peace Studies, Earlham College
Richmond (IN), USA

Background. Trained in law, philosophy, psychology, sociology, and educational theory. Teaches philosophy, peace studies, human development and social relations, education and management. Provides consultation to an educational research group in Santiago, Chile (CIDE) and an ecological ethics association in Ontario, Canada. Has written many articles and books on education and the social sciences. Special concerns: Worldwide economic well-being, Third World development, especially in Latin America.

His article. A legitimate global management economics would be concerned with mobilizing resources to meet human needs and to keep the environment balanced. A world system of this type would be based upon legitimate values and standards on which most people can agree. The author outlines such a system.

The disagreement is not about whether poverty should be abolished, but how economic systems should be organized to abolish it, and where the resources are going to come from.

World Values for Economic Justice

by Howard Richards

Let us assume we want global institutions:

•that can keep the peace and manage the productive factors of the earth in such a manner that every human being attains a decent standard of living, and ecological balance is maintained,

•that are regulated by principles to which most people consent, and

•whose authority is supported by the legitimacy of their values and standards.

Widespread consent would help make these global institutions legitimate, and legitimacy would increase the probability of such institutions becoming operational.

How are such institutions legitimized? What needs to be done to achieve and maintain consent to establish a viable world order? What sorts of principles need to be part of such an order, to maximize the likelihood that it will come about and that it will work?

Global Management Economics

For creatures like ourselves, who need standards and values for the sake of our safety, who are psychologically capable of acquiring reverence for justice, who have imagination and personal and collective histories, and who live in society . . . the general acceptance of workable standards and values would be — if it could be brought about — a feasible way to facilitate worldwide cooperation.

Against this approach to world order, an objection immediately arises. It could be argued that the world is now so bitterly divided on ideological issues that it is useless to try to achieve even a minimal working consensus on principles of justice that would have a strong psychological appeal to the world's people and guide the necessary functional cooperation.

I would argue that there are not very many important ideologies in the world today. The most widely influential system is Marxism; a second important ideology is that of the Judeo-Christian tradition, with which are associated the ethical values of Occidental culture; a third is the system of Western science. One may not agree with this list. One may wish to add more value systems, such as Islam, Buddhism, Hinduism, or rearrange the list by adding, subtracting, or making a distinction. Or one may wish to say that one of these world views is the truth while the others are "ideologies."

What is essential in my position is that the important value systems are few in number and that all of them came out of the same classical and medieval tradition. Scientists did not, in fact, begin to construct a worldview notably distinct from that of religious tradition until about 1600. And Marxism took form in an atmosphere saturated by Western scientific and ethical values around 1850. The worldviews of Islam, Hinduism and Buddhism are fundamentally compatible with Marxist, Judeo-Christian and scientific values.

Under the circumstances, then, it is understandable that in spite of a lot of loose talk about the impossibility of reaching agreement on normative principles, the nations of the world, acting through their representatives in the United Nations, have in fact reached agreement on a great number of normative principles. The Universal Declaration of Human Rights expresses agreement on many moral values, and seeks to translate them into effective principles of law. Declarations of the principle of nonaggression and the renunciation of war as an instrument of national policy, which imply the right of every nation to settle its own internal affairs without foreign interference, command universal assent. In the field of economic and social rights, the nations of the world have made and ratified agreements which affirm the right of every person in the world to decent living conditions.

Consensus on Global Values

On the whole, then, if we are looking for a consensus on principles of justice, we do not have far to look; we already have at least a basic set of standards and values expressed in documents signed by representatives of nearly all the world's people and ratified by their respective governments.

It is in the area of economic justice that the world's people have been slow in arriving at a consensus. There is, of course, consensus that every child coming into the world deserves a reasonable standard of material well-being. The disagreement is not about *whether* poverty should be abolished. The disagreement is about *how* economic systems should be organized to abolish it, and *where* the resources are going to come from. The failure to put into practice principles of justice already perceived as legitimate can be partly attributed to failure to reach consensus in the areas of resource allocation and economic organization.

If prisoners are tortured in jails, in violation of recognized human rights, the torture is usually excused by the claim either that torture is necessary to defend capitalism against revolutionaries, or that it is necessary to defend socialism against revolutionaries. Warfare usually takes place now on the pretext of a similar claim, as does interference in the internal affairs of foreign states. In this way doctrines about economic justice — a topic on which global consensus has not yet been reached — are used to excuse violations of settled values.

It follows, then, that a science of global management economics, in which issues in normative economics were satisfactorily treated, would contribute to world peace in the key area which is still subject to bitter ideological disputes. Conversely, to the extent that violent conflict continues on issues of resource allocation and economic organization, global management economics can be studied, but cannot be applied on a worldwide scale.

Some world leaders are now aware that consensus on issues of economic justice is necessary and convinced that it is possible. In December 1974, the United Nations General Assembly approved a Charter of Economic Rights and Duties of States, which was strengthened later to declare that the developed countries have a duty to make technology and financial resources available to less developed countries. The Law of the Sea conference has affirmed that the resources of the ocean floor are a common heritage of all humanity.

There is, in short, a manifest tendency toward reaching ideological consensus in the major area that is still in dispute: economic justice. If such a consensus is eventually reached, it will not, of course, by itself bring about world peace, but an obstacle to building peace will have been removed.

The Nature of Global Values

My argument that there are no insuperable ideological obstacles to world peace consists of exhibiting in summary form some principles of economic justice, which have the following characteristics:

•They are in accord with (in fact, usually extensions of) the standards and values that are now being put forward on an international level.

•They are put forward in a manner acceptable to Christians, Marxists and persons holding Moslem, Occidental, scientific, pragmatic or utilitarian positions.

•If implemented, they would permit the management of the productive factors of the earth in such a manner that every human being attains a decent standard of living, and ecological balance is maintained.

•They are simple and they lend themselves to formulations that appeal to moral sentiments which already exist in some people and might be fostered in others.

Here are some principles:

A decent standard of living for everyone. "Decency" holds different meanings to different cultural groups. This principle does not call for equality.

Ecological stability. This principle states a condition for the survival of humankind, and expresses a duty to future generations.

The slowing of population growth. This is a corollary to ecological stability. It is consistent with treating population policy as part of, rather than a substitute for, development. Reduced population growth is a logical extension of tendencies implicit in the World Plan of Action adopted, on the initiative of the Latin American delegate, at the World Population Conference at Bucharest in 1974.

A full-employment principle. All available manpower, and all other resources, should be productively employed. It is not only anomalous, but unjust, that people and machines lie idle, for no good reason, while basic human needs are not met.

An efficiency principle. Cost/benefit ratios should be minimized. A new economics will view efficiency in human terms, seeking measures of benefit in terms of human needs and values. Example: Frances Moore Lappe established that the world deficit in protein can be overcome by shifting to the directly human consumption of protein-rich grains and legumes instead of feeding grains to cattle. Cattle consume many times more protein than they produce, and hence are usually inefficient. There are, of course, exceptions ... such as cases where cattle can graze land not suitable for crops. The point is that the criteria for authentic efficiency are given by comparing alternative ways to use resources to serve human needs and values, in a sustainable relationship to the environment.

A transfer principle. Surplus should not be used (except insofar as it may be necessary to provide incentives to achieve desirable kinds and levels of production) to increase the welfare of those who are above a minimum standard. Rather it should be assigned to the benefit of those who are still below a minimum level of decency. This principle leaves plenty of room for disagreement among economists concerning which incentives and how many are needed. It also lets economists and others continue to debate whether there should be redistribution of goods from the comfortable to the poor when the result would be to decrease the welfare of the comfortable.

An ownership principle. The protection and management of the environment through international institutions require the principle that property rights are subordinate to the social function of property. Most people alive today not only believe this principle, but live by it. Even US citizens, probably the staunchest advocates of private ownership and individual rights, are familiar with the social function of property on a local level. It operates when the state acquires right-of-way by eminent domain to build a road, when a school district levies property taxes, when a city enforces zoning laws, and when a local court requires property owners to abate a nuisance which endangers the health or safety of their neighbors. All but the most narrow-minded realize the value of placing social well-being above property rights in such cases.

Now we all need to recognize the legitimacy of the same principle on an international level, and as a limitation to sovereignty. For example, it is both necessary and right that the pollution of coastal waters by individual nations be restricted in order to protect the oceans, which are an important source of food and an indispensable part of an interdependent global ecosystem. Further, as implied in discussing the full employment principle, neither property rights nor sovereignty should be used to justify idleness and waste.

World Regulation — Two Basic Rules

Global values such as the seven listed above could help reach the goals stated — peace, decent living standards and ecological balance — even though they represent only a limited degree of consensus. They would provide an effective framework for the healthy growth and peaceful behavior of our social systems.

What is needed, however, in addition to the values above, is a means of managing the affairs of Earth in the best interests of the people. Within the framework of the global values, I suggest that only two norms are needed, although their detailed application may be highly complex.

• The level of decision-making should be high enough so that the responsible decision-making body can evaluate a system from a overall perspective, and

• Subject to this first principle, the level of decision-making should be as low as possible.

It perhaps goes without saying, and need not be stated as a principle, that change for its own sake is not desirable, and that existing decision-making structures should be modified only where there is a good reason to do so.

The two norms may be called responsibility and subsidiarity. Let's look at each of them.

Responsibility requires that a political-economic body or system has the obligation to serve human needs and values in the course of its activities. When it fails to meet this obligation, it ought to be judged and corrected.

Subsidiarity, as applied to global institutions, implies that each nation chooses for itself what type of internal economic organization it prefers, subject to the requirement that it make a proper contribution to global economic justice. The moral requirement that economic activities be subordinated to human needs is not easy to reconcile with the principle of subidiarity. In particular, it is not easy to say to what extent, if any, there should be an international authority empowered to oblige poor countries to use their resources effectively to meet the needs of their people, and empowered to oblige rich countries to make sufficiently large transfers abroad.

Whatever the morally correct reconciliation of responsibility and subsidiarity may be, however, there is much that is not being done that can be done without resolving this thorny issue. For example, we do not yet have an explicit consensus on the general guiding principle that the resources of the entire earth are to be used to meet the needs of its inhabitants. Nor do we have fully developed research and staff capabilities that could show the way toward even voluntary compliance with the minimal requirements of justice.

Subsidiarity does not provide a magic formula which will make it possible to avoid protracted negotiations concerning how small the transfers of the rich nations can be, and still be proper, nor to what extent any nation has a right to be inefficient and to leave resources idle, thus jeopardizing the welfare of the poor. Subsidiarity does, however, provide a framework in which negotiations can be conducted.

In summary, I propose, first, that economics take a comprehensive view of human nature and of the importance of norms to human conduct, that normative economics become the central core of the discipline.

Second, I propose the objective of attaining decent living standards and ecological balance; some principles to guide economic decision-making (the full-employment principle, efficiency, transfer, and the social function of property); and two complementary principles, responsibility and subsidiarity, for deciding who decides.

This second proposal could be broadened, but I believe it is on the right track.

Now let's look at some practical applications of these ideas. The applications are in four areas: the work of researchers in economics, multinational corporations, subsystem management, and funding international organizations.

By economic researchers I mean the people who work for the Economic Commission for Latin America, the UN's Food and Agricultural Organization economists, the other specialists who work for UN agencies, university professors, staff members of the Organization for Economic Cooperation and Development, members of the various national agencies for international development, and fellows institutes that study economic problems. In short, I am thinking of all research workers who might plausibly see themselves in the role of acting as staff members of global institutions that do not exist yet, but which are foreshadowed in institutions that do exist.

A global management economics should be concerned with mobilizing resources to meet human needs, and the indicators of economic success would be those that measure whether human needs have been met. Indicators like gross national product should be discarded in favor of measures of nutrition and health. We should develop measures of the extent to which psychological needs are met.

A comprehensive view of human motivation should lead to more interdisciplinary work in which economists cooperate with anthropologists, sociologists, and industrial psychologists in the study of economic behavior. Nor are economic studies separable from political and historical studies that deal with questions such as why Japan and China have been fairly successful in managing their resources to meet their needs, while India until recently has been less successful in that respect.

My suggestion for multinational corporations is quite specific. Corporations doing business in more than one country should be chartered by the UN, and their stock should be held by foundations dedicated to the welfare of the world's poorest people. This is somewhat less radical than it may seem at first, since the day-to-day operations of a corporation are much the same whether the stock is held by private individuals or by charities. I make this specific suggestion for its shock value — because it is a good idea, although perhaps not the best idea on the level of values, while it is completely impractical on the level of power politics. This shows, once again, that ideological diversity is not our problem. The problem is not that humans disagree about values; it is that we lack the will and intelligence to put values into practice.

Capitalist and Communist Subsystems

In socialist nations and blocs, ideology often obstructs wise economic management. Such obstructions appear when there are objections to the use of interest rates in planning capital investments on the mistaken ground that Karl Marx would turn over in his grave, or when, as in Hungary, some people object to the introduction of market pricing because it subverts morals. In such cases ideology limits the available alternatives; it acts as a constraint that rules out solutions to concrete problems which are, at times, feasible and optimal.

In capitalist countries, the ideological problems are different. To achieve full employment and to smooth out the effects of business cycles, some experts advocate putting money into the economy and other experts (or sometimes the same experts at other times) advocate taking money out. This unfortunate conceptual confusion has led us to the point where many intelligent business executives believe a doctrine which maintains that "the only effective way economists have to eliminate an inflation is to cause a recession."

For socialism and capitalism, one's strength is the other's weakness. The way to merge the strengths and erase the weaknesses is to pose the issues at a more fundamental level. How can we meet human needs? On this more fundamental approach it seems evident that the amount of money pumped into or out of the economy can have at most an indirect effect on whether or not resources are mobilized. To regulate an economy wisely where resources are mobilized by means of the profit motive, what one must regulate is the profit motive. That includes at least these five steps:

1. Insofar as the function of profits is to motivate investment, profits which are more than what is needed to provide an incentive for investment should in principle be taxable. And so on for the other functions of profit, asking in each case if what profits do, needs to be done, and if it needs to be done that way.

2. To use the profit motive to channel investment into useful production and jobs for the unemployed, it may be helpful to discourage alternative uses of the investment dollar, such as buying government bonds, investing in foreign countries, and nonproductive speculation.

3. Many companies find that they can maximize profits by producing less and selling at a high profit per item, but they could still stay in business if they produced more and sold more at a lower profit per item; in this case antitrust action and other types of government intervention can move business toward greater activity at lower profit margins.

4. Government has a great many means at its disposal for lowering risks and increasing profits for corporations — everything from direct subsidies to government contracts to tax breaks. If we recognize that our economy largely depends on this type of cooperation between business and government and will continue to do so in the future, even if, and perhaps especially if, a reduction of military spending makes it possible for us to shift government spending toward the production of food and other useful items for our own poor and for the developing nations, then we will see the importance of developing new forms of accountability and strengthening the old ones. Utopian capitalisms which dream of a world where corruption in government is impossible because there is no government, and corruption in business is impossible because the invisible hand of competition disciplines everyone, only postpone the issue. The issue is ethical accountability in cooperative relationships.

5. One should also consider that there are often limits to the extent to which the profit motive can be successfully regulated. In that case a humanistic sense of priorities requires, for example, public safety nets and public employment.

Nations and multinational blocs today demand autonomy. They can and should remain sufficiently autonomous and self-contained that some of them can be capitalist, some of them communist or socialist, and others mixed, without these differences in economic organization among them preventing the functional cooperation that is necessary if peace, ecological balance, and decent living standards for all are to be achieved.

We need to be concerned, however, that there is regulation of economic life by legitimate values of some sort at the subsystem level. Global peace will not be stable in a world that is immoral or amoral in its subsystems.

With respect to the funding of the activities of global institutions concerned with food, energy, the environment, finance and disarmament, each member nation might be assessed not by a percentage of GNP, but rather on the basis of an index which would measure potential product — that is, an index of the humanly useful and environmentally sound goods that it might produce in a year if it managed its resources well in that year.

This is an application of the full-employment principle — that is, that idle resources should be used, and used to serve those whose basic needs are unmet.

Partial financing of some international activities in that way would provide an incentive for the humanly efficient use of resources, since nations would be taxed according to a reasonable estimate of short-run potential. It would require the measurement of a subsystem's ability to meet needs, and the evaluation of its failures.

Global values geared for wise management of a healthy global economy are definable today. A general consensus is within reach and it would get us on course toward a peaceful future.

(Updated, adapted from a May/June 1976 article in "Center Magazine," a publication of the Center for the Study of Democratic Institutions. Printed with permission.)

Chapter 20
Science Transfer to the Third World

by Abdus Salam
Founder, Third World Academy of Sciences
Trieste, Italy

Background. Received the 1979 Nobel Prize for theoretical physics. Has run the International Center for Theorectical Physics (Trieste, Italy) since its beginning in 1964. In 1983 founded the Third World Academy of Sciences. Currently pursues his science, education and development efforts chiefly from Italy, UK, and his native Pakistan. Has received numerous awards and honors. Is involved with many international associations for peace, development, and science. Has written several books and some 250 articles.

His article. In the colonial world of a century ago, poor countries were kept under rich countries' political and economic thumbs. Many improvements have come about since the crumbling of colonialism in this century ... but it is still a long, uphill march to equity and self-sufficiency. Third World countries need science and education for longterm economic health, but they receive mostly technology to satisfy their immediate needs. The author tells of the struggles for science — his personal struggles as well as those of the Third World bent on modernization.

If one were being machiavellian, one might discern sinister motives among those who try to sell us the idea of technology transfer without science transfer.

Science Transfer to the Third World

by Abdus Salam

*T*he Third World has come to realize that science and technology are its sustenance and its best hope for economic betterment, so why, barring a few of its countries — Argentina, Brazil, China and India — has the Third World taken to science as only a marginal activity? And why has Third World science development been kept at a low priority in the aid-giving agencies of the richer countries, in the agencies of the United Nations and also unfortunately in the scientific communities of the developed countries which might naturally have been expected to be the Third World scientists' foremost allies? More important, how do we correct the situation? These are the questions I address in this article.

The Neglect of Basic Sciences in Developing Countries

Let us be clear that science in developing countries has indeed been neglected by developed countries, by the UN and by the developing countries themselves. Of the ample evidence I submit two exhibits.

First, the developed world, while sharing the fruits of technology, seem reluctant to share the seeds. Policy makers, prestigious commissions (like the Brandt Commission), as well as aid-givers, speak uniformly of problems of "technology transfer" to the developing countries as if that is all that is involved. It is hard to believe but true that the word "science" does not figure in the Brandt Commission report. Very few within the developing world appear to stress that for long term effectiveness, technology transfers must always be accompanied by science transfers — that the science of today is the technology of tomorrow and that when we speak of science it must be broad-based in order to be effective for applications.

I quote the words of Steven Dedijir:

"Ninety per cent of world research potential is concentrated in about 35 countries with about 25% of world population. Hence the imperative necessity for a Third World country to find the most effective policy to bring about rapidly a macro science transfer on which to base its development. Without such a science transfer a Third World country will continue to be technologically, and hence economically and politically, one-sidedly dependent, more simply said, exploited in its international exchanges."

I would even go so far as to say that if one was being machiavellian, one might discern sinister motives among those who try to sell to us the idea of technology transfer without science transfer. There is nothing which has hurt us in the Third World more than the slogan in the richer countries of "relevant science." Regretably this slogan was parrotted in our countries unthinkingly to justify stifling the growth of all science.

Second, much of the Third World hardly knows where to begin. Science is transferred by and to communities of scientists. Such communities in developing countries need building up to a critical size in their human resources and infrastructure. This building up. calls for wise science policies, with long-term commitment, generous patronage, self-governance and free international contacts. Further, in our countries, the high-level scientist must be allowed to play a role in nation-building as an equal partner to the professional planner, the economist and the technologist. Few developing countries have promulgated such policies. Few aid agencies have taken it as their mandate to encourage and help with the building up of the scientific infrastructure.

A Nation's Scientific Infrastructure

What is the infrastructure of sciences I am speaking about? It consists of four levels:

•Science education (in all countries),

•Science interest within government and industry (in all countries),

•Cooperation between basic and applied scientists (in the more advanced countries), and

•More basic science research (as the infrastructure grows).

Education. First and foremost, we need scientific literacy and science teaching — at all levels — and particularly at the higher levels, at least for engineers and technologists. This calls for teachers who are inspiring, and we cannot be inspiring teachers of science without experiencing and creating at least some modicum of living science during some part of our careers. This calls for well-equipped teaching laboratories and (in the present era of accelerated science) the provision of the newest journals and books. This is the foundation of a scientific infrastructure which every country needs. For now, much of it must be provided by the developed world.

Interest. Next should come demands by the developing countries on their own scientific communities — consisting of their own nationals — from their government agencies and budding industries, for selective advice on which technologies would be relevant and worth acquiring.

Cooperation. Next, for a minority of the developing countries, there is the need for basic scientists to help their applied colleagues' research work. For any society, the problems of its agriculture, of its local pests and diseases, of its local materials base, must be solved locally. One needs an underpinning from a first-class base in basic sciences to carry out applied research in these areas. In a developing country the craft of applied science is much harder than the craft of basic science, simply because one does not have available next door, or at the other end of the telephone line, experts who can tell you what you need to know of the basics, relevant to one's applied work.

Fang Yi, the Chinese Minister of Science and Technology has given another reason for support of basic sciences. Noting that major technological advances will become more and more dependent on breakthroughs in basic research he has made the point that " 'some foreign countries' will be less willing to publicize their basic research in the open literature. China should therefore pay ever more attention to such fields of basic research." "Nature," Vol. 307, 2 February 1984.

Research. And finally, at the advanced stages of a country's development, is the need for basic scientific research for the riches it might unexpectedly yield for technology. Many examples of this come to mind.

Consider some of the breakthroughs in my own field — the field of unification of fundamental forces of nature. In this context, Faraday's unification of electricity and magnetism, accomplished in the last century, is certainly one of the most striking examples. When Faraday was carrying out his experiments — showing that while a stationary electric charge produces an electric force on another charge in its vicinity, a moving electric charge produces a magnetic force — no one could have imagined that this simple discovery in a laboratory in a dilettante part of Piccadilly in London would lead to the entire corpus of electrical generation technology.

One critic claimed, "Electricity is universally allowed to be a very entertaining and surprising phenomenon, but it has frequently been lamented that it has never yet, with much certainty, been applied to any very useful purpose . . . (while) it is easy to point out the humane and important purposes to which music has been applied . . . Many an orphan is cherished by its influence, and the pangs of child-birth are softened and rendered less dangerous . . . "

The story of the unification of electricity with magnetism continues with Maxwell, who immediately followed Faraday. From purely theoretical considerations, Maxwell suggested that an accelerating electric charge would produce electromagnetic radiation. A few years after Maxwell's death in 1879, Hertz in Germany verified Maxwell's predictions and found that the spectrum of Maxwell's predicted radiation consisted not only of light waves, but also of waves of longer wave length — radio waves — as well as waves of shorter wave length — X-rays. Thus, from a simple theoretical calculation made by an obscure professor flowed the marvels of radio, television and the modern communication systems, as well as the ability to see through a human body with X-rays.

A century after Maxwell, in the 1960s, my colleagues at Harvard — Glashow and Weinberg — and I independently took the next step of postulating a unification of two further forces of nature — electromagnetism and the weak nuclear force of radioactivity.

In January 1983, the great joint European Centre for Nuclear Research (CERN) at Geneva provided direct confirmation of our theory. It did so with technical brilliance and about $50 million. Accelerator laboratories like the one at CERN are founts of the highest technology in micro-electronics, in material sciences, in superconductor as well as vacuum technology. While I am not suggesting that the developing countries should create such accelerator laboratories, I rejoice that the Fermi Lab at Chicago has decided to set up a special Institute linked to the Laboratory, to make this area of science and related technology available to Latin American physicists. And the Cern laboratory has made available to us — the Trieste Centre — the services of some members of their microprocessor team who have already conducted three six-week colleges on microprocessor physics and technology at Trieste at the highest level, for 350 of the developing world's physicists. During June 1984, this team held a four-week microprocessor college in Sri

Lanka for 62 physicists from Southeast Asia and in June 1985 in Colombia with 38 physicists, to be followed by colleges in China (this year) and in Africa (next year) on the same subject.

To summarize then, technology in modern conditions cannot flourish without science flourishing at the same time. This was emphasized recently to me by a Turkish physicist from the University of Samsun who recalled that Sultan Selim III had introduced studies of algebra, trigonometry, mechanics, ballistics and metallurgy in Turkey as long ago as 1799, creating special schools for these disciplines with French and Swedish teachers. His purpose was to modernize his army and rival European advances in gun-founding. Since there was no corresponding emphasis on research in these subjects, Turkey did not succeed. In the long run, in the conditions of today, technology, unsupported by science, simply will not take or flourish.

Where Does Third World Science Stand Today?

In 1951 when I returned to teach in Pakistan after working at Cambridge and Princeton in high energy physics, in a country then of 90 million, I could call on just one physicist who had ever worked on a like subject. The most recent issues of the "Physical Review" available were dated before World War II (1939). There were no grants whatsoever for attending symposia or conferences; the only time I did attend a conference in the United Kingdom I spent a year's personal savings.

After 35 years, the situation in Pakistan has improved. For a population of around 80 million now, there are some 46 research physicists, experimentalists and theoreticians in Pakistan's 19 universities.(By US norms these numbers for this population base would be 100-fold larger — 5,000 scientists). These physicists still face the same problems regarding journals, publication dues and attendances at conferences; Pakistan is still not a member of the International Union of Pure and Applied Physics, since our science adminstrators do not think we can afford $1,500 of dues.

Our physicists are still told that all basic science — even the segments necessary for "applicable" physics — is a frightful luxury for a poor country. However, compared to Pakistan — and a privileged group of some 30 other countries which I shall mention — the situation in the remaining 60-odd other developing countries is as stark as it was in Pakistan of 1951.

First and foremost is the problem of numbers — of a critical size. The total number of research-trained physicists in many of these countries can be counted on the fingers of one hand — the choice of sub-disciplines in which they may have received training has been conditioned more by chance than design. They make up no communities.

The creation at Trieste of the International Centre for Theoretical Physics in the 1960s came about when some of us from the developing countries urged agencies of the United Nations, and in particular the International Atomic Energy Agency (IAEA) and the United Nations Educational, Scientific and Cultural Organization (UNESCO), to assist in ameliorating this situation regarding theoretical physics research. We were met with incomprehension even from some of the developed countries where physics flourishes.

One developed country delegate to the IAEA went so far as to say, "Theoretical physics is the Rolls Royce of sciences — the developing countries need only bullock carts." To him a community of even as few as 50 physicists, all told, trained then at a high level, for a country like Pakistan with a population then approaching 120 million, was simply 50 men wasted. Even leaving aside any involvement in research, the fact that these were the men responsible for all norms and all standards in the entire spectrum of Pakistan's education in physics and mathematics was irrelevant to this gentleman. He himself was an economist, who had wandered into a scientific organization like the IAEA. He could fully understand that we needed more high-level economists, but a few more research-trained physicists and mathematicians of quality — that was wasteful luxury.

In 1964, four years after the proposal was first mooted and after intense lobbying, the IAEA did agree to create a physics institute. However, we were voted a meager sum of $55,000 to create an international center of research. Fortunately, the Government of Italy came through with a generous annual grant of one third of a million dollars and the Centre was set up in Trieste. The international physics community had all along supported us; the Centre's first Scientific Council meeting was attended by J.R. Oppenheimer, Aage Bohr, Victor Weisskofp and Sandoval Vallarta. Oppenheimer drew up the Centre's statutes.

The Centre started operating in 1964. UNESCO joined as equal partner with IAEA in 1970. The Centre has flourished since then, with the support of even those who had doubted its validity at first. The bulk of its funds — now amounting to $4.5 million — come from Italy, IAEA and UNESCO. It also received an extra contribution of $4.3 million from the Dipartimento per la Cooperazione allo

Sviluppo of the Ministry of Foreign Affairs of Italy in 1985 and received $4.5 million in 1986. Smaller ad-hoc grants have come from time to time from the United Nations Development Program (UNDP), the United Nations Financing System for Science and Technology for Development, the United Nations University, the OPEC Fund, the US Department of Energy, the Ford Foundation, the Intergovernmental Bureau for Informatics (IBI), Canada, Kuwait, Libya, Qatar, Sweden, Germany, Sri Lanka, Netherlands, Japan and Denmark.

Over the 22 years that the Centre has existed now, it has shifted from emphasis on pure physics towards basic disciplines on the interface of pure and applied physics — disciplines like physics of materials and microprocessors, physics of energy, physics of fusion, physics of reactors, physics of solar and other non-conventional energy, geophysics, space physics, biophysics, neurophysics, laser physics, physics of oceans and deserts, and systems analysis — this, in addition to the staples of high energy physics, quantum gravity, cosmology, atomic and nuclear physics and mathematics.

Such a shift to the interface of pure and basic applied physics was made simply because there was not and still is not, any other international institute responsive to the scientific hunger of developing country physicists.

During 1985, over 2,700 physicists came to work at the Trieste Centre — 1,670 of them from 109 developing countries. Those from developing countries spend about two months or more at the Centre, participating in its research workshops and extended research colleges. Since 1981, we have held six of these colleges in developing countries — Ghana, Bangladesh, Colombia, Sri Lanka, Sudan and now China; these were 4-8 week research colleges on solid state physics, monsoon dynamics, desertification, solar physics and microprocessors.

We have pioneered an associateship scheme which guarantees that top physicists in developing countries can come to the Centre, at times of their choosing, for a period ranging between six weeks to three months, three times in six years, to work in a stimulating environment of their peers, to charge their batteries and then to return to their teaching and research positions. We do not pay salaries — only travel and stay. There are 346 such associates at present. We have a network of 195 institutes of physics in 61 developing countries federated with us with cost-sharing arrangements.

Through a Book Bank scheme, we have distributed, from individual donations, a total of 6,000 proceedings and books and 14,000 copies of recent yearly journals to some 300 institutions in 80 countries, and we have started a scheme to collect and distribute unused surplus equipment donated by developed country laboratories. With an Italian Government grant of $1 million annually, we have already placed 185 experimental physicists for one-year research positions in Italian universities and industrial laboratories since 1982. Another 65 physicists took up their grants in 1986. In its humble way, the Centre has enhanced the subject of physics in general, and physics communities in developing countries in particular.

Stages and Growth of Sciences in the Third World

Based on the experience gained in physics, we could divide the developing countries (other than Argentina, Brazil, China and India) into three categories. The first category would consist of nine countries — Bangladesh, Korea, Malaysia, Pakistan, Singapore and Turkey (in Asia), plus Egypt (in Africa) and Mexico and Venezuela (in Latin America). These countries have a population of physicists, currently approaching criticality, as well as a few centers of high quality for physics where teams of scientists can perform independent research. By and large, these centers are capable of awarding Ph.D. degrees for physics within the countries themselves.

In the second category, there would be some 25 countries which consist of Iran, Iraq, Jordan, Kuwait, Lebanon, Libya, Saudi Arabia and Syria (in the Middle East); the People's Democratic Republic of Korea, Indonesia, Philippines, Sri Lanka, Thailand and Vietnam (in Southeast Asia); Algeria, Ghana, Kenya, Morocco, Nigeria, Sudan, Tanzania (in Africa); Chile, Colombia and Peru (in Latin America) and the Fiji Islands (in Oceania). These countries have a modest population of physicists though at any given university the numbers working are rather small. There are no research groups as such, though in some cases individuals are highly active. As a rule, Ph.D. degrees are not awarded within the countries concerned. I mention these two categories, because with organized help from the rich world's scientific communities, these countries could take off in a short span of time.

The remaining 64 countries are below the "poverty line." Among them are some exceptionally bright individuals, whom we elect as associates of the Trieste Centre for the day when active research starts in their countries — but there is no organized physics research.

I stress once again, that these are impressions based on our experience with physics communities. No other significance should be read into them.

WHAT MUST BE DONE?

In the end, the growth of science in our countries is our problem. But in the meantime, I shall speak of help from the scientific communities and others in the developed countries. There is no doubt that outside help — particularly if it is organized — can make a crucial difference.

What the World Science Community Can Do

First, regarding the work of individual physicists, this could take various forms. For example, the physical societies of developed countries could help by donating 200-300 copies of their journals to deserving institutions and individuals. They could waive publication and conference charges. In this context, the International Union of Pure and Applied Physics (IUPAP) has helped the Trieste Centre defray postage costs for distribution of old runs of journals; the American Physical Society has helped us with shared subscriptions to 34 physicists from 13 least developed countries.

The research laboratories and the university departments in developed countries could also help by building up Federation links with their opposite numbers and by financing organized visits of their staffs to the institutions in developing countries. They could create schemes like the associateship scheme I have already described at the Trieste Centre (whereby a high-grade physicist working in a developing country becomes part of our staff by being accorded the right to come to us three times in six years), at least for their own ex-alumni.

May I be forgiven for thinking in the following terms — that the physics institutions in developed countries may consider contributing in their own ways (in kind) according to the norms of the well-known United Nations formula, whereby most developed countries have pledged to spend .7% of their GNP resources for world development. In the end, it is a moral issue whether the better-off segments of the science community should be willing to look after their own deserving but deprived colleagues, helping them not only materially to remain good scientists, but also joining them in their battle to obtain recognition within their own countries as valid professionals, who are important to the development of their countries and the world.

What the United Nations Can Do

Let me now come to the question of the long-term help the United Nations agencies can give with respect to building up scientific infrastructure, in their own areas of competence. I wish, in particular, to emphasize the role of the modality I am personally most familiar with — international centers of research.

There is no question but that the developing world today needs international research institutions like the Wheat and Rice Research Institute (on the applied side) and centers like the International Centre for Insect Physiology (ICIPE) in Nairobi (on the science side). Without internationalization, science cannot flourish. Conforming to standards, keeping abreast of new ideas, and enjoying a continual transfer of science by men who created it and who come to such centers, moved by their idealism ... none of these benefits can be guaranteed without internationalization. Recently there have been created an international mathematics center at Nice, an international science center in Sri Lanka, one in Turkey and another in Venezuela. An international physics center, directed towards Latin America, was formally inaugurated in Colombia by its President two years ago. Also the United Nations Industrial Development Organization (UNIDO) is on the way to creating two international centers in the field of biotechnology, one located in Trieste and one in India.

In biotechnology, we observe that modern advances in genetics started with the unravelling of the genetic code by Watson and Crick. Revealing as it does the basis for all known life, this has been one of the most synthesizing discoveries of the twentieth century, possibly of all times. I take pride in the fact that Walter Gilbert, who took a Ph.D. with me in theoretical physics at Cambridge in 1956 and then turned over to genetics, was among those who discovered elegant techniques for deciphering the genetic code. For this work, he received a Nobel Prize in Chemistry in 1980. In 1981 he founded a company, Biogen, which exploits, among others, techniques of genetic manipulation to manufacture human insulin. Again we observe the mutuality of high science and high technology.

To return, however, to the UNIDO initiative, the executive director of UNIDO, Dr. Abd-El Rahman Khane of Algeria, who, on a visit to Trieste, had been impressed with our example of interfacing the basics of pure with applied physics, conceived the idea that the time was ripe for creating one or more similar centers for biotechnology for the Third World. On UNIDO's call, a competition was instituted. This brought offers from Italy, Spain, India, Pakistan, Egypt, Thailand and Cuba. Three inter-ministerial meetings were held to choose the location. In April 1984, Delhi and Trieste were finally selected as the locations of a joint center.

To my mind, one of the most significant features of the biosciences situation is the fact that so many of the Third World countries were so keen to make credible offers for it from their own resources. I was sorry at the majority decision of the assembled ministers to refuse to accord to the losers of the competition — Egypt, Thailand, Pakistan and Spain — the status of even affiliated centers. These countries desperately wanted even a subsidiary status to share in the benefits of an internationalization of their local efforts. I hope this will soon be rectified and these other offers will also be accepted. The point I wish to make is that even countries with moderate traditions of scientific research are beginning to show an interest in hosting United Nations-run centers of science.

In this context, to highlight the role which agencies like the World Bank or the International Monetary Fund (IMF) can play, consider the following quote from a recent history of the World Bank by E.S. Mason and R.E. Asher:

"UNESCO has been providing sensible advice on educational planning for years, before the World Bank entered the field . . . Sometimes, some parts of this advice were accepted but there was a notable increase in attention given to educational planning when it became clear that some projects had some chance of being financed by the World Bank."

Besides educational planning, besides help with development of scientific agriculture, I would also wish that the World Bank could take it upon itself to emphasize to the developing countries that the fastest route to financial prosperity today lies with areas of science-based high technology — for example, of micro-electronics, computer software and the like, and that the major investment needed in these areas is investment in creating scientifically highly-literate people. The day that the entrepreneurs (either in the government or the private sectors of developing economies) begin to understand this, our economic salvation will start.

To summarize, my feeling is that almost every developing country has a scientific and technological problem which needs scientific expertise. I strongly feel that the United Nations system must take a lead with this legitimate movement towards internationalization of science within the developing world for the developing world. The research centers do not have to be within the developing countries. Some years back, Dr. Henry Kissinger, the then US Secretary of State, on behalf of the US government, promised to the Third World a multiplicity of institutions which would include institutes to improve access to capital technology. He mentioned, in particular, an International Energy Institute, and International Centre for Exchange of Technological Information and an International Industrialization

Institute. I am sure some day soon, the US administration will carry these promises out, adding to each Institute its due quantum of science.

What Nations Can Do

Finally, let us turn to the role of the national aid-giving agencies.

My plea to the development agencies everywhere would be that they may take a long-term attitude to the growth of science. They exert an immense leverage which they must use to ensure that an adequate infrastructure is built in the countries they help and that the scientific communities there are enabled, and allowed to play their rightful roles in the process of development.

One proven method of science transfer is the creation of an international foundation for science for giving grants to individual scientists in the developing countries. An international science foundation with these aims was in fact created at the suggestion of Roger Revelle, Pierre Auger, Robert Marshak and myself in 1972 in Stockholm. This Foundation is currently supported by Sweden, Canada, USA, Federal Republic of Germany, France, Australia, the Netherlands, Belgium, Nigeria, Norway and Switzerland. Its funds are given for research in the areas of aquaculture, animal production, rural technology and natural products, to individual researchers in developing countries, in grants not exceeding $10,000 per grant. Unfortunately, the total funds at the disposal of this Foundation are only $2,000,000. A similar function is carried out by the Bostid organization in the US which is supported by the aid organizations. These initiatives do not cover other natural sciences, nor is there any provision of funds for building up of scientific infrastructure.

With the Brandt Commission's recommendations on technology transfer in mind, in August 1981 I took the initiative of writing the following letter to the Heads of States participating in the Cancun Summit:

"I understand that technology transfer, with emphasis on problems of energy, will be one of the items for discussion at the forthcoming North-South Heads of States meeting in Mexico. Unhappily, most developing countries need help in building up scientific infrastructure at all levels and Science Transfer must accompany technology transfer if the latter has to take root in our countries. The scientific community in the North can, and I am sure will, be willing to help in building up the corresponding community in the South, provided it is mobilized for this."

I suggested the creation of a North-South Science Foundation to build up a movement towards Science Transfer, with funds similar to those, for example, disbursed by the Ford Foundation ($100-200 million a year). This foundation should be run by the world's scientific community for research and training for research, in basic sciences in developing countries.

I received polite replies of support to my plea from all Heads of States from the developed countries. From among the Heads of developing countries, however, only India's Mrs. Gandhi replied. (This unconcern perhaps emphasizes once again the marginality of the scientific enterprise in the Third World).

So let me re-emphasize the vital importance of developing a North-South science foundation, particularly since the Ford Foundation, in a letter to the Secretary of the then recently founded Third World Academy of Sciences, has told us that scientific research in developing countries is no longer a priority area for the Ford Foundation itself.

Where Are Our Priorities?

In sciences, as in other spheres, this world of ours is divided between the rich and the poor. The richer half — the industrial North and the centrally managed countries, with an income of $5 trillion, spend 2 percent of this — more than $100 billion — on non-military science and development research. The remaining half of humanity — the poorer South, with one-fifth of this income of around $1 trillion — spends no more than $2 billion on science and technology. On the percentage norms of the richer countries, they should be spending ten times more — some $20 billion.

At the UN-run Vienna Conference on Science and Technology held in 1979 the poorer nations pleaded for international funds to increase their present annual expenditure of $2 billion to $4 billion. They obtained promises, not of $2 billion, not of $1 billion, but only one-seventh of this. Even this has never been realized and the UN Funding System for Science and Technology for Development is without adequate means.

Contrast this with the situation in the military sphere. Each nuclear submarine costs $2 billion and there are at least 100 of these in the world's oceans. About 500 centers like mine at Trieste could be funded for a year for the price of one nuclear submarine.

To summarize, simply, we must adjust our priorities now, while we still have that ability.

Special thanks to IFDA (International Foundation for Development Alternatives).

PART FIVE:
DEALING WITH CONFLICT

*C*onflicts occur at all levels of life and go by many names. "Disease," for example, is conflict that occurs in the body, "arguments" erupt between individuals, "crime" happens in society, and "war" occurs among nations.

There are two ways to deal with conflicts — resolve them as they occur, and minimize them over an extended period of time. For example:

•Diseases can be resolved through curative medicine, or minimized over the long term through preventive medicine and wholesome living.

•An argument between a husband and wife can be resolved by talking things over, but if bickering and fighting become a way of life the couple may seek outside counseling to learn to communicate more clearly and more regularly, to minimize the conflicts.

•Individual crimes can be resolved via justice and punishment, while crime in general can be minimized in society over an extended period of time by rehabilitating criminals and teaching wholesome values to young people.

•War between nations can be resolved by truces, treaties and other "peacemaking" processes, or it can be minimized through "peacekeeping" efforts such as national stability in economic and social matters, and alignment of nations to a mutually agreeable set of global values and international laws.

The final chapters in the book explore some of the work being done today in dealing with conflicts. Although the emphasis is on international conflict resolution, we also get a glimpse at the symptoms of social conflict (crime), and receive some tips for handling the squabbles and misunderstandings that occur in our own day-to-day dealings with the people around us.

Real-world experience. Diplomat John Burton, looking back over his 44 years of international peacemaking experience, observes that nations must be secure before the world can be stable. Conflict resolution is a process vital to achieving national security. Dr. Burton reveals the key ingredients for resolving conflicts successfully, describing the role of the facilitator.

Leading-edge research. Tobi Dress, an attorney and educator, looks at the leading edge of modern research into conflict resolution, explaining the need for a third party in three proven processes — mediation, conciliation, and arbitration.

A theoretical approach. Social scientist Louis Kriesberg explores an emerging model or paradigm of the diverse social structures of the modern world, and their interactions.

Symptoms of social conflict. Richard Lamm, former governor of Colorado, employs statistics to show the alarming rise in US crime since the 1960s, then describes an innovative way to free up space in overcrowded prisons while at the same time giving young offenders a last chance to straighten up before receiving a prison sentence.

The most dangerous conflict. Educational advisor Rene Wadlow takes a close look at the most volatile situation of international affairs — Mideast tensions and conflicts. He lays out the steps that might and might not succeed in dampening this likely fuse to World War III.

Chapter 21
Three Qualities of a Secure Nation

by John Burton
Founder and Director, Center for the Analysis of Conflict
Canterbury, UK

Background. Diplomat, scholar, theorist, and author of over a dozen books on international affairs and conflict resolution. One who practices in the real world what he writes about. Participant in many international conferences: Food and Agriculture (1943), ILO (1944), UN Charter (1945), Paris Peace (1946), Delhi (on Indonesia, 1949), Bandung (1955), others. Leadership positions in several international research groups since 1966. His career has spanned Europe, the USA and his native Australia.

His article. The author mixes his international peacemaking experiences with a look at the 25-year evolution of peace theory into effective peace processes which are now being applied to conflicts at many levels — from family and neighborhood to national and global situations — with equal success. This article gives us a glimpse at the inner workings of facilitated international talks, which are usually held in private. We emerge with tips on pursuing personal peace as well as world peace.

It is not the job of facilitators to advocate solutions, but to throw light on conflictual relations generally, to help in the analysis of the conflict in question, and to offer creative options for consideration.

Three Qualities of a Secure Nation

By John W. Burton

*T*he 1986 Summit meeting between Leaders Ronald Reagan and
Mikhail Gorbachev, in my view, contained the first signs of political
realism between the Superpowers since the Cold War. This realism
occurred when the USA President introduced consideration of
"regional conflicts." The greatest threat to the security of the Soviet
Union and the United States — and perhaps all humanity — is the
ideological superpower competition for the allegiance of other
nations in a post-colonial world in conflict. Solving this problem of
US-USSR contention is a pre-condition of arms control and of
improved political relationships.

Of course, the President's proposals were limited to apparent
interventions by the USSR, not the USA. Furthermore, there was no
plan or process introduced to resolve local and regional conflicts.
These limitations need to be dicussed.

At the root of the world situation is the issue of national security,
which in its broadest sense means freedom from conflict, danger,
deprivation and other destabilizing influences.

There are three prerequisites or steps to achieving national security by
non-military means — internal stability, conflict resolution and
consensus.

Domestic Stability

By far the most frequent source of threat to a nation, its people, its
authorities, its system of government, its values and interests, is
domestic.

At present there are few wars among nations, but some sixty or so wars going on that are domestic. We are familiar with those which are given media attention — Cyprus, Sri Lanka, South Africa, Lebanon, Israel-Palestine, Northern Ireland, El Salvador, Nicaragua, Philippines, Haiti and others. We are aware of these well reported conflicts, but less familiar with many covert domestic wars in which there is as yet little or no overt violence to report due to effective repression.

Surprisingly few modern nations are really secure. Of the members of the United Nations, probably only about forty per cent have legitimized status. Many unstable nations have regimes with elected presidents who are merely a facade for rule by a military, land-owning or some other interest group. In each case the so-called national defense forces are there to defend against internal threat, not potential or actual external aggression. These are all potential overt conflict situations, and all invite the confrontation of the competitive great powers.

In the pursuit of national security the first prerequisite, then, is that nations, great powers and small states, are themselves confident and internally secure.

Conflict Resolution and Change

Achieving a secure state inevitably requires changes in a nation's socioeconomic and political structures, and these changes rarely come about without conflict. The second prerequisite to national security is a set of processes that will achieve those changes and resolve the on-going conflicts. My conception of resolving conflicts:

•Pertains to conflict at all social levels, from family to international relations. There are not only common underlying elements in conflicts at all levels, but conflict at one level spills over into others.

•Focuses on resolution and not on settlement, the latter of which implies a coerced outcome.

apter 21
Three
ualities
of a
secure
nation

•Centers around analysis. In order to arrive at a resolution of a problem there must be analysis.

•Is carried out by skilled facilitators who can provide an adequate theoretical base for analytical diagnosis, on which to build alternative relationships.

•Direct interaction between opposing parties and facilitators based on tested procedures and techniques.

Traditionally our institutions have been authoritative and adversarial — courts, parliaments, industrial management and law-and-order processes all have these features. This applies both to planned and to free enterprise societies. These institutions reflect the history of societies. The rule of kings and feudal lords has given way to more political participation, but the institutions of government still reflect the old, classical notion that there are those who have a right to rule, and others who have a moral obligation to obey.

As part of this traditional elitist system, disputes with authorities or between peoples are settled on the basis of legal norms that do not always take into account human needs. Behavior that is outside legal norms is usually not understood and simply labelled "deviant."

At long last we are discovering — along with the discovery that national military defense in thermonuclear conditions is dysfunctional — that settlement of disputes, domestic and international, by adversarial, power-bargaining and coercive processes is impossible where there are important values at stake.

In Search of a Universal Solution

For over 20 years there has been a search for processes that enable a deep analysis of conflictual situations, and sophisticated means of resolution. At last there is something to report.

It was not until the early 60s, in the area of industrial relations, that the traditional law and order view of social control was challenged. Since then, little by little, it has been discovered by experience at all social levels, that stable relationships emerge only out of reciprocity between authorities and those over whom authority is exercised, and in particular reciprocity in according identity and recognition. Whether the conflict involves a supervisor and employee, or a parent and child, or a government and citizens' group, or the UN and member nation, both parties must give and take mutually. Accordingly, different processes and institutions of conflict resolution are required, processes that re-establish such reciprocity by determining the institutional and policy changes that make this possible.

By the 60s it was clear that the UN was failing in its objectives, that conflicts were remaining unresolved. A group of international lawyers at the David Davis Memorial institute in London reviewed the global situation and concluded that the explanation lay, not in faulty institutions or processes available to deal with conflicts, but in the unwillingness on the part of national authorities and other parties to use them.

The first stage in the saga of conflict resolution was an examination of this assumption. Was it true that parties to disputes preferred the costs of conflict to a resolution by some appropriate processes? What was amiss: willingness to seek a settlement, or the institutional means available? If the latter, what was required in institutions of conflict resolution that would make them acceptable and sought after?

A Test Case in Southeast Asia

At the time there was a continuing violent conflict in Southeast Asia between Indonesia, Malaysia and Singapore. All three governments had refused an invitation by the Prime Minister of Great Britain, Harold Wilson, to confer. Each had preconditions and objections. In 1965, with the approval of Wilson, a group of scholars at the Centre for the Analysis of Conflict (CAC) at the University of London, with which I was associated, asked the three heads of government each to nominate persons who would meet in an exploratory and problem-solving framework.

They called this framework controlled communication. The term referred to the role played by a panel of facilitators which was to ensure a dialogue free of bargaining and negotiation, and which would be deeply analytical. On the basis of this the facilitators would help evolve some acceptable options.

Two weeks later, in December 1965, a five-day discussion took place. Representing Malaysia there was a close diplomatic friend of the Malaysian Prime Minister, Mr. M. Sopiee, and the Deputy High Commissioner for Malaysia in London, Mr. Lim. From Singapore there was Mr. K.C. Wan, who had a military role. From Indonesia there were Mr. Sukarno from the Information Ministry and Mr. R. Sukartiko from the Foreign Office. At the request of the participants they were joined at a later stage by Mr. Tom Critchley, who had been the Australian representative in both Indonesia and Malaysia, and also Mr. Tom Dalyell, M.P., who was in touch with the British Prime Minister.

pter 21
Three
ualities
of a
secure
nation

The facilitating panel was comprised of ten scholars who were invited because of their research interests and experience. It included many British scholars and one American, Professor Roger Fisher.

Success!

The analytical meetings lasted over a week, during which time discoveries were made about the origins and nature of this conflict. There was some follow-up by the Centre. In due course all three Governments advised the Centre in simultaneous and similar messages, thus indicating their direct communication, that no further assistance was required.

Upsetting the assumption that parties preferred to fight rather than attempt to resolve their problems, and demonstrating that parties to a dispute will, in fact, discuss their disputes in an academic framework, did not necessarily suggest a practical alternative international institution or procedure. Further explorations were required to determine what was in this academic framework that made the process acceptable, and how this ingredient, whatever it was, could be introduced into non-academic institutions. Further exploration was necessary.

Another Test

In 1966 the United Nations official in charge of Cyprus negotiations, Ralph Bunche, could not persuade the Greek and Turkish Cypriots to meet together. Both had a pre-condition: that their particular versions of the Constitution should be the basis of negotiation. Once again London's CAC, with the knowledge of the United Nations Secretariat, in September 1966 asked the Greek-Cypriot President, Bishop Makarios, and Turkish-Cypriot Vice-President, Mr. Kutchuk, each to nominate persons to the same type of exploratory discussion. They met in London October 17-21, 1966.

On the Greek Cypriot side there was the Cypriot representative in London, Mr. Costas Ashiotis, and a leading businessman and friend of the President, Mr. Chris Economides. On the Turkish Cypriot side there was an associate of the Vice-President, who was subsequently the formal negotiator at the UN discussions, Mr. Umit Sulayman, and an educationalist, Mr. Niazi Ali.

The panel included 10 scholars. Conscious of the fact that this was an important research enterprise, the London group sought the assistance of relevant scholars in the United States. Searching through the literature, three scholars seemed to be most relevant. Indeed, they proved to be so and have been valued colleagues ever since. They were Professors Chadwick Alger, now at Ohio State, Herbert Kelman now at Harvard and Robert North of Stanford.

The five-day dialogue was an intense one, not only for the participants from Cyprus where the opposing parties were then involved in a high level of violence, but also for the panel members who were exploring something new and challenging. There were many disagreements among them. There was no shared theoretical framework and no shared experience. It was first and foremost a research exercise.

Nevertheless, some important discoveries were made, in particular, that both sides sought to identify with the whole island, and that neither side wished to be joined directly to, or controlled by, their respective national protectors, Greece and Turkey. Despite requests by both sides for further discussions, the Centre withdrew from this research exercise when the United Nations once again entered the situation.

Developing the Universal Solution

The next stage in the saga of conflict resolution has proved to be, by far, the most important. This was a deliberate research stage: the development of a generic theory of conflict. At this time there were some "islands of theory," but no adequate theory, explanation or basis for prediction that could guide a panel in assisting participants to discover acceptable options.

In a problem-solving workshop of this kind, the quality of the interaction and of the outcome depend almost entirely on the input from the facilitating panel. It is this role of the panel that distinguishes the process of facilitated conflict resolution from arbitration, traditional mediation and other forms of facilitated interaction.

While it is not the job of the facilitators to advocate solutions, their most important contribution is to throw light on conflictual relations generally, to help in the analysis of the conflict in question, and to offer creative options for consideration. For this an adequate theoretical framework is required.

Some years of "a-disciplinary" research followed, thanks to substantial grants from the Carnegie Foundation office in Geneva, and to certain most supportive Quaker-oriented trusts in the United Kingdom. Work in the industrial, police and school areas gave some insights, and work in Northern Ireland was most instructive. An important input into this international relations research came from sociologists, especially the work of Steven Box of Canterbury, England, and Paul Sites of Ohio, USA.

Chapter 21
Three
qualities
of a
secure
nation

The Global Test

The next step was to take these new ideas to scholars in other cultures and systems, and to test their relevance. It was possible to arrange discussions that lasted many days with members of the Soviet Academy, in particular members of the Institute for Economics and International Relations, and members of the US-Canadian Institute. In February 1974 we had an extensive, but not very productive, discussion in Moscow where what we term in the West the "political realist" approach was pronounced.

In January 1977 there was an unexpected return visit. One Soviet scholar introduced the discussion by saying that on our previous visit he had argued that all small wars must end, that the great powers could control middle-sized wars, and that war between the great powers was impossible in the thermonuclear age. Since then it appeared that small wars do not end, that middle-sized wars bring the great powers into conflict, and that thermonuclear war seemed to be possible. What was it that we were saying about conflict resolution?

There followed two visits to Moscow, one in September 1978, and another in February 1980, where conceptual notions were examined in the most searching and constructive atmosphere that I have experienced in any academic seminar. During a further visit for a different purpose in 1983 it was clear that failures in negotiations had led to a lot of research and re-thinking at this Academy level.

It was now time to return to the applied field of international disputes.

Recent Test Cases

Facilitated discussions are held in private and usually no public reference is made to them. I have made reference to two earlier situations only because they were of concern twenty years ago. There are two more recent situations in which the parties, for their own reasons, sought some limited publicity on the process and its outcome, and mention can be made of these.

In 1983, and twice subsequently, there were meetings initiated by members of the same London group, to discuss the Falklands/Malvinas problem. These were held under the auspices of the Center for International Development and Conflict Management at the University of Maryland, directed by Dr. Edward Azar. Members of the House of Commons Foreign Affairs Committee of the United Kingdom and Members of the Congress of the Argentine, together with some advisers and a representative of the Islanders concerned, were invited to participate. Three meetings took place and an agreed statement of principles was arrived at. This has been discussed at an official level by both sides. Another meeting was to have taken place in London early in 1987.

At this stage I considered it appropriate and necessary to set out in some detail the rules or procedures that had been discovered to be effective. These were criticized by a seminar of scholars and practitioners, under the chairmanship of Ambassador John McDonald of the Foreign Service Institute of the Department of State. With his encouragement it was redrafted and is now being published by the Foreign Service Institute.

A Consensus on Problem Solving

I have detailed two prerequisites of national security. The first was domestic cohesion and stability. The second was the process whereby this is attained.

There is a third prerequisite which we should note. This is a challenge to the power-political consensus which assumes national authorities to be the locus of power and which traditionally has led nations to adopt counter-productive national security policies; and the corresponding creation of a consensus that is based on the politically realistic assumption that power finally resides with the individual and the identity group — which is only sometimes the nation-state — through which the individual operates. Not until this shift in thought has a consensus backing will there be a public understanding of the nature of conflict, the nature of national security, the nature of identity struggles, the nature of terrorism, the nature of the critical problems we face in superpower relationships, and the nature of the processes required to handle them.

Conclusion

I began with a reference to President Reagan's initiative in calling attention to regional problems. Perhaps a future step could be discussion of the processes whereby situations in which political change is taking place can be handled without leading to competition between the USSR and the USA. It may be possible to arrive at:

1. Agreement that, as a prior condition of any support by the Soviet Union or the USA to any faction or state involved in a dispute, regional disputes be referred by the parties to some appropriate facilitation process.

2. Agreement for the establishment of an appropriate facilitation service for such purposes.

3. Agreement on norms of intervention by the USSR and the USA in support of authorities or factions in disputes if and when facilitation fails.

Chapter 21
Three
qualities
of a
secure
nation

4. Agreement on conditions under which arms and other support are legitimate.

5. Agreement to establish Facilitation Institutes in both countries for the purpose of research and coordinated activities in the area of facilitated conflict resolution.

If human civilizations do survive, and if they do expend adequate resources on another two decades of applied research into conflict resolution, then the President's focus on local conflicts will indeed have its place in history. In the meantime, survival by combatting problems, not by combatting others, must be our main concern.

Chapter 22
Alternative Conflict Resolution
in an Adversarial Age

by Tobi P. Dress
Attorney, mediator, administrator
Los Angeles, USA

Background. Attorney and educator specializing in conflict
resolution, arms control and disarmament. Career has evolved from
national associations (Presidential Clemency Board, Interstate
Commerce Commission, and Federal Trade Commission) to
international bodies (CARE, International Relief and Development
Organization, and International Senior Citizens/International Senior
Forum for Peace, a nongovernmental organization in consultancy
status with the UN). Currently doing business mediation and an
adjunct professor of Law at Loyola Law School where she is developing
a course in the Law and Policy of Arms Control and Disarmament.

Her article. Conflicts should be resolved with planning and strategy,
not handled haphazardly on a crisis-by-crisis basis. We must develop
sound processes and practices to resolve conflicts effectively at the
personal, social, national, and global levels. Many methods used
today generate win-lose outcomes, and in so doing they fuel tensions
instead of soothing them. Third-party intervention systems hold great
promise for resolving conflicts among people, cultures and nations,
and they involve skills that every individual and every world leader
can learn and apply.

*What is needed to resolve conflicts is a
system which can identify strengths and
weaknesses of all positions, so that
disputants can release the tight grip on
their positions and absorb additional
information.*

Alternative Conflict Resolution in an Adversarial Age

By Tobi P. Dress

*I*n the Allegory of the Caves by Plato we are shown a solitary man chained to the wall of a concrete cave. Because of the light filtering in through the cracks in the concrete, he sees the figures of other human beings moving along the other cave walls. The man sees only shadows but believes them to be actual people, because he lacks more complete information on which to base his belief. His belief is a reasonable one based on the information available to him.

Much like the rest of us, he believes that he is seeing people in their full forms and experience, when in fact he is seeing only a glimmer of them, the parts of them revealed by the particular light of place, time and circumstance.

As we in today's society extend outside of our families and nuclear communities, we relate to other people virtually every day of our lives with less than full information and varying degrees of misinformation about those with whom we relate. Therefore in order to form relationships we make numerous assumptions, and we speak, act and interact based on those assumptions. This is inevitable; we have little choice as we extend and reach out to more and different people.

But our relations are greatly strained by the gaps in our information and by the mistrust and lack of certainty that we experience in our relationships and communications with others. The end result of our troubled attempts to reach out to others in business, in personal matters and as nations, is the uncomfortable sensation we call conflict.

Such conflict is inevitable and will always be with us. Nevertheless, there is no greater threat to our survival and personal well-being than the desolation that can be caused by conflict, whether person to person or nation to nation.

Despite its recurring nature, conflict is a continual source of concern and surprise to institutions and nations worldwide.

Isn't it remarkable, then, that while we have highly developed information systems, intelligence technologies, military strategies, and even space-travel technologies, we have no standardized, planned conflict-resolution technology?

Conflict resolution should not be haphazard, accidental, left to chance or mobilized in a hurry on a crisis-by-crisis basis. As the twenty-first century approaches it is essential that we develop and utilize strategically sound methods, technologies and institutions for conflict resolution and management. These should be as well-planned and well-funded as our other leading technological priority systems. This article

•Explores the nature and causes of conflicts, which can be helpful as well as harmful

•Observes that many methods of resolving conflict in practice today are last-resort, adversarial systems which often fuel conflict situations rather than relieving them,

•Explores current, progressive alternatives that can be employed successfully at all levels to resolve conflicts among people, groups and nations,

•Encourages political leaders, business executives, community leaders and academicians to learn these proven processes and to use them at every level of government, industry and community,

•And last, but certainly not least, offers them to you to resolve conflicts in your personal interactions.

The Nature of Conflict

The nature of conflict is illusory and its reasons are often unclear. It is a fact that we all experience conflict. As consumers we often have conflict while purchasing goods and services; as business people we experience conflict with clients, staff and suppliers; as family members we routinely face logjams in our relationships with loved ones; as nations we are confronted with economic, legal and political clashes of interest, which often result in the bearing of arms before other resolution mechanisms have been fully explored.

The reasons for conflict, among individuals as well as among institutions and nations which are comprised of individuals, are both internal and external, ideological, practical and situational. They may result from actual clashes of interest, from misunderstandings, or

Chapter 22
Alternative
conflict
resolution
in an
adversarial
age

251

from real or perceived threat. Conflict will always be part of our lifestyle, because we seek interaction and liaison with others without fully knowing their needs, fears and expectations. Interpersonal and international conflict will continue to accelerate as we continue reaching further into new spheres to relate and do business.

We make two types of assumptions whenever we interact with others. First, we make general assumptions about relating itself. For example, we believe that the words we use convey certain meanings which are understood by the other party. We assume that the other party has the same ideas of good faith that we have. We assume that a look, nod or handshake has the same implications for the other person that they have for us. However, words, tones and gestures may have vastly different connotations to different people. This is true even in families and local neighborhoods, and becomes an even more prominent factor in relating when we deal with people from other communities, cultures, professions and ideological systems.

Secondly, we make assumptions about the people with whom we communicate. As we relate with them, we watch, listen and assume, and what we don't know, we fill in. We do so without information about their histories, needs, fears and expectations, just as they are doing with us.

So inevitably, our communications and relationships are often based on very shaky foundations and are fortified with beliefs that may be real or may be illusory. Yet we, as individuals, groups, nations, are largely unaware of our lack of information.

Yet this very lack of information without awareness, coupled with the assumptions we make as we interact, create a distortion in perception.

It is reasonable and necessary to make assumptions and fill in gaps in order to communicate. However, if without justification, based on fears, biases and perceived threat, we fail to perceive or acknowledge our lack of information, we invite hostility. Often we nurture our misinformation, our incorrect or exaggerated assumptions, our belief systems based on partial knowledge. Others then feel misunderstood, damaged, humiliated or short-changed, and conflict emerges as a signal that several misconceptions have converged.

This is the point of friction, the sharp edge of two different perceptions or two clashing interests colliding head-on, which forms the tense, uncomfortable, disquieting phenomenon of conflict.

Naturally, at that point, when we most need to examine our premises and clarify our communication, we instead want to flee from the situation, want to end it without scrutiny, want to justify our position about which we are becoming increasingly more insecure, and destroy the other party who has engaged us in this untenable situation.

We see the conflict as something to be avoided at all costs, rather than handled, as though conflict is a contagious and deadly disease and it is best not to get too close to it.

This avoidance adds an additional dimension to the syndrome, compelling us to continue justifying and strengthening our positions rather than taking responsibility, seeking new information or working towards clarification of points of dispute.

Oddly enough, it is at this point of friction that conflict can be a stimulating, educational, meaningful encounter. When conflict is generated and then avoided, it looms larger and larger and ever more unmanageable. But when it is tackled and dealt with by the parties in an appropriate setting and context, it can be diffused without loss of face to either party and can lead to useful change, insights and growth.

To realize these benefits of conflict, we need to do two things. We need first to reverse certain automatic assumptions about conflict, and we need to employ the correct processes for diffusing it.

In our society we have an almost universal belief that conflict is negative. The word alone evokes fearful and defensive feelings and has dramatic connotations.

Yet conflict, in and of itself, is not negative; nor is it positive. Conflict is neutral. It is the way it is handled that assigns it a positive or negative value. Conflict can be educational and stimulating, can generate new levels of communication and thought and can be a necessary catalyst for growth or change. It can spawn new ways of thinking and new solutions for solving recurring issues.

Why, then, is it automatically assumed to be negative?

apter 22
ernative
conflict
solution
in an
versarial
age

This assumption is made for many reasons. First, conflict is almost always uncomfortable for the parties involved, and while in this state of tension, as suggested above, we are more concerned with extracting ourselves from the situation than with resolving it fairly. The outcome of the dispute, which was actually the reason for the dispute, now becomes secondary to the dispute itself. Conflict also carries with it a stigma for the parties involved. It creates a cause for blame of oneself or others, and is closely associated with personal failure. We mistakenly believe that if we experience conflict there is something inadequate about our feelings, conduct or abilities to interact as adults and professionals, rather than realizing that differences of opinion are as endemic to modern society as traffic congestion.

In addition to the tense feelings generated by the conflict itself, the crucial aspect of potential loss is involved, which adds the element of fear. The result of possible "loss" of a conflict can have critical repercussions in our lives, including loss of property, money, a job or job status and reputation. It may jeopardize relationships and alignments. And worst of all, it may cause us to lose face. So the idea of conflict includes implied threats of great loss and unwanted disturbance of our status quo.

Most interestingly for our purposes, there is a third major reason that conflict is always presumed to be negative. Not only is conflict associated with uncomfortable, unwelcome feelings, and not only does it bring with it a threat of possible loss, but ironically, the resolution mechanisms we use to resolve conflict are often adversarial and inflammatory. As such, they often tend to exacerbate, rather than ameliorate, the conflict and in fact may cause additional unwanted feelings and situations. This is the element we are most concerned with here, because this added stress on a conflict situation is often an unnecessary additional element.

Current Conflict Resolution Systems

The primary processes now used to ameliorate conflict are largely systems which are designed to select or determine a prevailing party, which necessitates having a defeated party. Current conflict resolution mechanisms can therefore be destructive in their consequences and ramifications.

These mechanisms include use of litigation on a domestic basis, and use of power politics, international sanctions and force, on an international basis. Despite the complex and intricate strategies involved in both litigative and military exercises, both of these systems often conclude conflicts but do not necessarily resolve them. For conflict to be shifted, transformed or neutralized, it must be resolved rather than merely concluded.

Let us look at the similarities between use of judicial adjudication and use of the bearing of arms for solving conflicts. Most critically, they both imply the necessity for a winner and a loser, and they seek to defeat the position of the opponent or object of conflict, often destroying the opponent in the process. Further, they leave a defeated, unsatisfied party who is likely to harbor retaliatory feelings. An individual or a nation in a retaliatory posture can be a very dangerous and volatile generator of renewed hostilities.

In fact, methods of concluding conflicts which are adversarial and are structured to produce a winner/loser syndrome are not as effective as processes which do not require determination of a prevailing party. They can create excessively bad feelings and pain, and in fact they are often unrealistic. This is repeatedly true in the case of litigation and trial since there is rarely a case in which one party's position is infallible while the other party's position is entirely incorrect. There are almost always merits and flaws on all sides of every legal dispute.

What is needed to resolve conflicts is a system which can accommodate all of the points of view presented, can identify strengths and weaknesses of all positions, and can diffuse the tension between the disputants so that they can release the tight grip they have on their positions and absorb additional information. This can help to clarify the reasons for each other's positions and can lead to joint solutions and a final elimination of conflict in a way that does not encourage retaliation.

Third-Party Intervention Systems

Third-party Conflict Resolution is such a system. There are various types of Third-party Conflict Resolution interventions — each will be described below — but in each case the process is one in which a neutral third-party joins the disputing parties in an attempt to find resolution to the dispute in question. Ideally this system does not defeat either party and does not exclude facts or evidence which the parties believe to be important. It allows all parties to feel they have been heard and that their positions have been fully taken into account. These processes are less formal than judicial adjudication and often allow the parties to come to their own decisions regarding judgments and awards. They are based on mutual disclosure and communication in a setting which is confidential and which cannot later be used in any way against either party.

During each of these intervention processes, the parties are encouraged to state their positions, reasoning, and evidence in the presence of the opponent and the neutral third-party. They are given ample opportunity to explain and clarify their positions and to state the facts and supporting data they feel backs up their case. Once the parties have thus brought the facts as they see them into the open and feel that they have been heard, they become receptive to additional information. This condition permits them to re-examine their positions in light of new facts. The exchanges that follow often lead to new and useful realizations, realizations which may lead to further exploration of alternative solutions which can satisfy both

apter 22
ernative
conflict
solution
in an
versarial
age

255

parties. The technique is directed toward resolution, not decision, so that even when conflict is not totally resolved, both parties still gain considerable clarity and insight into each position. They then have a better opportunity to achieve a realistic appraisal of the conflict, the stakes involved and possible solutions.

The intriguing thing about this type of process is that it is largely the same whether the dispute at hand is between two neighbors or two nations. It can be successfully used in disputes that are inter-personal, business related or international. This is because every situation of conflict boils down to the perceptions of individuals and their beliefs about their rights and responsibilities and the rights and responsibilities of their adversaries in the conflict situation. These beliefs and assumptions of right, responsibility and privilege, when held up to a screen of scrutiny through verbal communication, almost always undergo transformations of perception as new information is woven into the fabric of the fact pattern.

Defining the Processes

So far we have identified general information about conflict and its positive as well as negative qualities. We have discussed the ironic fact that conflict resolution processes that we now use are largely adversarial and therefore exacerbate the very conflicts they seek to solve. We have further suggested that there are processes available and in place that, when used responsibly and effectively, provide a new option for, and new dimension in, conflict resolution. Before moving into the definition of these processes, it is important to note that using the word "new" for these mechanisms is somewhat misleading. For centuries conflicts and disputes have been solved on a community level around the world through use of the third-party intervention mechanisms described here. The institutional contexts for the processes may be considered new, but the processes of non-violent intervention are as old as the use of force.

There are three primary types of third-party intervention — mediation, conciliation and arbitration. All of them depend for their effectiveness on the neutrality of the third-party and the confidentiality of the process.

In the mediation process the role of the mediator is to assist the parties in airing their positions and the facts as they see them. The mediator reflects back the information presented and then meets individually with the parties. During these private meetings the mediator can help each of the parties realistically assess the strengths and weaknesses of their positions and can help them identify what kind of outcome each can realistically expect. With the additional information generated in this process, the mediator encourages the parties to decide between themselves how they will resolve the conflict. If this process were used routinely at the outset of major conflicts, many interpersonal, local and world tensions could be nipped in the bud at the start.

Conciliation is a less structured process than mediation when used domestically. (Internationally it is more formal than mediation and is a process of mediation and inquiry.) It may be the process of a friend intervening between two neighbors in a dispute. Conciliation may even be done on the telephone as a sort of shuttle diplomacy between disputing parties. It is a preliminary process in which the parties agree to try to settle their differences through assistance of the third-party before taking further steps. As with mediation, for conciliation to be effective the parties must determine the final resolution of the case. Like mediation, it can be used at the outset of any misunderstanding and can often end the tension before it becomes hostile.

Arbitration, on the other hand, is the most formal and structured of the non-judicial third-party intervention processes. However, it is considerably less formal than the court system and information is not excluded according to strict rules of evidence, as it is in litigation. So arbitration is something of a hybrid between the concepts of mediation and litigation. The arbitrator serves not only as a facilitator, but also as decision maker. After hearing the presentations of both sides with any evidence presented, the arbitrator is vested with authority to make a decision or award in the dispute. The arbitration may or may not be binding, depending on the terms outlined in the contract or agreement which the parties initially signed.

The importance of understanding these processes and being aware of the options available cannot be overstated. Educators, attorneys, business executives, diplomats and policy-makers will benefit greatly by being aware of these processes and having systems in place to use them.

Equally important, however, is the understanding that they are not infallible and are not necessarily suitable for every conflict situation.

The biggest problems so far with third-party intervention processes are the lack of standardization and uniformity of training and licensing that still exist. Although various licensing procedures have been explored for mediators, as yet there are no uniform licensing processes. While arbitrators are governed by various procedures and regulations, there is no specialized training for arbitrators. Therefore a great deal rests on the ethics, credentials and abilities of the

apter 22
ternative
conflict
solution
in an
versarial
age

individual third-party intervenor.

Even with their inherent imperfections, greater use of third-party mechanisms to resolve conflicts at all levels would result in decreased tensions, less court backlog and greatly improved international relations.

Turning briefly to the issue of international-relations, the primary form of communication used for international conflicts, other than bearing arms, is negotiation. While negotiation is a powerful tool and is sometimes effective, it places the negotiating parties in a dilemma since they each come into the negotiation with a position and a bottom-line. Without anyone there to mediate the discussion, negotiations often end up being merely a precedent to greater tensions or warfare. In most negotiations more could be accomplished

---

Superpowers: Compatibility or Conflict

Values can be defined as the abstract forces that compel us to behave the way that we, as living beings, behave. Not just our personal beliefs and social customs, but also our basic, biological compulsions like hunger and desire, and the many rules and regulations that our groups encourage us to obey.

Given that broad definition of *values*, we can define *conflict* as the result of incompatible values between any two or more people or groups (or, to be more general, between any two or more living things, or groups of living things).

Having the incompatible US and Soviet nations on the same planet is like having a cat and dog together in the same room. The two animals fear and distrust each other because of their basic incompatibilities, and will fight at the first sign of aggression. Likewise, the superpowers are divided by fear and mistrust due largely to economic, political, social and religious incompatibilities . . . and each is ready to launch its nuclear missiles at the first indication that the other side has done so.

The solution is, if they have to live together (and they do — the two animals are in the same room, and the two nations are on the same planet) the solution is to make them compatible. This can be done by having them align to a higher set of values. When a dog and cat are part of the same household and their behavior is directed by a sensible set of family values, the two animals can learn to coexist peacefully as their biological values become secondary.

if there were a bridge between the two adversaries.

It is inexplicable that the mediation system is so rarely used as a tool in international relations. One reason may be that international policy makers believe that assistance of a third-party will compromise their autonomy. The question of perceived lack of neutrality can also be a major factor.

However, world bodies can gain valuable information, test their positions, save face, avoid sanctions and armed conflict and profit more from mediation than they can from the negotiation process. In addition, this process does not compromise autonomy but may, in fact, help to clarify and solidify it for all parties because it clarifies boundaries, limitations and expectations.

Designing a set of mutually agreeable values for the two superpowers must be a combined effort not only of the USA and USSR, but also of their multinational groups and allies — Comecon and Warsaw Pact (on the Soviet side), NATO and perhaps EEC (on the US side), and, of course, a world representative such as the United Nations (in the middle).

If we hope to eliminate the chance of conflict between the superpowers, we must see them become compatible. As long as they are incompatible there is a likelihood of conflict . . . and as long as they have nuclear weapons, *nuclear* conflict is possible.

The Soviets took a bold step in 1987 by announcing a plan to decentralize. The move would involve radical social and political changes and would represent a big step toward compatibility with the West. Perhaps the USA will follow suit in the coming years and take a large, conciliatory step toward the East . . .

Eventually the two powers may have to sit at the table with a world-class referee and lay their social, political and economic cards on the table. Hopefully the game will not end with one winner and one loser, rather the two hands will be combined to produce the best possible hand for both players. Such a meeting would be a turning point in human affairs, marking the beginning of the end of the threat of nuclear war.

Meanwhile, US-Soviet exchanges of culture, teachers and other aspects of society, are moving us gradually toward a safer, more compatible world.
— Adapted from existing Earthview Press publications.

pter 22
rnative
conflict
solution
in an
ersarial
age

These processes also maintain good will, help to keep communications lines open in crisis situations, and can reduce levels of international tension.

As individuals, families, institutions and nations, we can now take the opportunity, during this most transitional period in history, to look at conflict in a new and fresh way, from a different angle. We need to understand it, confront it, manage it and actually benefit from it. We need to have more confidence in our ability to resolve tense and confrontational situations through communicative processes.

By developing skills in the use of peaceful conflict resolution we and our leaders can turn impasses in communication from tense interpersonal and international battles into doorways for improved exchange and dialogue.

Third-party resolution is not the final and only solution to world peace or even peace between individuals. Sometimes parties involved in conflict do not really want resolution, but prefer a conclusion in the traditional sense or have another motive for perpetuating a conflict. Some conflicts are so complex or heated that informal resolution may not be the most appropriate vehicle. However, third-party resolution can be an excellent tool for discovering the cause of most problems, and when we know the cause and roots of a problem a solution is usually not far off. Third-party Resolution techniques focus on discovering causes of conflict, not placing blame.

Plato's cave people were bound by lack of access to information. We are fortunate to have extensive access to information, if we choose it. Mediation is not only a tool for resolving conflict, but an information source for parties to a conflict.

We can't turn back to a small town world where neighbors solve problems over back fences, if indeed such a world ever existed. But we can make sure that we, as individuals and social groups, and that our leaders and representatives, become aware that there are options available to be used in situations of tension and crisis. If our world leaders are willing to expend time and money to develop technologies for information, intelligence, space and combat, we should urge them to consider improved conflict resolution technologies as a matter of equal priority.

We are an evolving species. We have now evolved to a point at which communication in adversity should be at the head of our international and community agendas. Our world can no longer survive by solving conflicts with what has been.

Chapter 23
Notes of a Social Theorist

by Louis Kriesberg
Director, Program on the Analysis and Resolution of Conflicts
Syracuse, USA

Background. Professor of sociology and member of many national and international associations dealing with education, sociology, and peace. Has lived in Mexico, Germany, Israel, France, and his native USA, with visits through Europe, USSR, the Mideast, India, Kenya and Central America. A prolific writer, with 8 books, over 50 articles, and dozens of papers, book reviews, and newspaper articles on peace and social issues to his credit. Honors include President, Society for the Study of Social Problems, Fulbright Research Scholarship (Germany), and Phi Beta Kappa.

His article. An emerging model of social structures is introduced which casts some light on the complex causes of international conflict. The author blends his personal experiences and historical research to observe tensions in the Middle East and between the superpowers . . . and to see what makes those tensions rise and fall.

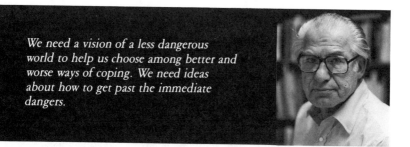

We need a vision of a less dangerous world to help us choose among better and worse ways of coping. We need ideas about how to get past the immediate dangers.

Notes of a Social Theorist

by Louis Kriesberg

Writers in the functionalist, Marxist, conflict, symbolic interactionist and other traditions have broadened their perspectives and in doing so have become more and more alike. Consequently, one can discern the outlines of a newly emerging model relevant for peace-making. The model is based on four sets of ideas:

1. Complex structures. Individuals and groups are actors which form complex social structures.

2. Complex interactions. These actors collaborate, contend and compete with each other — person to person, group to group, and person to group — in a variety of complex social processes.

3. Intentional behavior. The individuals and groups act purposively.

4. Distributed influence. Different actors have varying amounts of influence on the outcomes of different situations.

Complex Social Structures. Individuals and groups are multiple in two senses. First, many actors exist in parallel, on the same plane, such as national governments. The second sense is more interesting. Actors overlap, crosscut and are embedded or nested in each other.

An individual, for example, may occupy many statuses and play many roles simultaneously. One person may be a mother, a woman, a Catholic, a Kenyan, an agricultural worker, a political party member and so on. Each status or role is part of a collective identity and/or organization which may act as a unit.

The world structure is constituted by many non-coinciding systems — a very loose, bi-polar military system, a world market system with core, semi-peripheral, and peripheral countries, and overlapping sets of national, religious, ideological and civilizational adherents.

Complex Interactions. The second set of ideas in the emerging paradigm pertains to the multiplicity of processes of interaction. Individuals and groups indulge in a variety of forms of interaction — conflicting, exchanging, competing, collaborating, assimilating and so on. By multiplicity I mean that all these forms of interaction are occurring simultaneously among different sets of actors. Thus, while national officials are bargaining with local government heads and competing with officials from other nations, they are also collaborating with officials from still other countries and with several groups within their constituency. Even while collaborating in some regards, they are competing in others with the same interaction partners.

Of all the various forms of interaction, conflicts deserve a large share of our attention today. Conflicts are waged by coercion and by such noncoercive inducements as persuasion and positive sanctions, the latter of which can be used to divide the enemy, gain allies, rally constituencies, and forge communal interests with the adversary against an even greater shared threat.

Conflict processes are part of most social relations, as are cooperative processes. But this article is concerned with particular conflicts between actors who regard themselves as adversaries. Such specific conflicts are based upon social situations in which actors believe they have incompatible objectives.

No international conflict is merely two-sided. This is obvious in the complex web of fights in the Middle East, but it is also true of struggles between the Soviet and US governments. Allies, allies of adversaries, and potential allies affect the course of a struggle, if only by the way the primary adversaries take them into account. The multiplicity of actors lies not only among units of the same level. Significant actors transcend, cross-cut, and lie within governments and countries. There are international governmental organizations such as the United Nations and international, nongovernmental organizations (NGOs) like the IBM (International Business Machines) corporation and the International Sociological Association, and domestic groupings like army bureaucracies and trade unions.

To understand the course of conflicts it is particularly important to recognize the multiplicity of actors within and among countries. The linkage between domestic and foreign policy is of fundamental importance in explaining the transition from peace to war and from war to peace. Developments within countries have their own dynamics which are only partially influenced by external developments. For example, in the USA, survey data reveals that public support for increased arms spending began to rise in the early

1970s, after the historically unusual opposition to increased arms spending in the late 1960s. This shift was occurring when detente was in full bloom and elites were generally even less supportive of increased arms spending.

What policies a government pursues and the characterization of the national interest are shaped by the interplay of many domestic groups and factions. The multiple interaction paradigm helps avoid the reification of the state or nation and makes it more likely to attend to the diverse actors who constitute the state and country.

Intentional Behavior. The third core idea in the emerging paradigm is that people act purposively. They attribute intention to their conduct and this gives it meaning and direction. Such values as religious belief, political ideology and prevailing ways of thinking play important roles in providing possible actions and justifications for them.

Government officials and other adversary organization leaders largely determine which conflict is primary for their constituencies. In making those interpretations they themselves are likely to be affected by their own interests and values. Leaders who are heads of state and government tend to reify the nation-state and identify themselves with it.

Distributed Influence. The fourth and final aspect of the emerging paradigm is this: although the parties are unequal in their ability to shape developments, none of the actors is fully able to control them. Correspondingly, there are general regularities in the outcomes of courses of actions as well as a problematic character to the outcome of each particular series of occurrences. In short, events and structures are the resultant of complex interactions among actors.

The differential capacities for affecting the outcomes of a set of interactions may be referred to as power differences. The reference to capacities indicates that power or influence is relative and contingent upon the issue in contention. Furthermore, even when power differences are asymmetrical, influence is not completely one-sided. The party with lesser capacity has some.

The multiplicity of actors also means that each actor has possible allies or coalition partners. Having alternatives through relations with additional actors modifies the relative power positions.

Of course, the structure of relations cannot be regarded only in terms of power or influence. The resultant of multiple interactions establishes networks of collaboration and exchange as well as common identifications and bonds of obligation. These all channel future interactions.

National governments are major international actors and so are NGOs such as multinational corporations. Viewing these major actors as a resultant of multiple actors relating through multiple processes lends a dynamic cast to our conception of those structures. It increases our sensitivity to the inability of any one actor to control events. It helps account for the sometimes abrupt escalations and deescalations of international conflicts.

Real World Scenarios

Now we can apply this four-point paradigm to international affairs of recent years to analyze world conflict and perhaps draw some conclusions about the future. Several questions about deescalation should be kept in mind:

•What conditions and skills of the initiator lead to reciprocation of the initiatives?

•Under what circumstances and through what processes do deescalatory initiatives result in explicit agreement?

•What determines how enduring the agreement is, if one is reached?

•What are the shared gains and the relative gains of the deescalation for the many parties involved?

Partial Nuclear Test Ban Treaty. This treaty was signed in 1963 by the USA, USSR and UK. What led to this important conciliatory step between great powers?

Prior to the treaty there had been many informal meetings of Soviet and Western scientists to discuss technical and other issues relating to a comprehensive test ban. These meetings, held under the auspices of Pugwash, provided a means of communicating possible solutions to problems emerging in the formal inter-governmental negotiations and in developing common understandings among the expert advisers in the USSR and in the Western countries.

In the USA, public concern had grown over the effects of radioactive fallout on the atmosphere. At the same time, the Soviet break with the People's Republic of China (PRC) made Soviet adherence to the agreement easier and indeed even attractive as a way of pressuring the Chinese and appealing to Third World countries.

Among the most noticeable and effective steps in the conciliatory process in general, and the Test Ban Treaty in particular, are strong, open, unilateral gestures such as speeches and visits. The Test Ban Treaty followed a chain of interactions greatly enhanced by President John Kennedy's American University speech in June 1963. In that speech, Kennedy acknowledged a kind of parity with the Soviets and suggested the possibility that the USA might share responsibility for the Cold War. He also announced a halt of nuclear tests in the atmosphere as long as the Soviets also did not conduct such tests. The speech had followed privately conveyed indications from Premier Nikita Khrushchev that he was interested in such an agreement and wanted an initiating gesture. Khrushchev immediately responded to the speech with reciprocated gestures. Negotiations for the treaty were conducted quickly and successfully. The deescalation was based on some interests shared by major leaders in the USA and USSR, and the agreement allowed each group to gain domestic advantage.

US-USSR Detente of the 1970s. In the USA, anti-war sentiments and growing open-mindedness toward communism during the 60s and early 70s led to detente. It was made more attractive to the Soviets by the US movement toward normalized relations with the PRC. It was also facilitated by the Federal Republic of Germany's initiation of Ostpolitik.

Multinational corporations based in the USA supported detente moves by the US government because of their interests in expanding trade with the USSR.

Egyptian-Israeli Peace Initiatives, 1977-79.

For President Anwar Sadat, the idea of gaining support from the USA significantly contributed to taking peace initiatives in 1971 and 1977. Support from the US government elites and public generally was seen as a way of inducing the Israeli government to make the desired concessions.

Public opinion in Egypt also played a significant role in President Sadat's 1971 peace initiative since he thought that as a leader he had to appear active and that war was not possible. Public opinion in Israel too played a very important role in President Sadat's decision to break the psychological barrier in the Arab-Israeli conflict. He thought that his action would profoundly affect the people of Israel and other countries, and therefore make possible certain agreements that were not otherwise conceivable.

President Sadat's dramatic visit to Jerusalem in November 1977 was an outstanding example of a grand gesture. The event and the way

Sadat conducted himself profoundly affected the Israeli public and to a lesser extent the US public. These shifts were essential for negotiating and concluding a Peace Treaty.

That Israel had new leaders who could be strong enough to make domestically difficult concessions was also a consideration in dealing directly with the government of Israel. Sadat's act was public and irrevocable.

Sadat's conviction that the USA and not the Soviet government was critical in gaining his goals from Israel shows that he sought a non-coercive strategy. The forthcoming Geneva Conference promised to reintroduce Soviet influence in any negotiations; it also promised to give the most rejectionist Arab governments and groupings a veto power that would isolate Egypt.

Conclusions

The involvement of many actors who coincide in interests, who cross-cut each other, who overlap each other, and who may be internal to and encompassing of each other is a crucial factor in the de-escalation of conflicts. De-escalatory initiatives occur when one or more of the primary adversaries shifts its view of what is the primary struggle. That shift in assessment is a consequence of a new view of the balance, or correlation, of forces — a new view of which groups must have the highest priority to be placated or to be overwhelmed.

Public gestures in the peace process can be critical. Their absence probably contributed to the failure of President Sadat's peace initiative of February 1971, of the Rapacki Plan for a nuclear free Central Europe, and of President Johnson's and Secretary of Defense McNamara's effort in 1967 to begin substantive negotiations for ABM and SALT agreements.

Obviously major conflicts do not readily de-escalate. They often persist for long periods of protracted hostility. They sometimes escalate into extensive violence, or the mutual threat of violence, as in the Cuban Missile Crisis. Successful de-escalation has often come about through the use of non-coercive inducements and a change in objectives toward more mutual benefits for the adversaries and less of a one-sided gain.

Efforts toward de-escalation usually do not move quickly and smoothly to a mutually desired de-escalation. Peace initiatives by one party are often not reciprocated. They may be discounted as insincere tricks. In Egyptian-Israeli and US-USSR relations, we can find more failed than successful efforts at de-escalation. Many factors must converge for success:

•Officials in both governments must perceive some benefits from de-escalation.

•There must be a shift in each government and at least some concurrent movement in domestic support.

•The actions of each government toward the other must be viewed as mutually appropriate.

•The leaders of each government must believe it is in their interests to pursue the policy.

•The international setting at large must be conducive.

A change to reduced hostility, like a change to increased tension, requires the convergence of many factors. In conflict no one party is in charge. The course of a conflict is the resultant of many kinds of interactions among actors. Consequently, a change in the direction of a fight requires the concurrence of many conditions.

Understanding changes in social patterns cannot be adequate if isolated from the societal context in which they occur, and the societal context itself is greatly affected by the global context and intersocietal transactions. Nor is the global context simply background. Persons and groups interact across the world. For example, jobs in one city of one nation are affected by corporate investments in cities in other countries.

Our growing understanding of changes from war to peace and from increased to decreased tension contributes to answering the basic question of social theory: How is order maintained?

The world system is often viewed as anarchic, a setting in which every major actor is struggling with each other. Yet, lacking a common moral order and overarching institutions, most countries, most of the time, are not doing violence to each other. Is it that they hold each other at bay by threats of devastation? I think not. One of the bases of the order is that each country has a great deal of autonomy. What leaders in each country want cannot in good measure be given by leaders in other countries. The domestic conditions are the resultant of largely domestic factors. This is still true despite the increasing integration of the world system.

This is also true within nations. Many social actors within a society are also autonomous to significant degrees in many areas. Hence the problem of control is not as difficult as it would be if a high degree of coordination and integration were necessary.

This growing knowledge of the conditions for de-escalation and the processes which affect it can be applied by:

•decision makers at all levels of society, from national leaders to corporate managers, wishing to de-escalate a conflict, and

•mediators called in to assist the de-escalation process.

The knowledge may contribute to the control of escalation by affecting public and elite views. If a leader's constituency desires non-coercive approaches to conflict, involving significant reliance on persuasion and rewards, the leader will be freer to employ them.

The knowledge may also contribute to the demystification of the nation-state. Awareness of the many different standards and values at work in the world will lessen the significance of any single one. Awareness of the multitude of actors involved in any conflict gives adversaries a broader view. That awareness can uncover new common interests and outcomes which yield mutual benefits to the adversaries.

The knowledge provides evidence of the important role of public opinion in conflict escalation and de-escalation. This is true in Western democracies (as in the case of the USA waging war in Vietnam) and probably is true as well in authoritarian societies at particular junctures. Public opinion is mobilized not only in social movements and protest organizations but also by political leaders for political action.

We need the vision of a less dangerous world to help us choose among better ways of coping that move us to a safer world. We also need ideas about how to get past the immediate dangers.

**Chapter 23
Notes of
a social
theorist**

We have got into our present, life-threatening situation for a multitude of reasons. No one actor caused it. Many actors, generally with good intentions, interacted to bring us here. Many different people can and must contribute to moving us toward a less dangerous world. To our good intentions must be added more knowledge and the better understanding that social theory can provide.

Adapted and updated with permission from the journal "Sociological Review" Vol 32 No 3 (August 1984), ©Routledge & Kegan Paul Ltd, 1984.

Chapter 24
A New Approach to Prisons

by Richard D. Lamm
Professor, Attorney and Government Official
Denver, USA

Background. Man in transition. This year ended longest-running term (12 years) as state governor of Colorado. Earned a reputation as a frank, futuristic official. In the words of British educator Peter G. Boyle, "If Americans were less concerned with 'walking tall' and took a look at their immediate vicinity, they would see the problems Governor Lamm is pointing to."* Winner, *Christian Science Monitor* "Peace 2010" essay contest. Author of 5 books. After his governorship, a visiting professor (Dartmouth University for six months, Innsbruck, Austria, for six weeks . . . .)

His article. US crime has soared in recent decades, and prisons in most states are overcrowded. Building more prisons is the most obvious, though not necessarily the most effective solution. This article advocates that young, nonviolent offenders should have an option — a traditional prison sentence with hardened criminals or a shorter sentence in a new program of intensive discipline which could mold a new set of values for young offenders and help motivate them to avoid future trouble. The new program would also reserve more prison space for hardened criminals.

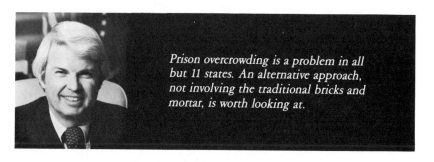

Prison overcrowding is a problem in all but 11 states. An alternative approach, not involving the traditional bricks and mortar, is worth looking at.

* Rocky Mountain News, August 17, 1986

A New Approach to Prisons

by Richard D. Lamm

*C*rime, it is said, doesn't pay — but it does exact a price from the law-abiding. Citizens foot the bill for crime through loss of the sense of freedom and security and, more tangibly, in real tax dollars.

In an effort to keep these costs under some kind of control, public officials across the USA — including Colorado lawmakers — have called for longer, tougher sentences for many crimes. But the officials aren't always willing to authorize payment for the bricks and mortar it takes to keep sentenced convicts locked up. As a result, prison and jail overcrowding now is a problem in Colorado and all but 11 other states — a problem that may not be affordably solved by traditional approaches.

Current projections show that to meet future prison needs, Colorado needs 16 more prisons, at a cost of about $35 million per prison, by 1996. And that's just to build the prisons; costs of overseeing the occupants will run an estimated $16,000 per year per prison bed.

With more than 450 Colorado convicts now waiting for space in state prisons — crowding county jails as they stand in line for state detention — I have asked the Colorado Legislature to look into building more prisons, and also to investigate new programs to meet demand for prisons and rehabilitation at lower cost.

Now is the time to begin to address the problem, because it is not likely to get better with time. The reality is that the USA's rate of violent crime rose 233 percent between 1960 and 1983. The reality is that our prison population has grown faster than the general population, with 111 prisoners per 100,000 people in the USA in 1975, growing to 188 prisoners per 100,000 people by 1984.

The reality is that protection from crime costs money — money that must also cover competing and increasingly pressing needs.

Other states, too, have gone to stopgap measures to house prisoners. In Massachusetts, there are inmates living in storage rooms and classrooms. In Tennessee, the backlog of prisoners in county jails got so bad that one sheriff, tired of housing state convicts in his county jail, chained 12 convicts to a fence at a nearby state prison. The sheriff had his own federal court order barring overcrowding in his own full jail. The 12 inmates finally were housed in another county jail.

Overcrowding often means substandard prison living conditions that federal courts have declared unconstitutional, as cruel and unusual punishment. Some prisons, complying with court orders, have had to release offenders early.

And overcrowding turns up the heat under the pressure cooker many prisons become. In Texas, which has one of the most understaffed and overcrowded prison systems in the USA, it has been calculated that a Texas prisoner is six times more likely to be killed in prison than outside one.

The Colorado General Assembly, like many legislatures across the country, recently passed bills that crack down harder on crime. But it made no provision to house the additional criminals, who cannot all go to our already-overloaded prisons. That doesn't address the problem; it leaves the job half undone.

In Colorado, a $35 million medium-security prison is scheduled to open in June 1987. But building new prisons is an expensive and slow process. A 500-bed facility, like the prison under construction in Ordway, Colorado, can cost anywhere from $8 million to $78 million to build, depending on its security level. It usually takes about two years from the time a prison is funded to the time a prison is ready for occupancy. We need to explore solutions other than high-security warehousing.

The Ordway prison will be full, or nearly full, the day it opens, because Colorado has more than 450 prisoners backed up in county jails. And, within five years, Colorado's inmate population will have doubled to more than 7,000. Our prison space is woefully inadequate for such a population boom among prisoners.

To help keep the Colorado prison population at a reasonable level, the criminal justice system has taken a number of actions. Those include decriminalizing public drunkenness and possession of lesser quantities of marijuana, deferred sentences, deferred prosecution, wider use of probation, renovation of the existing correctional centers, construction of modular units, and double-bunking. A new diagnostic center is being planned, a new prison is being built, and two cellhouses are being renovated.

During my 12 years in office, I asked for and received funds to build three prison facilities. Those institutions, which will be able to house 1,220 prisoners, will make a significant dent in our overcrowding problem. Another program I instituted deports illegal aliens from Colorado prisons. That program has saved taxpayer money and helped reduce overcrowding.

But much more needs to be done. An alternative approach, not involving traditional bricks and mortar, is worth looking at.

Last year I announced a proposal to implement a "boot camp" program for Colorado's young, non-violent offenders. Such offenders would be given an option of a traditional sentence in a correctional facility, or a much shorter sentence in a Regimented Inmate Discipline program, where they would do hard work in a highly disciplined environment, similar to military training, or "boot camp." The program would save prison space for older, more hardened, more serious criminals. Experience in other states shows the hard work in boot camp motivates young offenders to stay out of future trouble.

Boot camp participants, none older than age 26, would have to be non-violent offenders. They would spend 90 days working hard and doing strenuous physical exercise. The environment is strict and disciplined. There is a dress code and the inmates have limited movement. Participants are rewarded for positive behavior. And boot camp does not eliminate all time spent behind bars — those who choose to do their time in a boot camp would first spend about 30 days in a state prison diagnostic center.

Compared with the $35 million estimated construction cost of building a new prison, a boot camp for 480 prisoners would cost only an estimated $1.5 million to set up.

A few other states, including Georgia and Oklahoma, have tried boot camps. In Georgia, the "shock incarceration" boot camp program is housed right outside the Dodge Correctional Institute. Young offenders can see the future looming over them, should they opt not to change their ways.

The Georgia program was designed to house 50 inmates, but so many offenders have chosen the option, the program was expanded to hold 100 inmates. Georgia now plans a second facility.

Participants in a boot camp concept program are chosen through a placement process. The diagnostic staff selects offenders who are likely to benefit from the experience. Volunteers must be healthy enough, both mentally and physically, to participate in all boot camp programs.

Those would include daily classes including education and vocational study. Assigned work is tailored to fit each individual's needs and those of the facility. In addition to the physical exercise required, volunteers are allotted free time daily to use for recreation, hobbies, sports or group participation.

Boot camp programs ideally are located where there is access to supplies, hospital services and emergency medical facilities. The programs typically have psychological care staff on contract, can offer non-denominational religious services, and should have jail or detention facilities available.

Once an offender finishes the boot camp program, a review board determines the next step. A participant's sentence might be reconsidered to time already served, or an offender might go on probation, parole, intensive supervision, or be transferred to a minimum-security or community corrections facility. Any of those avenues reduces costs below those of traditional prison confinement and eases the overcrowding problem.

The Colorado General Assembly voted down a Colorado corrections boot camp in last spring's legislative session, but offered no other substantive overcrowding alternatives. It is time to take another look.

A boot camp program cannot replace our current prison system. There will always be a need to keep certain, dangerous prisoners away from the public. But boot camp adds flexibility to a prison system that long ago lost whatever elbow room it had.

Other new approaches have been given a go in other states. North Carolina is experimenting with a community work program tailored to each offender. A privately owned prison in Chattanooga has helped to alleviate the overcrowding problem in Tennessee. Some states are imprisoning offenders at home, electronically monitoring them using an ankle bracelet. Others are trying victim restitution programs, where offenders and victims meet and agree on a way of making some recompense.

In a New Jersey program, problem teenagers spend one day listening to intimidating stories told by lifers at the Rahway State Prison. Over 23,000 kids have been through the Lifers Juvenile Awareness Program in its 11 years in operation. The program, which was featured in a television program called "Scared Straight," is designed to shock problem teenagers off the prison-bound path.

Our choices are tough, but at least they're still ours to make. Ignoring prison overcrowding is a luxury we don't have. Failure to address the situation will lead to forced action through the courts — or to explosive behavior among the inmates we must keep secure.

Protecting ourselves from harm costs money, but it's not all that painful. We pay insurance premiums for our homes and cars. We buy safety equipment to engage in numerous sports. We all contribute to our national defense against potential war.

So, too, we must face up to the costs of protecting ourselves from crime — and begin thinking of new ways to keep those costs as low as possible. Our quality of life depends on it.

Chapter 25
Dampening the Mideast Fuse — Resolving Conflicts from Afghanistan to Libya

by Rene V.L. Wadlow
Editor, *Transnational Perspectives*
Geneva, Switzerland

Background. Member of the editorial committee of *Geneve-Afrique*. Represents the International Fellowship of Reconciliation and the World Association of World Federalists to the UN — Geneva. 1964-78, professor and director of Studies of the University Institute of Development Studies at the University of Geneva. 1961-64, an educational advisor to the Ministry of Education of Gabon, equatorial Africa.

His article. The Middle East is a burning fuse for a US-Soviet World War. What conditions are fanning the fuse, and what steps must be taken to disarm it? Penetrating solutions are proposed by a world-minded editor who has followed closely the growing turmoil of the region, from the Soviet invasion of Afghanistan to the US bombing of Libya.

There will be no permanent reduction of conflict in the Arabo-Islamic heartland until there is a reweaving of the social, political and economic fabric . . . until there is a willing and creative interaction with the rest of the world.

Dampening the Mideast Fuse — Resolving Conflicts From Afghanistan to Libya

by Rene V.L. Wadlow

*I*n an article "The Fuse: A Chain of Nations in Conflict" in the *Bulletin of Peace Proposals* (Number 2, 1980) Alan and Hanna Newcombe compared adjacent nations in conflict to a fuse of the bomb which is a US-USSR world war.

"The diffusion of war from nation to nation along the chain is facilitated by certain properties of the chain: geographic adjacency, high military preparedness, substantive conflicts between successive neighbors, a chain of two-against-one alliances which cause each nation to see itself surrounded by enemies, the nuclear or near-nuclear status of many nations along the chain."

The Arabo-Islamic heartland is one such fuse. The zone is in a condition of rapid socio-economic change and political flux. There are two active wars: the USSR vs Afghanistan and Iraq vs Iran. The social weave of Lebanese society has been badly torn and replaced only by violence and sordid bargains between clan chiefs. Tensions between Israel and Syria remain high. There is little progress either to integrate the Palestinians into Israeli society or to create a separate Palestinian state. Chad is divided, with Libya having annexed the north of the country. North-South tensions in Sudan are again acute, and the Horn of Africa is the scene of numerous struggles. The societies of Arabia — Saudi Arabia, the United Arab Emirates, Yemen and the other Gulf states — are fragile, ill-adapted to the modern world, torn by opposing socio-cultural currents. Factions from this Arabo-Islamic heartland are considered prime movers of terrorism both within the heartland and reaching out to Europe.

Both the USA and the USSR consider this zone of instability important to their national interests. Each has tried to make allies but this is the only world area in which there have been reversals of alliances without a total change of regime. Given this instability of alliances, both superpowers keep large war navies off both ends of the heartland — the Indian Ocean and the eastern Mediterranean. The navies play a watching role: replacing land bases. Both superpowers have trained rapid deployment forces so as to be able to get troops into the area as quickly as possible.

Moreover, the Arabo-Islamic heartland is by far the first importer of major conventional weapons and associated military services. Hostility is the order of the day and "my enemy's enemy is my friend" is the first rule of the conflict game. Thus:

•Israel and Syria both support Iran against Iraq while being hostile to each other in Lebanon.

•Iran helps the Iraqi Kurds, and Iraq helps the Iranian Kurds while each state carries out a campaign of mass destruction of its own Kurdish population.

•The Soviets hold the relighting of the Baluchistan revolt in Pakistan as a key card to prevent greater Pakistani support of the Afghan resistance movement while resisting ethnic separatist movements at home.

•In this chain of conflicts there is already one full nuclear-weapon state involved — the USSR.

•Israel is thought to have nuclear weapons capacity, and both Iraq and Pakistan have advanced nuclear programs which could be redirected to military purposes if a political decision were made.

•Iran had, prior to its revolution, an extensive nuclear program which could be recreated.

•Iraq has made and used chemical weapons, indicating that other states in the area with a similar level of technology could also do so.

•Highly sophisticated weapons and aircraft have been sold to countries in this chain, and the Soviets are using increasingly sophisticated weapons against the Afghan resistance and civil population.

Each conflict is a human tragedy in itself with longer range consequences. The loss of life in the Iran-Iraq war is comparable to that of World War I when battlefield deaths were higher than in World War II. As with France and Germany after 1918, the loss of men in their most active years will have long-range social and political consequences in both Iran and Iraq. The systematic destruction of civil life in Afghanistan and the deliberate creation of refugees by the destruction of civilian centers will have long-range consequences even if a negotiated withdrawal of Soviet troops were possible.

Despite the real risk of violence spreading from one conflict to the next and ultimately provoking the USA and the USSR into a major war, efforts to bring any of these conflicts under control have not been successful. Is there anything new which can be done to dampen this fuse effect?

The first step, it seems to me, is a wider awareness of the fuse effect. By looking at only one conflict at a time, the fuse effect has not been given policy consideration. Each state in conflict is naturally preoccupied by its own conflict, and the USA and the USSR are too involved in partisan ways to have an overall strategy.

The United Nations, as yet, has little independent vision other than that of the states involved so that it has not been able to play a coherent role. The minimum that the UN could do is to educate the states involved about the fuse effect so that the states could plan to counteract the dangers of the conflicts linking and spreading. Such planning assumes a degree of rationality that has not yet been evident, but all policy proposals are set out with a hope that decision-making is done on a rational basis.

A wider awareness of the fuse effect should lead to a holistic vision of the problem. The lack of a holistic vision is one of the major weaknesses of nation-state policy-making. A holistic vision would stress three inter-related aspects:

•the wide geographic area and the impact of the extra-regional great powers;

•the many regional factors that interact — the social structures, the economic production, ethnic loyalties, religious convictions, political power struggles, external influences;

•the long time dimension.

Especially in the Arabo-Islamic heartland many attitudes and structures are not easily changed. The continuing impact of the structures of the Ottoman Empire on the area is important. The Ottoman Empire was built on self-governing religious-ethnic communities loyal (or at least subservient) within a multinational empire. The Pan-Arab movements, which were important in breaking up the Empire, were not based on the idea of a nation-state. Rather they stressed the idea of the "Arab Nation" temporarily divided by outside forces into the existing states. A unified "Arab Nation" rather than a federation of existing states was the aim. Running parallel to the Pan-Arab movements has been a Pan-Islamic philosophy which stressed the community of believers rather than loyalty to an established state. Thus the states within the Arabo-Islamic heartland have no legitimacy, and popular loyalty is directed toward a leader rather than toward the state. Leaders often have transnational appeal — as did Nasser, or as does Khomeini.

While attitudes inherited from the past are strong, the socio-political structures of the past have been irrevocably undermined. No area of the world can be cut off from the trends of the future which include world economic integration and transnational cultural and ideological currents.

Thus there is a need for what is likely to be a slow and painful reweaving of the social fabric of the Arabo-Islamic heartland, a social weave that will include many different ethnic groups and religious currents, a weave that will integrate people at very different stages of modernization. This weave of a new society will have to integrate Israel, which is a regional power, in the same way that Israel will have to integrate the Arabo-Islamic culture as a legitimate component of Israeli society.

Likewise a dynamic and renewed Arabo-Islamic heartland will have close relations with the European Community whose economic and cultural drive is a factor of world stability and a motor for Mediterranean regional integration.

The weave of a new Arabo-Islamic society will contain three types of strands: 1) new attitudes, 2) new institutions of consultation, compromise and cooperation, 3) new governmental policies based on compromise and cooperation.

For such a new social fabric to be woven, the USA and the USSR must undertake a policy of continuing consultation and of self-imposed restraint. Such self-restraint would be an agreement to refrain from expanding or establishing new military bases in the region, to refrain from expanding the naval buildup in the eastern Mediterranean, the Red Sea and the Indian Ocean, to avoid the proliferation or development of nuclear weapons in the area, and to scale down the supply of weapons to the area. Such an agreement of US-USSR self-restraint is the minimum needed to stop the processes of socio-political disintegration.

Closely linked to such a policy of self-restraint is the need to create regional institutions in which all states of the area may participate fully. For the moment, the United Nations is the only such universalistic body. Thus efforts must arise from the United Nations, complemented by regional organizations, national action and the forces of as yet unstructured world public opinion.

For such new policies of compromise and cooperation to be able to take hold, there must be a reduction of violence in the area, especially violence which has a highly destabilizing effect.

The Soviet invasion of Afghanistan at the start of the new decade of the 1980s has transformed a rather traditional struggle for power within Afghanistan into an international conflict. The shock waves from the Soviet attack have had wide impact which will continue until there is a withdrawal of Soviet troops. In an issue of *Transnational Perspectives* devoted to "Afghanistan: Proposals for Peace" (Volume 9, Number 1, 1983) I set out what I believe to be a growing consensus as to the necessary elements in a realistic Afghan settlement.

1. A Regional Security Conference. The Soviet actions have transformed an internal conflict into an international one. Other countries, especially Pakistan and Iran, feel insecure. Therefore a Regional Security Conference is a necessary prerequisite for an internal settlement within Afghanistan and for Soviet troop withdrawal. Such a Regional Security Conference would bring together the representatives of the permanent members of the UN Security Council, Pakistan, Iran, India, perhaps Turkey which has had historic links with Afghanistan, representatives of the current Afghan government and the resistance movements. All the bilateral tensions among the states of the region cannot be resolved at one conference, though it is sure that better relations between India and Pakistan and an end to the Iran-Iraq war would be useful steps toward security in the whole area. Such a security conference would re-affirm the territorial integrity of Afghanistan, its non-aligned status, as well as the willingness of all to let the Afghans settle their internal disputes without direct intervention.

2. An orderly return of refugees. There are currently over four million refugees in Pakistan, Iran and smaller groups in other countries. There must be a procedure supervised by the United Nations for the orderly return of refugees so that all can participate in finding a basis for a government of national reconciliation. The refugees must be disarmed by the UN representatives as they return so that violence will not be a major factor in an internal settlement.

3. A broadly-based, highly decentralized Government of National Reconciliation.

Afghanistan is a country of great cultural diversity and a wide range of local conditions. Therefore political and social decision-making must be made at the most local level possible. There should be policies of local self-reliance based on existing regional and ethnic structures. Such local self-government will mitigate against the "winner-take-all" mentality of centralized political systems. All governments directed from Kabul, no matter what the ideological tendency, have met resistance from some of the provinces. Thus the internal solution within Afghanistan can come only by reducing to the greatest extent possible the power of the central government and by shifting decision-making to the local unit. Each village can thus decide its land tenure patterns, its educational policies, the changes in social relations wished, the degree of socialist or Islamic ideology it desires. The struggles for political and social power will shift. An effort to control the policies of the central government will become an attempt to control local and regional decision-making. The result will be a recognition of local diversities. If the central government in Kabul has very reduced power to set policies for the whole country, there will be less incentive to try and capture power in Kabul. It will be easier to have a government of national reconciliation made up of representatives from all regions, ethnic groups and political tendencies.

The withdrawal of Soviet troops and the establishment of a broadly based government of national reconciliation would help to delink the adjacent conflicts and thus dampen the fuse.

There will be no permanent reduction of conflict in the Arabo-Islamic heartland until there is a reweaving of the socio-economic and political fabric, until there are democratic and representative institutions put into place, until there is a willing and creative interaction with the rest of the world. However ending armed conflict and creating a regional security community in which all people feel safe is a basic requirement for the reweaving process to take place.

THE FINAL CHAPTER: CONSENSUS

To help pull together the diverse ideas of this book, several main ideas were extracted from each chapter, compiled into a questionnaire, and mailed off to the authors ... in hopes of achieving a degree of consensus on solving today's problems.

Despite three obstacles — the complexity of the ideas, the limitations of the written word, and the fact that everyone views life and the world a bit differently — the survey produced many important and interesting results.

The original survey contained 120 major points. The authors (all but four participated) rated their reaction to each issue on a seven-point scale:

I strongly agree (3 points)
I think so (2 points)
It makes sense (1 point)
No opinion (0)
I'm skeptical (-1)
I think not (-2)
I strongly disagree (-3)

Herein are the results of about half the issues — the half that drew the heartiest agreement. The number in parentheses after each issue indicates the total points after all authors' responses were tallied up. A "66" would indicate that all authors were in complete agreement with a given issue. The highest mark recorded was "65" which, though not a "perfect" mark, nevertheless indicates very strong consensus. Not surprisingly, that consensus was on the need to apply world-level efforts toward ending wars, resolving international conflict, and eliminating the arms race.

Authors were invited to write in additional comments wherever on the form they happened to have had strong opinions. Some of their comments are added below *(in italics)*.

From the Book Introduction

Society is in levels — individuals, families and companies within municipalities, within provinces or cantons or counties, within states and nations. To achieve peace, we need to pursue it at all levels. (53) *Marc Nerfin is uncomfortable with the term "levels," which implies a hierarchy. He prefers "spaces."*

From Part One

One vital step toward peace is to improve communication at all levels of human life — within us, among us and throughout world society at all levels. (63)

People tend to assume, often mistakenly, that their messages are clearly understood by others. Faulty communication and misinformation can cause conflict. (51)

Clear interpersonal communication requires a neutral, objective attitude on the part of the listener. It also requires on the part of the speaker the cultivated psychological skill of forming a message so that listeners will comprehend, accept, believe, and be ready to cooperate when necessary. (55)

Desirable values for better communication don't always come naturally to people; they must be cultivated purposefully and systematically in young people. That should be one job of the schools, among other institutions. (58)

Young people should learn at least two languages — their native tongue and an international language — English, Russian, Spanish, French or Chinese. (45) *Marc Nerfin would add Arabic to the list.*

onsensus Telecommunications technology will continue to play a growing role in effective worldwide communication, with such advances as fiberoptic telephone networks, computers, and communication satellites. (43) *Five authors warned, however, that the improved communication could enhance peace or stimulate conflict, depending on the types of information dispersed on the burgeoning global network, how it is regulated, and by whom.*

There is a need for international or global communication standards (such as the ISDN standards now being developed by an international body — CCITT) that will allow computers built and programmed in one place to communicate with any other computers. (43)

From Part Two

Another vital step toward peace is to learn the nature of wise, humane regulation ... again, at all levels of human life — from self-control, parental responsibilities and corporate management at the more basic levels of society, to sensible regulation of nations and humanity at large. (53)

Self-control. As Gandhi said, we must stop this desire to endlessly increase our wants. For peace and comfort, and for a future of our planet and species, we need training to promote generosity, wisdom and love. (46) *Howard Richards says, "This is true, but I wonder whether people are ready to hear it and whether it will be understood. Some people may reject the idea as mere sentiment." Caesar Voute adds, "It is difficult to change human nature." Tobi Dress, expressing concern about words like generosity, wisdom and. love: "They mean different things to every person. Everyone thinks their actions are based on these ideals."*

We should all cultivate a peaceful way of life:

• Avoid frustrating others.

• Break the chains of aggression around you with honesty.

• Redefine power as competence, not domination.

• Don't corner people during negotiations; provide "yesable" propositions. (45)

Cultivate in children a sense of responsibility in order to avoid authoritarianism. Inner-directed responsibility is far more legitimate, appealing and effective than duty imposed from the outside. If individuals are not trained to look to the good of others, then an external power steps in to curb the greed and bring about collective good. (49)

Qualities of legitimate regulation. As stated in Ashby's Law of Requisite Variety, regulators of a group (whether in city government, in corporate management, or in national government) must reflect the variety of the system they regulate in order to be of service to it (or to be legitimate). (45)

Regulation and decision-making occur at all levels. Most should occur at the lowest, most local level (personal, family, community). (58)

There are two basic rules for deciding who should regulate what. Legitimate regulation is initiated 1) at the lowest or most local possible level, but 2) high enough as to be responsible for all those (and only those) who are affected by the decisions. (49)

It has become an interdependent world. (57) *John Fobes points out that it has been an interdependent world. Now it is becoming moreso.*

For solving some problems in the modern world, sovereignty of nations is not appropriate. (52) *John Fobes reiterates, "Sovereignty never really existed." Archie Bahm feels the statement would be more properly worded, " . . . sovereignty of nations must be challenged." Tobi Dress notes that newly independent Third World countries "cherish their newly acquired sovereignty."*

Public and private institutions are needed at every level. We need international institutions with the authority to cope with global problems while preserving basic sovereignty and cultural diversity. (58)

Global standards and values would do at the world level what building codes, zoning ordinances and traffic lights do at the community level, and what household rules do at the family level. They would provide greater peace and order in the dealings of nations, transnational corporations, and other large social systems. Decisions of the World Court and many policies of the United Nations family of organizations are examples of global values.

If we were going to devise a detailed set of global standards and values to help regulate certain unstable aspects of the world situation, they should have certain characteristics to be legitimate. For example, they would:

1. Provide decent living standards and ecological balance worldwide. (52)

2. Be flexible enough to be tailored to local conditions. (53) *"Within reason," cautions Pat Mische. "Certain standards such as prohibition of torture should not be flexible."*

World cooperation is a prerequisite to relaxed tensions and detente. (43) *Hanna Newcombe expresses uncertainty as to which comes first — cooperation or relaxed tensions. Rene Wadlow agrees, "I think the two must be pursued. There are certain tensions that can be reduced now by negotiation; others need a process of cooperation."*

What areas of human endeavor might be subject to global standards and values . . . with the understanding that these standards and values, whenever possible, would meet the above guidelines?

•environmental problems (acid rain, pollution of oceans, destruction of the ozone layer, radiation fallout, destruction of rain forests, etc.) (61)

•world trade (51) *Howard Richards: "Needs regulation, not with the aim of having as much of it as possible."*

•energy (54)

•ending wars, resolving conflicts, eliminating the arms race (65)

•raw materials (49)

•food (57)

•international debt crisis (54)

•terrorism and international drug trafficking (57)

•*Chellis Glendinning adds "Women's rights" to the list.*

•Space technology. We need cooperative space programs to benefit all humanity. Space applications are by their nature regional and global in scope. We need a holistic approach to space rather than the random, piecemeal methods that have occurred since Sputnik. Two basic objectives for space research should be to promote trust and confidence among nations, and to promote cooperative development efforts. (49) *Jan van der Linden adds, "Some healthy competition is also good."*

Space technology applications of a global nature include 1) earth observation (surveying and mapping, resource inventory, observation of changing phenomena and routine processes), 2) satellite communications, 3) space manufacturing and medicine, and 4) navigation systems for ships and planes. (43)

Moral issues as well as intellectual, scientific and technological issues must be part of a global space plan. Space must satisfy the needs of humanity and global management on one hand, and equal rights and optimal opportunities for the individual on the other hand. (41) *Howard Richards: "I'm especially worried about the effect of satellite communications on local cultures."*

•Economics. Karl Marx and Adam Smith provided theories for the modern industrialized world (centrally planned economies and market economies, respectively), but these theories were based on realities of the past, not accounting for nuclear energy, chemical industries, environmental deterioration, and other modern realities. New economic theories are needed. (45) *Hanna Newcombe adds, "Also some ancient ones, like Buddhist economics." Gerald Mische: "Present theories have much that remains valid (marxist, capitalist, socialist, etc.)"*

What is needed for better international coordination and world governance?

Just as each of us has an inner map of reality to guide us in our day-to-day lives, and just as every cohesive social group or nation has its own map or model of reality accepted to some degree by its members, we now need to devise a world framework or paradigm or model that accurately reflects a complex, changing world marked by great diversity among nations, religions and cultures. (52) *Caesar Voute: "Pluriformity is difficult to include in one world framework or model." The Misches caution that there can be no "final," unchanging model toward which world order evolves; rather the model must follow along behind the development, reflecting the growing world order.*

The United Nations needs to be revitalized and/or restructured. (54) The UN should:

Focus on several vital areas by doing such basic things as monitoring nature and societies, facilitating the spread of ideas, promoting
education and understanding among cultures, and steering a world society in transition. (46)

Have an independent secretariat, as originally intended. (53)

From Part Three

Our beliefs lead our actions. We each have a unique inner map or

mental model of reality which helps shape our perspectives, attitudes and behavior. (58)

Nations also have an overall map of reality which citizens accept to some degree and use as part of their personal map, and this helps shape their perception of other nations and the world. Collectively held unconscious beliefs shape the world's institutions and are at the root of institutionalized oppression and inequity. (47)

Because of limited human knowledge of the overall scheme of things, all these versions of reality probably have some flaws. Many of the realities are incompatible with others ... and the incompatibilities often lead to conflict. Hence there are many changes and transformations that will inevitably occur at many levels of our lives as we move toward greater peace. (54) Several authors balked at the term "transformation," preferring such terms as "evolution" and "emergence."

When changes are needed in our personal view of our groups view of reality, sometimes crisis causes the vital change. Examples at the personal level are alcoholism and mid-life crisis. Examples at the world level are the debt crisis and the destruction of rain forests. (50)

We need to teach children about the UN and the world. Encourage them to devise and explore alternatives to modern realities. (53)

Most of the world is a patriarchal society dominated by male values. Women's reality of connection, communication, and relationship must be nurtured at this crucial point in history. (45)

For greater personal peace and social order, men and women each must work to develop their opposite side to become more complete individuals. This is a vital step toward humanity becoming a more complete social system — bridging the chasm between traditional masculine and feminine roles. (44)

We need to broaden our perspective on life. Most people think of the present and near future, not the distant future. They think of their immediate environment, community and to some degree maybe their nation and humanity, but not the nonhuman plants, animals and ecosystems. People centuries from now are real and we need to sense this. Ecosystems are vital to our present and future well-being, and we need to sense this. We need to regain our sense of oneness with the planet and all its living parts. (48)

From Part Four

Two world situations merit special attention — East vs. West, and North vs. South. (East refers generally to socialist countries with centrally planned economies. West refers generally to the capitalist-democratic, capitalist-socialist and other countries with market economies. North refers to East and West collectively. South refers generally to the Third World, or nonaligned countries.) (48)

Greater East-West and North-South economic cooperation is needed. (52) *Jan van der Linden: "But not only as handouts of money and physical resources, but as developmental aid and training."*

The modern economic structure throughout much of the North is based on a dangerous assumption that ever-increasing wants should be continually satisfied by ever-increasing production and organization. (43)

Reliance of industrialized countries on Third World resources causes fierce competition among the rich and mistrust between the rich and poor countries. (47)

Nations collectively should establish priorities for resource usage with health, food, environment and education placed higher than military and space research. (51) *Howard Richards: "Yes, but nations usually don't congeal their domestic economies enough to fix priorities."*

Nations collectively and independently should reexamine consumption levels and eliminate waste. (56)

In extreme poverty situations, more equal distribution is vital. (45)

A political-economic body or system has the obligation to serve human needs and values in the course of its activities. When it fails to meet this obligation, it ought to be judged and corrected. (47) *"By whom?" wonders Chellis Glendinning.*

Wise economic management means managing the profit motive to meet human needs. (44)

A growing economy is not necessarily a healthy economy. In reality, healthy growth is the result of wise planning and sound decisions made at the most local levels of society that can take into account the needs and concerns of all people and groups who will be affected by the growth. (42)

Technology is the fruit of science; science is the seed. Sending technology to the Third World without science helps keep the Third World dependent upon the industrialized world. (40)

According to recent figures, one nuclear submarine costs about $2 billion, enough to fund 500 Third World research centers for a year. If that is true, we need to adjust our priorities. (56)

Nations together should form a large North-South science foundation to fund research by Third World scientists. (40)

From Part Five

Most traditional conflict resolution systems (such as judicial systems in a nation, or military action among nations) are adversarial, based on win-lose outcomes. In reality, all sides usually have merits which should become part of the solution. A facilitator or neutral third party helping in confidentiality can make a fair, equitable, mutually agreeable outcome more likely, whether it is a husband and wife, or two neighbors, or two nations in conflict. (51)

We need to define and adopt nonviolent ways to solve conflict. We could all be benefitted by learning the skills of mediation, conciliation and arbitration for practical use in our day-to-day lives. There are common features of conflict at all levels. Skills of the facilitator should be learned. (56)

Young people should learn an awareness of conflicts and methods of solving them. We need standards for teaching and applying the skills of mediation, conciliation and arbitration at all levels of social life, · from interpersonal to global. (53)

Meanwhile, we must deal with the symptoms of conflict at all levels. In society those symptoms include growing crime rates and crowded prisons. There will always be a need to keep certain dangerous individuals away from the public. Many young offenders, however, deserve a second chance to change their values and behavior before being removed to prison life. Young, nonviolent offenders should have an option — a traditional sentence in prison with hardened criminals, or a shorter sentence in a special disciplined program similar to military boot camp. This could help motivate young offenders to avoid future trouble and reserve more prison space for hardened criminals. (45) *Howard Richards likes the realism of the boot camp idea, asserting "We need basic discipline." Hanna Newcombe would go a step further: "Better still, (have the offenders) do service for the victims."*

To resolve Mideast issues, we need to take an overall look at all the conflicts in the region, moreso than analyzing them separately. (46) *Hanna Newcombe: "Sometimes it's better to fractionate conflict."*

What Can We Do at the Grassroots Level?

Realize that our actions are important. Big changes occur when many people change their minds just a little. It takes a "critical mass" of individuals to move society. The future of the world rests not on one or a few sets of shoulders, but on ALL our shoulders. (49) *Gerald Mische points out, however, that "actions of a few leaders can also affect great change."*

Link up and network with others. Networks or cobwebs reach across levels and boundaries to enhance communication and cohesion. Concerned individuals need to cross national, cultural, religious, ideological boundaries to cooperate. Link up with national and international groups. (57)

Be active. Peace begins at home but can't end there, for the links of interdependence are too strong. Individuals must act. We cannot be "free riders" as the world strives for a just future. People can pressure their governments and link up locally with other world order thinkers. (48)

Other Issues of the Survey

The above issues are those in the original survey which received strongest agreement by the authors. A few other issues deserve mention. The idea that drew the greatest contrast was, "The UN should be transformed into world government by equipping it legally and materially with enforcement power." Some authors added enthusiastic comments of support (there were even a few stars and exclamation points written in). Other authors strongly disagreed, but added no comments. In the final tally, this issue received only 17 points because of several strong disagreements. Perhaps Caesar Voute summed it up most succinctly: "Too early." Or Jan van der Linden: "Step by step. First more consensus."

consensus

Nearly all authors see the need for more regulatory authority to be transferred from the national to the world level, but most were reluctant to commit to that general statement without qualifications, such as how the transfer will occur, what types of activities should be subject to the world-level regulation ... and, in the words of Pat Mische, "This must not be taken to mean a global swallowing of poorer countries, and their cultural obliteration."

There is a skepticism toward technology as a panacea to world problems because of its tendency to enhance or amplify *all* aspects of our nature . . . not just our creative, helpful side but also our destructive, compulsive side. Most authors generally laud the role of telecommunications in smooth worldwide communication, but at the same time worry that the messages and those who control them could pose great harm to many people if the information does not account for international, intercultural differences and is not in the best interests of humanity and the world. Almost as many authors laud the role of space technology in providing us a more objective view and better understanding of our planet, but at the same time worry that we may use the vast potentials of space to live out our distrustful nature and aggressive tendencies as well as our desire to cooperate in improving and expanding our lives and our world.

Author Joszef Bognar (Hungary) stated in his article that there is a degree of "backwardness in mechanization, in technology, and in sophistication . . . " in the East due largely to tightly centralized regulation. The statement drew cautious mixed reactions from authors in the West. Gerald Mische says it "depends how we define backwardness." Pat Mische adds that any "backwardness" may be due also to a "slow start; they were far behind the West at the turn of the century, with masses of poor illiterate." All told, this issue of backwardness received only 19 points.

MORE ABOUT
THE AUTHORS

Ahmad Abubakar has served as consultant, planning officer and official in the service of the Nigerian government. He currently is deputy director of the Centre on Integrated Rural Development for Africa (CIRDAFRICA).

Born Nov. 27, 1948 in Nigeria, he received a B.Sc. degree in economics from the University of Ibadan (Nigeria) and his M.A. degree from Vanderbilt University in Nashville, Tennessee. He also attended the International Institute of Management in Bucharest, Romania.

His career has included consultancy services to state governments, serving as senior planning officer and later deputy chief planning officer for the Bauchi state government; permanent secretary of the Ministry of Economic Planning; general manager of the Bauchi State Investment and Property Development Co.

Mr Abubakar also represented the Bauchi state government on the Committee of the National Economic Council (1982-83), which advised on solutions to then prevailing economic problems of Nigeria. He is a member of the Nigerian Economic Society, the Monthly Review Associates (USA), and the International Foundation for Development Alternatives.

He has attended numerous conferences and workshops on planning held in Egypt, India, Malaysia, Japan, Brazil and various countries in Africa.

Articles and papers include *The Economics, Politics, and Administration of Plan Implementation, CIRDAFRICA and Africa's New Development Strategy, Development Priorities and Needs of Rural Populations* (written for the 9th World Forestry Congress in Mexico, 1985); *Hadeja Local Government: Continuity and Change after 1976 Reform.*

Prachoomsuk Achava-Amrung, a native of Thailand, pursues a career in education and world peace activities that has been recognized internationally.

She received a B.S. degree in chemistry in Thailand, a master's degree in education administration and supervision and her Ed.D. in economics of education and research methodology, both in the United States.

Mrs Amrung has been chairman/president/director of many research projects and education organizations on the university level in Thailand and for the Thailand government including general supervisor of ministry of education, head of the departments of Education Research and Foundation of Education, dean of faculty of Education at Chulalongkorn University.

Active in world peace organizations, she has been a member and served in an official capacity in many organizations, including the International Association of Educators for World Peace (IAEWP), a non-governmental organization of the United Nations; Emergency World Council, the Netherlands; Bangkok Humanity Symposium; and in 1977 became a Registered World Citizen, Washington, D.C.

Mrs Amrung is also an author, editor, and translator of books and professional publications. Among honors bestowed upon her for her work and publications are:

First Class the Most Noble Order of the Crown of Siam (1974); Honorary Citizen of the City of Huntsville, Alabama, USA (1975); Biographee of the International Biographical Dictionary, United Kingdom (1976); First Class the Most Exalted Order of the White Elephant (1976); Biographee, Who's Who in the World, USA (1978); International Who's Who of Intellectual, IBC, UK (1981); official candidate, UNESCO Peace Prize (1983); and Honorary Doctorate degree in philosophy of education, Nigeria (1985).

She is married to Col. Kluen Achava-Amrung and has four daughters.

Archie John Bahm (rhymes with game), a humanist, has said, "Mankind's doomsday can be postponed if we reduce population, eliminate waste of resources and pollution, overcome obsolete religious fanaticism, and achieve a minimal world government. Growing demoralization may be reversed and loss of direction revitalized by adopting a needed world philosophy informed by a quantum-leap system-gesalt generated by understanding the intricately complicated interdependencies at all levels of existence made obvious by our contemporary crises."

Mr Bahm has written articles and reviews for many publications on ethics, philosophy and religion. He has been editor and publisher of the biennial *Director of American Philosophers* since 1962, and served as editor and advisory board member of numerous philosophical, humanist, and scientific journals and periodicals.

Born Aug. 21, 1907 in Imlay City, Michigan, Mr Bahm received his A.B. degree from Albion College, and M.A. and Ph.D. from the University of Michigan.

He worked briefly as a reporter before joining in 1934 the staff of the now Texas Tech University. From 1946-48 he was associate professor of philosophy at the University of Denver (Colorado), and then professor of philosophy at the University of New Mexico until 1973 when he became professor emeritus. He was a visiting lecturer in philosophy at the University of Rangoon 1955-56, and at the University of Rhode Island in 1964.

Mr Bahm was a Fulbright research scholar at the University of Rangoon (1955-56) and at Benares Hindu University (1962-63). He received the Humanist of the Year award in 1963 from the Albuquerque (New Mexico) Chapter of the American Humanist Association.

His memberships include International Metaphysical Society, American Philosophical Association, Metaphysical Society of America, Indian Congress of Philosophy (life member), Southwestern Philosophical Society (organizer, 1935), Mountain-Plains Philosophical Conference (organizer, 1947), New Mexico Philosophical Society (organizer, 1949), Phi Beta Kappa, Phi Kappa Phi, Phi Sigma Tau, and member of the 10th, 11th, 13th, 14th, 15th and 16th International Congresses of Philosophy.

More about the authors ***Jozsef Bognar,*** a native of Hungary, is an economist whose career has included teaching, writing and politics, for which he was awarded the Hungarian State Prize in 1970 as well as several Hungarian and foreign medals.

Born Feb. 5, 1917 in Szombathely, he was educated in Budapest, his studies including literature and philosophy at Eotvos Lorand University. He is a university professor of economics, president of the Hungarian Scientific Council for World Economy, director of the Institute for World Economics of the Hungarian Academy of Sciences.

Professional positions he has held include Minister of Information, Mayor of Budapest, Minister of Internal and Foreign Trade, President of the Institute for Cultural Relations; member of the Hungarian Parliament, chairman of the committee for Planning and Budget, member of the Hungarian Academy of Sciences, editor-in-chief of *Studies on Developing Countries* and *Trends in World Economy.*

Mr Bognar has been a member of (and held offices in) numerous societies, including Hungarian World Alliance, Hungarian Patriotic People's Front, Hungarian Economic Association, Club of Rome, World Academy of Art and Science, International Social Prospects Academy (Geneva), IFIAS Panel of Special Advisors, UNITAR'S Advisory Panel on Research, Scientific Committee Instituto di Studi e Documentazione sull 'Est Europeo, Trieste; editorial board of *Mondes en Development* and *The Asian Journal of Economics,* and honorary editorial advisory board of *World Development.*

He has published numerous articles and studies on economics in Hungarian and foreign publications.

John W. Burton — author, teacher, researcher and economist — was born Feb. 3, 1915 in Melbourne, Australia.

He received his B.A. degree in 1937 in Sydney, a Ph.D. (Economics in the Faculty of Economics)in 1942 in London, and a D.Sc. degree (1970) in international relations, also in London.

From 1937-1951 his career in public service for Australia included work for the commerce department; Australia House, London; research in the statisticians department; Department of Labour, post-war reconstruction; the Foreign Office, and High Commission Ceylon.

In 1960 Mr Burton began his research and teaching career, spending 1960-63 at the National University, Canberra (Rockefeller grantee). He has also been affiliated with the University of London, University of Kent, University of Maryland, and since 1985 the George Mason University where he is the distinguished visiting professor, Center for Conflict Resolution.

Among the conferences he has participated in are Food and Agriculture(1943), ILO (1944), United Nations Charter Conference (1945), Paris Peace Conference (1946), Commonwealth Prime Ministers' Conferences (1945-48, Delhi Conference on Indonesia (1949), Philippine Conference on Asian Relations (1950), and Bandung Conference (1955).

His published works include: *The Alternative* (Australian relations with Asia, published in 1954), *Peace Theory* (1962), *International Relations* (published in 1965 and reprinted several times, in Spanish in 1973); *Systems, States, Diplomacy and Rules* (1968, reprinted in Japanese in 1970); *Conflict and Communication* (1969); *World Society* (1972, reprinted in Dutch in 1974 and in the United Kingdom in 1977); *The Study of World Society: A London Perspective* (1974); *Deviance, Terrorism and War: A Study of Process in the Solving of Unsolved Social and Political Problems* (1979); *Dear Survivors* (1982); *Global Conflict* (1983); *Procedures of Facilitated International Conflict Resolution* (1986); and *Conflict Resolution, Theory and Practice* (1986).

Keith Clarke's engineering career has moved him among exciting, new technologies in their early stages of development — computer time-sharing, computer graphics, computer-aided design (CAD), videotex, and the ISDN standard. Born in London, England, in 1940, he studied electrical engineering at the University of Bradford and computer science at Imperial College, London.

After training with the General Electric Company at Coventry, his first job with Central Government in the Ministry of Technology led to a life-long interest in national and international technical standards, as he became involved in the burgeoning time-sharing industry, and was responsible for setting up the Ministry of Technology's Time Sharing Centre.

At Dollis Hill he worked on the introduction of computer graphics and CAD facilities in the Post Office Research laboratories. Soon afterward, Sam Fedida arrived at Dollis Hill and produced his pioneering report on "Viewdata" (which later became known around the world as "Videotex"). Involvement in the first experiments with this project gradually drew Mr Clarke deeper into the new technology as he rose through management positions to head the newly formed Viewdata Division in what had become British Telecom Research Laboratories. He engineered the installation of Prestel, the world's first videotex service and he was particularly concerned with the defense internationally of the UK and European videotex standards.

He is a fellow of the Institution of Electrical Engineers, the British Computer Society and the British Institute of Management. Professional publications and lectures number about 50 in the fields of computer time sharing, computer aided design, viewdata, cable TV and the ISDN.

Keith, his wife Barbara and their two children live in Martlesham, an attractive rural county of Suffolk, England. He enjoys family interests, in particular parent-teacher activities, and still finds time to indulge his hobby of "messing about in boats and exploring the extensive network of rivers and canals in England."

Tobi P. Dress, executive director of the International Senior Forum for Peace (ISFP), has distinguished herself in a career of law and peace activities.

She graduated from the Northeastern University (Boston) in 1968, received a B.A. degree in anthropology in 1970 from the University of Maryland, Juris Doctor degree in 1977 from the American University, Georgetown University, and was admitted to the District of Columbia Bar in 1978.

Ms Dress's area of proficiency include law and policy of disarmament, peace and arms control; conflict resolution/mediation; international non-profit management; and media/public relations for non-profit agencies.

Positions include executive director for the ISFP (a United Nations affiliate organization), adjunct professor at the Loyola Law School (Law and policy of arms control and disarmament); regional assistant director/acting director of CARE, Inc. (an international relief and development agency); attorney/managing attorney for the US Federal Trade Commission, attorney/policy analyst/mediator-conciliator for the Interstate Commerce Commission; attorney/researcher for the Presidential Clemency Board; consultant and assistant to the president of McCleod Corporation, and senior law clerk in the US Department of Justice, LEAA, office of general counsel.

She has participated in legal and peace conferences in the USA and abroad including Sao Paulo, Brazil and London.

Ms Dress's memberships and interests include the District of Columbia Bar Assn., Los Angeles World Affairs Council, Washington Independent Writers, Washington Women in Film, National Peace Education Fund, National Association for Female Executives, Amnesty International, Advisory Board of Odyssey House Drug Rehabilitation Program.

John Edwin Fobes a distinguished American diplomat and scholar, was born March 16, 1918 in Chicago, Illinois. He received a B.Sc. (cum laude) degree from Northwestern (Illinois) University and his M.A. degree from the Fletcher School of Law and Diplomacy in Medford, Mass. He was awarded a Doctor of Humanities, Honoris

Causa, from Bucknell University in 1973.

While serving with the US Army Air Force (1942-46), he rose in rank from private to major, and from 1945-46 he served in the UN secretariat in London and New York.

Following military service he was an analyst for the Bureau of the Budget in Washington, D.C., assistant director for technical assistance of the Marshall Plan, deputy director of organization and planning for the National Security Agency, adviser with the US delegation to NATO and European Regional Organizations (Paris), director of the Office of International Administration for the Department of State, program officer and deputy director for the US Aid Mission to India (New Delhi), assistant director-general and later director-general for administration, UNESCO (Paris), lecturer at the University of North Carolina, adjunct professor of political science at Western Carolina University, and president of Castalia Associates (Webster, North Carolina), consulting in the field of international cooperation.

He has been a visiting scholar at Indiana, North Carolina, Duke and Harvard Universities; chairman and vice chairman of the US National Commission for UNESCO, and consultant for the Intergovernmental Bureau for Informatics.

Chellis Glendinning is a psychologist and a pioneer developer of psychological approaches to living in the Nuclear Age. She founded the first organization of mental health professionals offering help for nuclear-related distress, and co-founded the international network Interhelp. She is the author of *Waking Up in the Nuclear Age* (1987) and numerous magazine articles and book chapters.

Ms Glendinning attended Smith College, was graduated (Phi Beta Kappa) from the University of California at Berkeley, and received her doctorate in psychology from Columbia Pacific University.

She was introduced to her life's work, involvement in social change, at an early age helping her political activist mother by licking stamps and collating packets. In the late 1960s she became involved in the peace movement and in the early 1970s in the feminist movement.

She was one of several who originated what has come to be known as Despair and Empowerment Work — psychological approaches to becoming active in a tenuous world. The work is now fostered by the organization Interhelp and practiced all over the USA, Japan, Australia and Europe.

Ms Glendinning is a Fellow at Peace and Common Security Institute (PACS) in San Francisco; on the board of advisors of Interhelp; the community board of advisors of the Peace and Conflict Studies at the University of California at Berkeley; and a Peer at the Elmwood Institute (Berkeley).

Willis W. Harman, engineer and scientist, is president of the Institute of Noetic Sciences (Sausalito, California). Founded in 1973 by Astronaut Edgar Mitchell, the Institute's purpose is to expand knowledge of the nature and potentials of the mind, and apply that knowledge to the advancement of health and well-being for humankind and the planet Earth.

Mr Harman also is senior social scientist at SRI International of Menlo Park, California. For 16 years, he says, he "had the unusual privilege of working essentially full time exploring the national and global future." The Future's Research Group he founded at Stanford Research Institute has worked on long-term strategic planning and policy analysis for an assortment of corporations, national governments and international agencies.

Mr Harman is professor of engineering-economic systems at Stanford University, and a member of the Board of Regents of the University of California.

He received a B.S. degree in electrical engineering from the University of Washington, and his M.S. in physics and Ph.D. in electrical engineering from Stanford University in 1948. He taught for several years at the University of Florida before joining the Stanford faculty in 1952.

He was a Fulbright lecturer on statistical communication theory at the Royal Technical University of Copenhagen in 1959.

Through the 1960s Mr Harman was active in the newly formed Association of Humanistic Psychology, serving as a member of the executive board and as a member of the editorial board of the Journal of Humanistic Psychology. He was a member of the Commerce Technical Advisory board serving the US Department of Commerce from 1973-77.

Mr Harman is the author of numerous texts and papers in various aspects of electrical and systems engineering, futures research, social policy and analysis, and the current societal transition.

He was listed as an "exemplary Futurist" in the World Future

Society's reference work *The Study of the Future* (1977). His many published works include *An Incomplete Guide to the Future*, *Changing Images of Man* (co-authored with O.W. Markley), and *Higher Creativity* (co-authored with Howard Rheingold).

Louis Kriesberg has had an impressive career as scholar, professor, researcher and author. Born July 30, 1926 in Chicago, Illinois, he earned a Ph.B. degree (with honors in the Social Sciences) in 1947 from the University of Chicago and an M.A. (Phi Beta Kappa) and Ph.D. from the University of Chicago, Department of Sociology. He also has attended Columbia University, the University of California at Berkeley, and School of Advanced International Studies at Johns Hopkins University.

Mr Kriesberg has been a professor in the department of sociology at Syracuse University since 1966, and has served on many university committees.

Prior to joining the staff at Syracuse University, he was a senior study director for the National Opinion Research Center, and research associate, for the Department of Sociology, the University of Chicago; a Senior Fellow in law and the behavior sciences, the University of Chicago Law School; a Fulbright research scholar associated with the University of Cologne, Germany, and a sociology instructor at Columbia University. Other professional positions include having served as book review editor, associate editor and board member of various publications.

Mr Kriesberg has been listed in *American Men and Women of Science*, *Who's Who in the East*, *International Scholar's Directory*, *Dictionary of International Biography*, *International Who's Who in the Sociology*, *Men of Achievement*, *International Soziologen Lexikon*, and *World Who's Who of Authors*.

He is a member of and active in many professional organizations among them the Consortium on Peace Research Education and Development, American Association of University Professors, Union of International Associations, American Professors for Peace in the Middle East, Inter-University Seminar on Armed Forces and Society, International Studies Association, and International Peace Research Association.

More about the authors

He has written extensively — books, research monographs, articles, and chapters in books — and has presented numerous papers at state, regional, national and international professional meetings.

Mr Kriesberg has lived in Mexico, Germany, Israel, France, and visited in Kenya, the USSR, Central America, Egypt and most European countries.

Ricard D. Lamm has served as governor of the state of Colorado (USA) three terms (1974-1986), and has spoken out on many quality-of-life issues and problems — high cost of medical care, overcrowding of prisons, air and water pollution, illegal aliens, to mention a few. He has delved into these problems in his recently-published books: *The Angry West* (written with Michael McCarthy); *Pioneers and Politicians* (with Duane A. Smith); *Megatraumas: America in the Year 2000;* and *The Immigration Time Bomb: The Fragmenting of America* (with Gary Imhoff).

Prior to being elected governor, Mr Lamm was a member of the Colorado House of Representqtives (1966-74), and active in the political organizations of Young Democrats and Denver Young Democrats.

During his years as governor he served as chairman of various committees of the National Governors' Association and was the head Governor of the association's task force on tax reform. He was also chairman of the Western Governors' Association and chairman of the group's policy office.

Mr Lamm was selected one of *Time* magazine's "200 Young Leaders of America" in 1974, and won the *Christian Science Monitor*'s *Peace 2010* essay competition in 1985.

Born Aug. 3, 1935 in Madison, Wisconsin, Lamm received a B.B.A. degree from the University of Wisconsin, his L.L.B. degree from the University of California in 1961, and was certified as a public accountant in 1960.

In his early adult years he worked as an oreboat deckhand, lumberjack, and stock exchange runner. Following service in the US Army as First Lieutenant (1957-58), he worked as an accountant, tax clerk, law clerk, certified public accountant, attorney, professor of law at the University of Denver, state representative, and was a visiting professor at the University of Colorado at Denver, Graduate School of Public Affairs.

Gerald F. Mische is president of Global Education Associates, a network of associates in over 60 countries. After working in a community development leadership project in Mexico, Mr Mische co-founded and was first director of the Association for International

Development — a non-profit organization that trained and placed people to work in 22 countries in Africa, Asia and Latin America from 1957-67.

Co-author of the book *Toward a Human World Order* Mr Mische has written many articles and monographs. He has lectured and conducted workshops on global interdependence and world order on five continents. He is a graduate of Columbia University's Graduate School of International Affairs.

Mr Mische is presently heading up a new Center for World Order Alternatives in New York City, which facilitates and coordinates worldwide dialogue, research and global networking on world order alternatives among the individual and institutional associates of Global Education Associates in over 60 countries. Transcending national, cultural and ideological boundaries, the GEA network links educators, religious leaders, economists, community organizers and representatives from business, government and labor in a unique global forum.

There are plans for a circle of "visiting scholars" from Asia, Africa, Europe, North and South America; an international core of "center associates" who, though not in residence, will actively participate in activities and programming; and a circle of "partner" organizations and institutes which will collaborate in the planning and sponsorship of particular projects of the center. The visiting scholars will include both academic and grassroots leaders. Some will be directly sponsored by organizations or institutions affiliated with GEA's global network. Others will be persons already doing research or postgraduate work in the USA.

Patricia M. ("Pat") Mische is co-founder of Global Education Associates, a network of men and women in over 60 countries involved in research and educational programs on global issues and alternative futures. She has authored numerous articles and several books on peace-related issues, including *Star Wars and the State of Our Souls* and *Toward a Human World Order* (co-authored with her husband, Gerald Mische).

More about the authors

Mrs Mische has an M.A. degree in International Education from Columbia University and has also done graduate studies at the University of London and the University of East Africa. She has given over a thousand presentations and workshops in countries around the world on peace, justice and other global concerns. In 1986 in the Philippines she participated in an Asian Consultation on World Order and also observed the Philippine elections.

Mrs Mische also founded and was the first director of an Institute for Peace, Justice and Human Values at Seton Hall University. She is a member of the Experimental Project on the Conditions for Peace, a think tank exploring security alternatives to the arms race.

She and Mr Mische have three college-age daughters.

Marc Nerfin, born in Geneva, Switzerland, has lived in Switzerland, Tunisia, Ethiopia, New York (USA), Cuernavaca (Mexico), Rome (Italy), and has visited half of the 159 member-countries of the United Nations. He has been in all the continents, and has visited most recently in Lesotho, Venezuela, Colombia, Chile, Brazil, Indonesia, the Philippines and in Europe.

He worked ten years for the UN and was at the center of the preparations for the 1972 Stockholm Conference on the Environment. He says he believes in the UN, "but also that global relations are too serious an affair to be abandoned to Princes (governments) or Merchants (transnational corporations)." He operates within a global citizens' network expressing itself, among others, through a bi-monthly publication, the *IFDA Dossier,* which is global in its circulation, the themes it covers and its contributors.

Born Sept. 26, 1930 in Geneva, Nerfin is a citizen of Founex, Vaud, Switzerland. He is a graduate of the College de Geneve (1949) and the Universite de Geneve (1955).

He worked as a journalist in Geneva, was a teacher and journalist in Tunisia, and worked with and for the UN, serving on committees and with officials as adviser, liaison officer, and executive assistant.

He became director of the 1975 Dag Hammarskjold Project on Development and International Cooperation. The following year he was named consultant to the Dag Hammarskjold Foundation (Uppsala, Sweden) as well as to various other national and international organizations.

Many of his articles on the UN and others of global interest have been translated in French, Spanish, Greek, Portuguese, Arabic, German, and Polish.

He is a member of the advisory editorial committee, *Development Dialogue,* a journal published by the Dag Hammarskjold Foundation; associate member of the Third World Forum; the Consultative Committee, Geneva, Institute of Postgraduate Development Studies; executive committee of the Latin American

Institute for Transnational Studies, Mexico and Santiago; executive committee of CODEV, Communications for Development Foundation, Malta; the Council of Swissaid, Swiss Foundation for development cooperation; and is secretary-treasurer of Christopher Eckenstein Foundation for the study of relations with the Third World, Geneva.

Hanna Newcombe has received acclaim and awards for her work on peace, among them one of the six "Women of the Year" awards (in 1985) from the city of Hamilton, Ontario (Canada), and the "Peace Hero" award in 1972 from the World Federalists of Canada (WFC). Also she, with her husband, Alan Newcombe, received an honorary LLD from McMaster University in Hamilton, and in 1974 they were selected for the Lentz International Peace Research Award.

Mrs Newcombe was born in Prague, Czechoslavakia in 1922 and came to Canada with her parents in 1939. She earned her B.A. degree in chemistry from McMaster University and was awarded the chancellor's Gold Medal for Academic Achievement. She received her M.A. and Ph.D. degrees in organic chemistry from the University of Toronto.

Due to her interest in international relations, Mrs Newcombe became a member of the UN Association, the Voice of Women, and the WFC of which she was national president (1981-83).

She and her husband, both of whom are Quakers (Religious Society of Friends), organized the Hamilton branch of WFC and helped raise funds for the Canadian Peace Research Institute. She was a volunteer for abstracting the peace/war literature for the Institute and later became editor of the Peace Research Abstracts Project.

In 1965 Mr and Mrs Newcombe founded the Canadian Peace Research and Education Association and developed the Canadian form of mundialization with Mrs Newcombe serving on the mundialization committees of Dundas and Hamilton.

She has been a member and officer of the National Political Action Committee of WFC; was president of the World Law Foundation; a member of the International Executive of World Federal Authority committee located in Oslo and served as its president in 1980; member of the official Canadian delegation to the second special session of the UN on disarmament; Council of the International Peace Research Association headquartered in Tokyo; executive of Consortium for Peace Research, Education and Development (COPRED), located in Kent, Ohio; member of the Board of Science for Peace, Toronto; alternate delegate to the People's Conference; a professor of the Institute of Mundialist Studies at La Lambertie, France, and member of the World Mundialization Council.

Howard Richards is professor of philosophy and education and sometime director of peace studies at Earlham College (Richmond, Indiana); consultant for the Centre for Research and Development in Education (Santiago, Chile); and Fellow of Holy Cross Centre for Ecological Ethics (Port Burwell, Ontario).

He studied at Yale University (1956-58) where he was awarded the New York Yale Club Prize for Outstanding Scholarship in 1957. He earned his A.B. degree in pre-law and a J.D. degree from Stanford Law School; an M.A. in philosophy from the University of California; an advanced certificate in education (in philosophy, psychology and sociology of education) from Oxford University, with honors; a Ph.D. in philosophy (his dissertation on Aristotelian justice and Marx's labor theory of value) from the University of California at Santa Barbara; and a Ph.D. in educational theory from the University of Toronto.

Mr Richards was a volunteer lawyer for Cesar Chavez of the National Farm Workers Association in 1961-65, at the same time serving as assistant to the president of the Center for the Study of Democratic Institutions, in Santa Barbara.

His professional experience includes dean of studies at Santiago (Chile) College; foreign adviser to the Chilean educational reform, and consultant to Center for Educational Research and Development in Santiago since 1972.

Many of his articles and papers on education have been included in such books and magazines as publications of the Chilean Ministry of Education; magazines published by CIDE; Stanford Law Review; Alternatives, a Journal of World Policy; Peace and Change; Cuadernos del Tercer Mundo (Mexico); Perspectives, a UNESCO quarterly review of education; Earlham College publications, notably the 1982 baccalaureate address; also small religious publications such as for the Benedictine Sisters of Erie, Pennsylvania; and the now defunct Logos which was published in Colorado Springs, Colorado.

His most recent book, *The Evaluation of Cultural Action*, was published in 1985.

Abdus Salam was born Jan. 29, 1926 in Pakistan and has distinguished himself worldwide with a career in science.

He earned a master's degree from Government College at Lahore, Pakistan; a B.A. and Ph.D. from St. John's College at Cambridge, England, and has received honorary D.Sc. degrees from 22 universities.

He was a joint winner of the Nobel Prize for Physics in 1979, and among his many other distinguished awards are the Lomonosov Gold Medal (USSR Academy of Sciences) in 1983; Atoms for Peace award (1968); Guthrie Medal and Prize (1976); Royal Medal from the Royal Society, London (1978); John Matteuci Medal from Accademia Nazionale di Lencei, Rome (1978); John Torrence Fate Medal from the American Institute of Physics (1978); Pride of Performance Medal and Award from Pakistan (1959).

Mr Salam has served as head of the mathematics department at Panjab University, was a lecturer at the University of Cambridge, professor of theoretical physics at Imperial College of Science and Technology, University of London.

He was the founder and director of the International Centre for Theoretical Physics, Trieste; was a founding member of the Third World Academy of Sciences (1983), and has held memberships and offices in numerous science organizations in Pakistan, Paris, London, USA, USSR, Rome, Baghdad, Morocco, Lisbon, Yugoslavia, and Korea.

His publications include *Symmetry Concepts in Modern Physics* (1966), *Aspects of Quantum Mechanics* (1972), and over 200 articles.

Jan Tinbergen, a renowned physicist and economist, has received many awards, honorary degrees, and in 1969 was awarded the first Nobel Prize in economics (together with Ragnar Frisch) for having developed and applied dynamic models for the analysis of economic processes.

He was born April 12, 1903 in The Hague, The Netherlands, and was reared in a scientifically intellectual and social environment.

He studied physics (1922-26) at the University of Leiden, and received his doctorate in 1929 with a thesis on "Minimum Problems in Physics and Economics," and soon shifted his interest to economics.

Due to strong social feelings he refused to serve in the army. In lieu of military service he worked in the prison administration in Rotterdam and later at the Central Bureau of Statistics in The Hague where he stayed until 1945.

Mr Tinbergen has received international acclaim for his work and research in economics. He worked for the League of Nations from 1936-38. In 1945 he was appointed director of the Netherlands Central Planning Bureau, serving until 1955 when he resigned to devote his time to problems of the developing countries.

He also served a year as visiting professor at Harvard University, and was elected to hold a new and full-time chair in development planning at the Netherlands School of Economics.

During the 1970s he served as adviser to the governments of various developing countries including India, Egypt, Turkey, Surinam, Syria, Iraq, and Libya, also to The World Bank, Organization for Economic Cooperation and Development, and numerous United Nations agencies.

Following are a few of his many published works:

Business Cycles in the USA 1919-1932 (1939); *Business Cycles in the United Kingdom,* 1870-1914 (1951); *On the Theory of Economic Policy* (1952); *Centralization and Decentralization in Economic Policy* (1954); *Economic Policy: Principles and Design* (1956); *Shaping the World Economy* (1962); *On the Theory of Income Distribution* (1956); *The Design of Development* (1958); *Central Planning* (1964); *Development Planning* (1967); *Income Distribution: Analysis and Policies* (1975).

Jan van der Linden, after studying physics and philosophy at the Free University of Amsterdam, was a science teacher at a high school for a few years. In 1951 he moved into industry and was engaged in management training and development, first at KLM Royal Dutch Airlines for 19 years, then at the Netherlands Cable Manufacturers (a susidiary of the Philips concern).

During this period, in the 50s, he also coordinated and represented *World Goodwill* and *Triangles* (both service activities of the Lucis Trust) in Holland; and after that started the Dutch secretariat of the *Meditation Group for the New Age,* a worldwide meditation project. He served on its International Committee until 1976.

Mr van der Linden studied psychosynthesis (a blend of psychology, meditation and exercise) with Dr. Roberto Assagioli in Florence, Italy and then organized the first workshops and training courses in Holland to introduce the ideas of psychosynthesis, both to the lay public and to professionals.

In 1976 Mr van der Linden left Holland, together with his wife, to join the staff of the School for Esoteric Studies in New York City, with which he had already been associated for more than 15 years. He has three daughters who live with their families in The Netherlands.

Caesar Voute, a citizen of The Netherlands, is a geologist whose career spans over 40 years as professor, consultant, lecturer, and author.

He has served as consultant on projects in 25 countries in Europe, Near and Middle East, Africa and Latin America. His writings include over 200 publications on general and applied geology; conservation of monuments, technology and society; military and peaceful uses of outer space, and remote sensing education.

Currently he is professor of general and applied geology at the International Institute for Aerospace Survey and Earth Sciences (ITC) at Enschede, Netherlands. The ITC was founded in 1951 upon the recommendation of a United Nations Cartographic Conference to provide technical training for the benefit of developing countries. It has over 7,000 alumni from more than 160 countries, 80% from the Third World and 20% from industrialized nations.

Born Nov. 20, 1922 in Magelang, Indonesia, Mr Voute is a 1949 geology graduate of Utrecht State University, Netherlands, and received his Ph.D. degree in 1961. He was a staff member of the university from 1946-51, and served as part-time lecturer/assistant professor of hydrogeology at Leiden State University, Netherlands, from 1956-71. Since 1963 he has been a full professor at ITC.

Mr Voute was appointed project co-ordinator of the Unesco Project Conservation of Monuments and Sites in Indonesia (1971-75). He has also served as a Netherlands delegate to the UN Economic and Social Commission for Asia and the Pacific (ESCAP); Second UN Conference on the Exploration and Peaceful Uses of Outer Space (UNISPACE 82); and the 23rd Unesco General Conference in Sofia.

More about the authors
He has been a member of numerous UN expert groups and lectured at UN workshops and seminars; was chairman of the UN expert meeting on the space applications for disaster management; past member of the remote sensing working group of the European Space Agency; chairman of the remote sensing education working group of the European Association of Remote Sensing Laboratories; honorary member of the Association of Hydrologists of India, and active in Pugwash Conference symposiums and workshops.

Rene V.L. Wadlow, since 1978, has been editor and publisher of *Transnational Perspectives,* a journal of world affairs largely devoted to questions of world security and regional armed conflicts. He is the representative to the United Nations in Geneva of both the World Association of World Federalists and the International Fellowship of Reconciliation, active on problems of disarmament and human rights.

From 1964 to 1978 he was professor and director of studies of the Institute of Development Studies of the University of Geneva. He served as principal editor of *Geneve-Afrique,* a well-known scholarly journal on Africa and as book editor of the *International Development Review.*

During this period he was involved in many development projects for different organizations such as the World Council of Churches, traveling to Africa and Asia. In 1977 he was a social science member of a team working in Hiroshima which prepared a report for the International symposium on the Damage and After-Effects of the Atomic Bombing of Hiroshima and Nagasaki, a report presented to the first UN General Assembly on Disarmament in 1978.

From 1961 to 1964 he was an advisor to the Ministry of Education of Gabon, Equatorial Africa working on educational reform, adult education programs and improved teaching methods. In Gabon he came to know well Dr. Albert Schweitzer as both had been active against atomic testing.

Mr Wadlow was born in 1934 in New Jersey USA, educated at Princeton University and the University of Chicago and studied rural development questions at the International People's College in Elsinor, Denmark.

Ofer Zur, Ph.D., is a psychologist, teacher and researcher in the area of the psychology of peace and war. His recent research focuses on the public myths and beliefs about the nature of war and the relationship between gender and war.

Mr Zur also developed a new scale of attitudes toward war. As a former military officer and oceanographer, he brings a unique combination to his teaching and writing.

He is a faculty member of the California Institute of Integral Studies (San Francisco), where he has been developing a new graduate program in Peace/War and Global Studies. He is also employed by Alameda County Criminal Justice Mental Health and has a private practice in Berkeley.

EARTHVIEW WORLD MODEL

(A CONDENSED VERSION)

The Earthview Model provides a framework for the Peace Series and is updated with each volume of the Peace Series. This is Update I, which includes information from Volume One. Earthview Press makes an effort to ensure that each chapter is generally compatible with the Model, which may involve editing the article or adjusting the model. The authors of each volume are not necessarily in agreement with all the ideas and principles of the Model, but they have final approval of the content of their respective chapters.

1. Life and Nations

1.1 **Life** is "nested" — systems within systems within systems — for example, cells within people within families within communities within nations . . . all within the human species. There are four basic types of living systems — *biosystems* (such as trees, dogs, insects and people), *regisystems* (such as insect colonies and coral reefs), *social systems* (such as families, clubs, companies, nations and religions), and *ecosystems* (such as oceans and forests. Each system is composed of *subsystems*, and each is itself a subsystem of higher-level systems.

To analyze any living system it is necessary first to conceptually divide the world in two — everything *in*side the system, and everything *out*side the system.

1.2 **Nations** and other social systems are made entirely of people and products, and are powered by energy. A nation needs to consume natural resources for nourishment, just as a person needs to consume food. Resources are not part of the nation's structure, as an apple is not part of a person. A person may *own* an apple, and a nation may *own* resources, but they do not become a physical part of the system until they are consumed and broken down into system products and energy. A crucial distinction.

2. Four Principles of Basic Well-Being

2.1 Consuming the proper amounts of the proper types of things from the outside world is one main factor in a system's well-being.

2.2 Structural order is also vital to life and is achieved by standardizing such physical characteristics as system boundaries, density, structural integration, and functional design of subsystems.

2.3 Behavioral order, too, is vital to life and is achieved with values — regulation, routines, reactions and objectives — which shape behavior to the needs of life.

2.4 Each system is a living link between the smaller systems within it and the larger systems of which it is part. For life in general to be healthy, each link needs to be reliable.

3. Fitting Current Disciplines Into the Model

3.1 **Economics** is to a social system (like a nation) what *nutrition* is to a biosystem (like a person). A nation needs to consume sensible amounts of wholesome resources to maintain sound economic health. (Relevant to 2.1)

3.2 **Sociology, political science, psychology** and other studies of society and politics, are to a social system what *biology* is to a biosystem — the study of structure and behavior within the system and around it. (Relevant to 2.2 and 2.3)

3.3 **Spirituality** involves the efforts of an individual to be a healthy, reliable link between the biosystems within and the social systems of which s/he is part. Spirituality involves inner work (to stay healthy and balanced), outer work (to be reliable and useful in society), and bridging the internal and external worlds with such things as meditation, morals, and a stable mental picture of the world. National spirituality involves a nation's inner work (domestic affairs), outer work (foreign affairs and ecosystem concerns) and bridging efforts such as aligning to multinational and global standards and values. (Relevant to 2.4)

4. Five Basic Obstacles to Peace

4.1 **Malnourishment** is a nutritional imbalance in a biosystem or an economic imbalance in a social system. The needs of the system are not being properly satisfied by the food or resources the system consumes. (Relevant to 2.1)

4.2 **Malformations** are structural defects in a living system. They can be the result of broken parts or development of a system according to faulty standards. (Relevant to 2.2)

4.3 **Conflicts** occur when two or more systems are not compatible in their behavior. They are the result of incompatible values. (Relevant to 2.3)

4.4 **Decadence** occurs when a system loses the will or ability to act as a healthy, reliable link between its inner and outer worlds. (Relevant to 2.4)

4.5 **Accidents** are unpredictable. They can occur at any time at any level of life for any number of reasons, to trigger any of the four obstacles above.

5. Basic Prerequisites of Peace Include:

5.1 **Clear Communication.** If people in the same family or nations in the same world don't share ideas and information regularly, they gradually grow apart, and eventually become incompatible.

5.2 **Equity.** Within any system, the basic needs of all subsystems must be met. In case of an overall scarcity, fair distribution becomes crucial to peace.

5.3 **Sensible Regulation.** Regulation (monitoring situations and deciding what changes to make and when to make them) should occur at the lowest or most local levels within a system, but high enough to account for all subsystems affected by the decisions. The most crucial situations facing us today require regulation at the world level. These situations, which threaten the future of everyone on this planet, include nuclear weapons proliferation and the rapid deterioration of oceans and rain forests which provide the very basis of life on our planet.

INDEX

ENDORSEMENTS

"The National Peace Council, the 'umbrella' organization of the peace movement in the UK, welcomes this valuable book — a constellation of ideas and concepts which can focus our thoughts on ways forward in all our varied works for peace."

— *Jan Martin, Acting General Secretary*
National Peace Council (London)

"Though there are no easy solutions for the problems afflicting us today, *Solutions for a Troubled World* analyzes many of the major problems and emphasizes some positive steps that can be taken. What is needed is not only better and more effective information but a rethinking of many of our values, a lessening of inequities, and more effective ways of dealing with conflict. On these issues this book has particularly valuable things to say. Reading should force us to come to grips with basic problems that each of us can do something about."

— *Vern L. Bullough, Dean*
Natural and Social Sciences
State University College at Buffalo (New York)

"Faith can move mountains, but so can dynamite. Faith can do more; it can enrich, ennoble and inspire the human heart to new endeavor; it can give strength to the weak, power to the helpless and courage to the defeated. Faith can transform the life of dull routine into a life filled with meaning and purpose.

"We must have a purpose in life if we are to expand our spiritual beings. We must offer something of ourselves to each unforgiving minute if we are to find the satisfying life. Our purpose must be something above and beyond the satisfaction of our own mere physical needs. It must include something of a greater depth and wider scope and embrace in its scope the ideal of service to our fellow man.

"It is the limitations of the human personality that largely account for the tragedies of the twentieth century and beyond. The arch enemy, War, is the outcome, not as in the past, of economic instability, but of psychological immaturity. Society is threatened not so much by famine, pestilence or material adversities, but by turbulent elements within itself. The majority of human beings that go to make up society are not yet emancipated from bondage of elemental instincts and unwittingly endeavour to destroy the only organism that can provide them with richer life. Our wisdom — our control and understanding of ourselves — has not kept pace with our technological and scientific progress.

"I endorse and support this book."

— *Olusegun Obasanjo, General*
Former Head of State
Nigeria

"This peace studies collection is unusually broad in the types of peace-related issues it covers, the scholarly disciplines represented, and the fact that the authors are drawn from all continents. Readers will certainly be stimulated to explore the issues covered in greater depth."

— *Elise Boulding*
Professor Emeritus of Sociology
Dartmouth College

"Mutual goodwill and the spirit of cooperation are both essential in present day life for the success of humanity. This applies to individuals living in a state as well as to nations in international life. I say so because the human race is threatened today by violence and terrorism in internal as well as international relations. (This situation) is dangerous to the peace of the individual, and can even destroy humanity in a major armed conflict. May I, therefore, pray to each individual human being as well as the nations of the world to accept the 'Mantram' of mutual goodwill and cooperation.

"Humanity is one and the same wherever it exists irrespective of national boundaries, caste, religions or political creed. All distinctions and boundaries must be eroded to join humanity as one race. All beings must pull toward a common goal.

"This goal was indeed well and firmly laid down in clear, categorical terms when wisdom dawned on humanity after centuries of trial and tribulation and two major world wars, and this wisdom is now contained in the United Nations charter. It appears essential in this context to spell out emphatically the principles of the UN Charter.

• "First and foremost: Non-use of force in international relations.

• "Second: Coexistence and toleration of rival views, creeds and religions, and nondiscrimination in every aspect of human relationship.

• "Third: Noninterference in domestic affairs of other states.

• "Last but not least: Respect for human rights and self-determination in political life.

"If humanity is to live in peace to make progress and bring prosperity to the world, it must adhere to these golden principles of internal and international life. If we disregard this wisdom of humanity embodied in the UN Charter we must perish and destroy all life on Earth. All individuals have, therefore, the sacred duty to do their utmost to respect the UN Charter . . . to build a better and safe world for all to live in.

"The spirit of *Solutions For a Troubled World* is in line with these goals and principles."

— *Judge Nagendra Singh, President
International Court of Justice*

"This fascinating book provides a compelling description of the many problems that plague our existence and then sets forth solutions to these problems. One's first reaction on finishing this highly readable book is one of admiration for the editor, who has succeeded in bringing together a remarkably diverse collection of authors, most of whom are global thinkers, yet all of whom have the unique ability to discuss the theoretical and then propose the practical. The dominant theme of the book deals with new and innovative ways to achieve a more peaceful world, moving from the level of the individual to the global. The interacting web of ideas and suggested solutions will heighten the ability of the reader to communicate with other like-minded persons who share a vision of a peaceful world. The authors present a portrait of an exciting view of the future."

— *John W. McDonald*
Ambassador and Global Strategist

"It is good to know that good people are looking over the troubled world, and to find leading world intellectuals collaborating on one book proposing solutions for it. I would recommend this book to anyone who is worried about our troubled world."

— *Dr. Kinhide Mushakoji, Vice Rector*
Regional and Global Studies
United Nations University

Other peace-related publications by Earthview Press:

World Model, 24 pages, provides a basis for all Earthview Press publications. 0-930705-02-5

Last Chance For Peace, 276 pages, explores various aspects of the World Model in depth. 0-930705-01-7 (pbk); 0-930705-00-9 (hcv)